Music Genres and Corporate Cultures

Music Genres and Corporate Cultures explores the workings of the music industry, tracing the often uneasy relationship between entertainment corporations and the artists they sign. Keith Negus examines the contrasting strategies of major labels like Sony and Universal in managing different genres, artists and staff, and assesses the various myths of corporate culture. How do takeovers affect the treatment of artists? Why was PolyGram perceived as too European to attract US artists? Why and how did EMI Records attempt to change their corporate culture?

Through a study of three major genres – rap, country and salsa – Negus investigates why the music industry recognises and rewards certain sounds, and how this influences both the creativity of musicians and their audiences. He explores why some artists get international promotion while others are neglected, and how performers are packaged as 'world music'. Negus examines the tension between rap's image as a spontaneous 'music of the streets' and the practicalities of the market, asks why executives from New York feel uncomfortable when they visit the country music business in Nashville, and explains why the lack of soundscan systems in Puerto Rican record shops affects salsa's position on the US *Billboard* chart.

Drawing on extensive research and interviews with music industry personnel in Britain, the United States and Japan, *Music Genres and Corporate Cultures* shows how the creation, circulation and consumption of popular music is shaped by record companies and corporate business style while stressing that music production takes place within a broader culture, not totally within the control of large corporations.

Keith Negus is Lecturer in the Department of Media and Communications, Goldsmiths College, University of London. He is the author of *Producing Pop* and *Popular Music in Theory*.

Music Genres and Corporate Cultures

Keith Negus

- has have all these findings changed in 15 years?
- He seems to have been on the tail end of the pre-Internet years, but didn't people see these changes coming? Anybody?
- How would such a study even proceed today? Are there reliable data on consumption + circulation? Even production?! (92)

London and New York

First published 1999
by Routledge
11 New Fetter Lane, London EC4P 4EE

Simultaneously published in the USA and Canada
by Routledge
29 West 35th Street, New York, NY 10001

Routledge is an imprint of the Taylor & Francis Group

© 1999 Keith Negus

Typeset in Sabon by Routledge
Printed and bound in Great Britain by
Biddles Ltd, Guildford and King's Lynn

British Library Cataloguing in Publication Data
A catalogue record for this book is available from the British
Library

Library of Congress Cataloguing in Publication Data
Negus, Keith,
Music genres and corporate cultures / Keith Negus.
p. cm.
Includes bibliographical references and index.
1. Sound recording industry. 2. Popular music–History and
criticism. 1.&;Title.
ML3790.N4 1999
781.64–dc21

0–415–17399–X (hbk)
0–415–17400–7 (pbk)

Contents

Acknowledgements

A substantial part of this book is based on research funded by the Economic and Social Research Council (ESRC) of Great Britain within the *Media Economics and Media Culture* programme (award ref. L126251046). I would like to thank all of those working for the ESRC who made this possible, along with the various anonymous referees and assessors whose comments and reports helped me focus my ideas and think about the project more clearly. I would like to extend very special thanks to Simon Frith, who as Chair of the programme provided intellectual guidance, practical advice and also important feedback, encouragement and suggestions in response to my questions and working ideas during and after the research.

Margaret Crawford took the administrative systems of Leicester University into unknown territory over a three-month period of planning and during my time away. She then endured and assisted with a number of desperate faxes concerning such things as unpaid hotel bills, changed itineraries and medicines for a spider bite. I would like to thank Margaret for patiently co-ordinating and sorting out many of the administrative details of the research and also for her help with a number of personal matters. Also at Leicester I would like to thank Annabelle Sreberny for much personal and professional support prior to, during and after the research. Thanks too to Oliver Boyd-Barrett, who prompted me to focus my thoughts on musical genres during a grey awayday in the Leicestershire countryside – Oliver unwittingly helped set in motion the pattern of events that led to the research and this book. Peter Jackson helped in the formulation of my research agenda by providing a number of insights into management thinking and notions of corporate strategy. Still at Leicester, I would like to thank the University for supporting this research and for prior financial assistance which enabled me to visit Japan and to conduct a number of interviews in the UK.

In Puerto Rico I would like to thank Emilio Pantojas García for welcoming me into the Center for Social Research as an *Investigador Invitado* and for providing me with both intellectual dialogue and the space to reflect upon the research material and to develop ideas. Very special thanks are also due to Angel Quintero Rivera (Chuco) for much personal and professional support and encouragement, for constructive criticism of my writings and dialogue about many ideas. I am grateful to Jorge Duany who suggested that I submit an article to the *Revista de Ciencias Sociales* and who subsequently translated it into Spanish (thus, an earlier version of Chapter 6 appeared in Vol. 4, *Nueva Epoca*, of the *Revista* and I would also like to thank the journal's anonymous referees for their comments and suggestions). Thanks to Jorge Giovanetti Torres and Liliana Cotto for discussions about culture and society in Puerto Rico and in the Caribbean more generally.

My time in New York City would have been less rewarding without the company and dialogue of Dave Sanjek, Bob and Annie Clarida and Kai Fickentscher: All assisted with urban orientation and aspects of research planning. Thanks also to Stuart Liebman and his colleagues and students at CUNY in Queens for providing feedback and encouragement in response to some tentative working ideas. Thanks to staff at Radio City Apartments for their flexibility, friendliness and assistance with communications to the UK. Special thanks to Nel Román for welcoming me to both New York and the extended family and for showing me parts of the city of which I would otherwise probably have had little personal experience.

In Tennessee I would like to thank Paul Wells for providing me with access to the library facilities of the Center for Popular Music at Middle Tennessee State University, the staff at the library of the Country Music Association, and Richard Peterson for dialogue, information and insights about country music and the city of Nashville.

Some of the material in Chapter 7 was researched during a trip to Japan in 1993, and I would particularly like to thank Masahiro Yasuda, Hiroshi Ogawa, Toru Mitsui and Tadd Igarashi, all of whom welcomed me into their homes and shared their music, ideas and food with me. Also thanks to Takuya Iwamura for help with arranging interviews and translation.

I would like to extend my gratitude to the following people who gave up their time to talk to me about their work, companies, genres or the music business in general. In the UK: Mike Allen, Roxy Bellamy, Mina Fukue, David Hughes, Hiroshi Kato, Jorgen Larsen, Eric Longley, Jonathan Morrish, Fran Nevrkla, Tina Poyser, John Preston, Steve Redmond, Peter Scaping, Jeremy Silver, Stuart Watson, Adam White. In the United States: Sarah Brosmer, Brian Chin, Bob Christgau, Kevin Conroy, Sue D'Agostino, Tim Dubois, Curt Eddy, John Esposito, Chet Flippo, Harry Fox, Lynn Franz, Joe Galante, Victor Gallo, John Ganoe, Jeff Green, Linda Greenberg, George Grelf, David Harleston, Ricardo Howell, Daniel Jason, Anne Latora, Joe Levy, Fran Lichtman, Roy Lott, Anne Mansbridge, Ruby Marchand, Kim Markovchick, Keith McCarthy, David McDonagh, Alastair McMullen, Bob Merlis, Antonio Moreno,

Marcus Morton, Havelock Nelson, Barbara Nuessle, Rigoberto Olariaga, Joanne Oriti, Jim Parham, Hal Peterson Jr, Dennis Petroskey, Ronny Pugh, Eddie Reeves, Paul Robinson, Nelson Rodríguez, Michael Rosenblatt, Terri Rosi, Rick Sanjek, Maribel Schumacher, Ajax Scott, Davitt Sigerson, Scott Siman, Gene Smith, Will Tanous, Neil Turkewitz, Renee White, Timothy White, Larry Willoughby, Walt Wilson, Tim Wipperman, and, in Puerto Rico, thanks to Lourdes Laboy. In Japan: Yoshihisa Honda, Kei Ishimura, Kei Ishizaka, Akira Kuwabara, Shigeo Maruyama, Kei Nishimura, Shigeki Ouchi, and Akira Yokota.

In researching, thinking about and then writing this book I have tried out a number of ideas in formal presentations, written work and during informal conversations, and I have benefited from feedback, suggestions and insights from a number of people. For reading many draft chapters and providing useful critiques, encouragement and suggestions I would like to thank Mike Pickering. Thanks to Dave Laing for discussing working ideas, pointing me in a number of useful directions, providing me with information and for spotting many of the errors in my drafts. For their critical and constructive comments in response to draft chapters I thank Reebee Garofalo, Dave Sanjek and Richard Peterson. Also, for char-acteristically perceptive insights and observations that have helped me in thinking through various working ideas, I would like to thank Paul du Gay, Eamonn Forde, Dave Hesmondhalgh and Sarah Thornton. Thanks to Rebecca Barden, Alistair Daniel, Sally Carter and Elizabeth Jones at Routledge.

My crash-landing back into Highfields after a year away was eased by the frequently crazy company of Eamonn, Hilde and Simon. Thanks too to Hari and Shoba for their friendship, wit and wisdom.

For much transatlantic love, support and practical help throughout the research project I would like to thank my brothers, Chris and Phil, and my parents, Maureen and Gordon. Finally, yet most importantly, I would like to thank Patria for her love, support and wisdom and for sharing the magic realism of an occasionally bizarre, sometimes frustrating and never dull story.

Introduction

I first made contact with a record company in 1974 when, with an aspiring school friend, I mailed the only copy of a badly recorded reel-to-reel tape to Donald 'Jumbo' Vanrenen at Virgin Records. Thinking back on this long-lost recording, produced with acoustic guitars and keyboards in one 'live' take in the back room of my parents' house, I am surprised that we even received a response, let alone the brief letter that accompanied the returned tape. I recall that our songs had 'promise' but that the vocals were 'weak', and we were advised to try and record using better-quality equipment. That was the beginning of a long association with the recording industry, during which I would spend many hours in the offices of record labels, production companies and song publishers, initially as one of the numerous musicians and songwriters attempting to 'make it' in the music business and then as an older and increasingly wiser sociologist attempting to understand the peculiar mixture of reckless abandon and cautious indecision that is such a feature of the music and entertainment industry.

A few years after that first tape, a number of us had made the transition from back rooms and bedrooms to performing regularly in pubs, community centres, youth clubs, parties and then more recognized venues. I had become a participant member of a passionate, competitive yet convivial and somewhat idiosyncratic music scene. My co-writing school friend soon joined X-Ray Spex, with whom he briefly achieved a certain degree of fame and a lesser degree of fortune before finding himself working in the office of a building society. After stints in numerous bands, I ended up performing with the lesser known and more embarrassingly named Coconut Dogs, who released a couple of singles and played numerous clubs, bars and provincial venues before sinking into ever deeper obscurity and the inevitable bust-up due to the stupid arguments that are euphemistically referred to as 'musical differences'. I then trailed a route through various 'solo' outings, typical early 1980s faddish synthesizer projects, and moved in and out of temporary bands while playing 'sessions' with a variety of people who provoked in me equal doses of elation and despair.

All this time, the music industry and various artist and repertoire (A and R) people, agents, would-be managers, publishers and wheeler-dealers were lurking in the background and occasionally stepping into the foreground. I was on the verge of signing a lucrative (compared to the dole) publishing contract for songwriting, but the company who were 'interested' in me suddenly had to make financial cuts as a result of the early 1980s recession, and my contact lost his job. I was about to sign up with a music business contact who was to be my manager and procure me that elusive 'solo deal'. But he suddenly disappeared. My telephone calls to his personal contact number, and then to his ex-production company, eventually provided me with the vague information that he had, rather suddenly, 'gone to Argentina'. I had much interest from another 'manager', and after a number of telephone conversations we met in a dingy bar adjacent to a London station. Here he presented me with a vision of how he saw my stage show and future direction. He evoked an image of me in a small theatre before an audience, the house lights dimmed, and then – after he uttered the phrase 'dry ice' – I stopped listening and my mind wandered on to other projects. I do remember taking the train back to the suburbs in a rather depressed state.

When I realized, during one of my more sane and sober moments, that (as Neville Shakespeare) I had told a journalist that I had 'turned my back on aspirations of fortune, fame and stardom' and was 'producing ecological acoustic piano music that might appear before the nuclear holocaust' (I still have the news cutting), it became apparent that something was not quite right. It was either the music business (and its peripherals) or the factories and warehouses where I had been working to support the 'earnings' from my music habit that were driving me crazy. In desperation I became a sociologist, devoted my time to attempting to understand what I had been through and tried to figure out why I was now sitting in a library in north London and not recording my latest album in Manhattan.

Armed with a degree in sociology and a grant to study for a Ph.D., I revisited many of the same offices and boardrooms (or maybe they simply appeared to be the same). I walked into rooms with a pencil in my hand, and stared thoughtfully at similar rows of desks, low comfy chairs, cool dudes, blank security guards and bored-looking receptionists. I hung around at the back of gigs, seeking out the packs of A and R staff, and listened in on their drunken conversations. I spoke to pop-paper people, sifted through the words in journals, trade magazines and biographies and connected all of this to a range of sociological ideas. If, in retrospect, one of my motives in studying the industry was undoubtedly therapeutic, I also had two fairly clear and well-formulated intentions. First, I would be able to impart some knowledge and wisdom to anyone brave or stupid enough

① passing on useful knowledge
② get in an academic job

to follow the same route, information that might be of some practical use to those – whether musician, industry worker or frustrated fan – who are subject to and have to deal with the music industry in whatever way. Second, I wished to contribute to academic debates and scholarship within popular music studies, a field of study that had begun creeping into class-rooms and 'corrupting' curriculums in sociology, cultural studies and related disciplines.

The book you have before you is my second attempt at understanding how the music industry works, approaching it from the perspective I have developed as a sociologist. It is an extended argument about how the creation, circulation and consumption of popular music is shaped by record companies and their corporate owners, along with numerous other people who participate in the making of what I have called 'genre cultures'. My concern is with the interplay and uneasy interaction between economics (music as commodity, various business strategies and organiza-tional structures) and culture (the practices, interpretations and ways of life of musicians, fans and industry workers) and the ways in which the two often blur and fuse. I am also interested in how genre categories inform the organization of music companies, the creative practices of musicians and the perceptions of audiences. In researching, thinking through and then writing about these issues, I have gradually become aware of how my own experiences of the recording industry and music-making have informed this project, influencing the issues I have decided to focus upon and the way I have thought about them. Looking back on the period that I have briefly alluded to, and reflecting upon this with slightly more than an 'if only I knew then what I know now' sentiment, I have realized that many of the intuitive assumptions I made about the music industry as a result of personal experience have informed the ideas I have developed in a more measured and self-consciously intellectual way in this book. I should also add that I have reassessed numerous previous assump-tions as a result of all this research.

There are two main ideas that I have been trying to think through in researching for and writing this book – genre and corporate strategy – and I want to highlight how these issues have a bearing on what we come to recognize as creativity. In Chapter 1 I will provide a discussion of these themes in terms of specific intellectual debates and theories. Here, without wishing to become too indulgent and self-referential, I want to include a few more words about my own personal experiences on the assumption that these are not unique, but comparable to what others may have endured through their involvement in writing songs, performing and attempting to obtain a recording contract. At the very least I would like to acknowledge that the ideas I am putting forward in this book have not simply been derived from a 'detached' scholarly process of research, thinking and writing, but have come together following a rather more chaotic pattern of learning over a longer period.

A central issue I am concerned with in this book is that of genre: the way in which musical categories and systems of classification shape the music that we might play and listen to, mediating both the experience of music and its formal organization by an entertainment industry. In retrospect, with one or two notable exceptions, most of my experiences as a musician were contained within a whole series of genre boundaries, codes and expectations (in a way that did not impact upon my musical consumption). Certainly all of my experiences as a member of bands who, to a greater or lesser extent, were focused on the goal of a recording contract, were lived within specific 'genre worlds'. From the first days of trying to form a band, the initial and recurring question was always 'What type of music do you play?', followed by 'What are your influences?' and 'What do you listen to?' This I would ask, or be asked, during meetings that occurred as a result of word-of-mouth communications, when answering advertisements in *Melody Maker*, in reply to notices placed in record shops or when responding to hand-scrawled announcements in newsagents' windows. The same type of question would be asked when we began to arrange gigs. It didn't matter if it was to be a performance in a pub, at a wedding, in an arts centre or as a support act with another band – the question was always the same: 'What type of music do you play?' Any attempt to refuse musical labelling by coyly playing the game of 'we don't like to classify ourselves' or 'we are unlike any other band' would not help us get bookings. It would usually result in a request to 'hear a tape' before a decision could be made.

Once we began playing in front of the public it soon became apparent that our audiences, and those of them who became fans and followed us around, would have their opinions about the category to which we might belong. During a break in a performance, or at the end of a gig, members of an audience would come up with various unsolicited opinions, making specific comparisons (I still recall: 'You play keyboards like the guy in Cockney Rebel' and 'The band sounds like XTC/The Boomtown Rats/The Beat/Split Enz'). There would be generic comparisons too ('New wave, but a bit of soul', 'You're too poppy for this place' or 'Heavy, great!' – the band members I was performing with when that last phrase was uttered were using amplifiers and PA equipment that would, against our best intentions, continually produce a distorted sound). Such opinions influenced the way in which the band interacted with the audience, how we performed and how we drew up our set lists. In a practical way we recognized the boundaries to genre expectations, how they interacted and overlapped. We got to know the venues in which we could be 'a bit poppy'; where we could get away with extended jams (improvisation); where we had to be a bit heavy (the rows of motorbikes parked outside the pub or club were usually a clue); and where we could – or more importantly, could not – inflict on the audience attempts at funk workouts or introduce reggae rhythms into rock 'n' roll standards.

If the responses and expectations of audiences were influencing our performances, then the assumptions about genre codes also had <u>an impact upon my own songwriting and style of playing</u>. Like many people, I was *composers* often simultaneously a member of groups performing different repertoires. For example, I was playing with a slightly jazzy, Steely Dan-influenced band at the same time as being a member of a punk band – and I don't think I was unusual, although it was often strategically necessary to conceal such double lives. I recall, during pre-punk days, a brief period when I had been playing with a heavy(ish) rock band, called – appropriately – Bullfrog Nightmare. I was asked to join the band because the members did not compose their own material and they had heard, somehow, from someone, that I could write songs. After a couple of weeks of rehearsals and conversations, I introduced my songs to the band. The response I still recall. My songs were 'good', had 'good lyrics and melodies', but were 'a bit too much like Paul McCartney' (if only! if only!). Somewhat irritated I went away, brought my limited knowledge of Deep Purple to bear on a riff stolen from Lou Reed, put it through a fuzz box, wrote about a rock band who cause minor havoc in a rundown hotel, and called it *Rock Mansion Hotel* – it was instantly accepted by the band; I had grasped the 'genre rules'. A few years later, I was asked to join another band who, in the wake of punk and new wave, were desperately trying to modify their awkward and, in retrospect, rather unique unblended mix of old r 'n' b riffs, Genesis-inspired whimsies and T-Rex boogies. Here I instantly found a place for my angry Elvis Costello pastiches. In other combinations I found an outlet for bad Stevie Wonder imitations; I learnt to 'stop thinking in chords' and 'follow the groove' when playing disco-jazz-funk; and I realized that punk rock finally allowed me to leave my keyboards behind and jump across the stage playing electric rhythm guitar (badly, naturally).

An irony I was always vaguely aware of throughout this time was the lack of any relationship between the genre performed by a band and the musical inclinations and record collections of the individual musicians. Individual preferences were often eclectic, defying any simple assumptions about a direct connection between musical 'taste' (or 'market') and social identities. This would also be apparent when meeting and getting to know the musicians in other bands. Most groups were a tense collusion and collision of factions, cliques and alliances, and the unit's style often the result of a degree of antagonism, compromise and occasional synthesis. This was always leading to arguments and resulting in bands continually splitting and re-forming. The alternative to compromise simply involved going crazy or going solo (and many of us tried both). I have subsequently come to believe that the most successful bands knew exactly what genre they were playing, recognized its musical and social boundaries and understood what their audience wanted to hear, see and be told. The most interesting bands musically (at least for me) were the strange, unpredictable mixtures and messes that were trying to please a range of audiences and band members simultaneously (and which are always to be found in a club or bar somewhere). These were not necessarily the most successful, either in commercial terms or according to their ability to communicate with large numbers of people. It was usually the former rather than the latter who obtained the recording contracts and it goes without saying that the ultimate genre question was – and is – asked by record companies. This is the way in which the music industry rewards and recognizes certain genre practices, sounds, combinations, cultures and not others. Some can be categorized, easily labelled and slotted into the cultures of production more easily than others. One of the central themes of this book concerns how the music industry and broader social networks act to divide and constrain these potentially fluid, multiple influences and genre crossings.

The issue of record company strategy is also central to this book. When I was signed to a record company, and during my numerous discussions with others on the receiving end of various 'deals', I would not have believed that record companies had coherent strategies (maybe back in the 1970s and early 1980s they were not so clear or obvious as they are now). Certainly my memories of being a member of bands signed to record companies bring to mind images of inertia and indecision, of things not happening, of the music business being disorganized and populated by 'untogether' people, and of label directors always changing their minds and changing their staff (a different A and R person in the seat every six months). I recall the days following the euphoria that accompanied the signing of a recording contract as a time of great expectations but nothing happening. The date for the release of the first single came – and went; the recording was delayed ('by forces beyond our control'). The release of the first single was postponed further because the distribution company had ceased operating and a new deal had only just been completed with PolyGram – but 'rest assured, they are "committed" to the band as the first release through this new deal'.

The single was at long last released – but there seemed to be little evidence of marketing or promotion (we had managed to get our own independently produced first single played on three different BBC Radio One shows). Word filtered along a chain from a friend of a friend who knew someone who worked as a secretary at the BBC: The 'independent promoter' who had been subcontracted to push our single was of the opinion that it was 'a piece of shit' and had got more attractive recordings to plug. We were told, more diplomatically, by the record company that it was 'not radio friendly'. Then senior staff at the record label began to reassess their obligation to release a second single before they even had to reach the impending decision to proceed through the first contractual 'option' clause and commit themselves to record an album. We were informed that there was a 'problem' with the credentials of the production duo (ex-members of a well-known 1970s rock band) who had agreed to produce our next single and whom we had met to discuss arrangements and studios. The directors of the record company were concerned that these producers had a reputation for not remaining sober in the studio. So what? Our collective response of 'this is rock 'n' roll' was not appreciated by the ones who held the purse strings (even if costs could be recouped from our future earnings). We were introduced to another producer, who came with the qualification of having played sessions with David Bowie. He told us some nice anecdotes, but we did not really hit it off with him musically. Who else would produce us?

Weeks went by and then turned into months. There were the beginnings of serious and emotional arguments between frustrated band members and record label. We were thought to be 'difficult'. It also became vaguely clear that the company had some financial problems. Eventually we 'settled' – we were paid off with a small amount of cash which we spent by going straight into a recording studio and 'putting down' some awful demos. These were not very good, recorded 'on the rebound' – not the best selection of songs, performed too fast with too many instruments in the mix and a lot of shouting or half-sung ranting accompanying the vocal line. I still recall the reaction of one A and R man at Polydor to whom we presented the tape a few days later. Pressing the stop button after listening for less than thirty seconds, he turned to us and, in a monotone which must have been perfected over many years, he said: 'The drum sound – it's last year's thing, maaan!'

At the time, and shortly afterwards, I believed that this entire mess was one big, unlucky, chaotic, cosmic accident without any underlying logic, reason or cause. I was later to reconsider this view and formed the opinion that this was just another typical series of occurrences within the music business, and symptomatic of how record companies function most of the time. I now believe that this was indicative of the inherent instability in the music business, the uncertainties that corporate strategies attempt to deal with, but also that these types of fiascos are the sort of events which corporate strategies help to create.

Reflecting upon this experience now, particularly when prefacing my own sociological account of the recording industry, it seems worth highlighting the tensions between these different understandings of the world of musical production. On one side is the academic tendency, developed from a training in modern sociology. This brings with it the assumption that the lives of people and things occur according to particular types of 'logic' – hence, the idea that there are identifiable patterns to music industry practices and recognizable motives guiding the habits and actions of musicians and recording industry personnel alike. As a humanist sociologist I have learnt to deal with my fellow human beings as rational and increasingly 'reflexive', self-consciously aware of our actions and the circumstances which limit or enable us to engage in one activity and not another. Like other sociologists I strongly resist the tendency to view behaviour in terms of an individual's hidden psychological motives or quirks. Instead, focusing on the combined actions of numerous groups and alliances, I seek to explain how such entities as the recording industry work in a systematic, coherent and orderly manner. Guiding my approach is the belief that this type of knowledge will be useful for academic colleagues, students, musicians, people within the recording industry, policy-makers and anyone who seeks to participate in or exercise some influence on processes of commercial music production.

Yet most of the time the music industry clearly does not operate as it should, or is supposed to. It doesn't work (continually producing huge numbers of 'failures' and disorder) even according to its own most basic criterion of success. In the process, it generates a large amount of confusion, incomprehension, misunderstandings, exploitation, conflict and anxiety. When great music does manage to escape from this vortex, it seems all the more inexplicable and even magical. It is here, at this point and during these moments, when notions of experiential confusion and immediate emotional response to the mysteries of the music rub up against, confront or simply diverge away from any attempt to offer a systematic analysis. 'Chaos' appeals to many people's experience of the music industry – not as a postmodern feeling of relativist anxiety (a consequence of complicated, multiple influences that are potentially knowable), nor as a psychological malady and neither as a social-psychological state of (equally explicable) disorientation. The musician's experience and industry worker's anxieties embrace chaos and confusion as a real explanation of social life and organizational existence, denying that the entire mess is amenable to any kind of systematic or 'academic' explanation.

Such is the challenge facing the sociologist, and it's one that I have become acutely aware of as a result of my own prior feeling of chaos and confusion. However, my position in this book is that while the recording industry might make us feel confused, this does not mean that we cannot relate such disorienting rhythms to very specific social processes, practices and organizational arrangements. While I am, and have always been, suspicious of simple and one-dimensional explanations of how the music industry operates (whether tales of corruption, the commercial rip-off or models of melodies passing along bureaucratic assembly lines), I do believe that it is possible, from research and study, to gain a useful insight into the complexity of people, organizations, companies and alliances and the historically changing motives, influences and agendas which shape the production of popular music. Throughout this book I will explain, in a more measured and comprehensive way, some of the corporate context that surrounds the tiny human dramas I have already alluded to, and highlight some of the reasons why record companies are such a characteristic mix of reckless speculation ('sign this band!') and nervous caution ('what shall we do with them?'). I will be using a number of sociological ideas to evoke a series of dynamics, social relationships and discursive practices which are characteristic features of music production. Bearing in mind the comments above, I have no intention of presenting the material in this book as a neat 'model', nor do I wish to reduce the diverse range of experiences I have drawn on to a closed 'system' of production. There will be a number of moments when I shall explicitly attempt to connect with feelings of confusion or incomprehension – for example, when discussing the consequences of corporate strategies for the problems faced by senior executives (in Chapter 2) and when highlighting the different ways in which music does, and does not, move across international borders (in Chapter 7).

While this book is informed, if only in an oblique way, by a series of personal experiences, it also draws from numerous sources and the writings of other authors which fall sometimes on one side, sometimes on the other, of a related division which grows out of the dichotomy dividing the experiential/immediate from the analytic/reflexive. Usually, this pits (often antagonistically) academic writing against varieties of journalism and fanzine material. In a similar way, writings about industry and management often diverge between the material found in weekly magazines, newspapers and popular paperbacks (with their immediate analysis, rallying calls and pronouncements about what big business might or should not be doing), and the more measured writing of academics who may have developed more 'critical' studies of the activities of those within industry and commerce.

For me, it has been impossible to deal with this subject (the production of music and the recording industry) without drawing upon and acknowledging these different sources and their various insights, claims and limitations. I don't pretend to have woven all of the material I have put together from these sources into an entirely academic, analytical, totally coherent and seamless pattern. It may be that, from a certain academic perspective, some parts of the book will be thought to be too descriptive and journalistic; certainly much of it will be considered too academic from the vantage point of many fans and journalists. These differing perspectives are not always discrete, and a number of authors have successfully written across these types of divisions. Such approaches also often converge, diverge, interact and inform one another. For example, many people within the music industry hold coherent 'theories' about what they are doing and why the music industry and people within it behave the way that they do. Theories of 'subcultures', of 'indies versus majors' and of record companies 'throwing mud against the wall' can be found in the writings of academics and in the everyday beliefs of those trying to make sense of what they are doing within the music business. Indeed, I have drawn on these ideas when using material derived from personal interviews with music industry personnel. This leads me to another issue and a further series of dilemmas and questions that I think it useful to raise here in these introductory words.

Over the years I have often been asked a very similar question about my research, a question that goes something like this: 'How do you know that people in the music industry are telling you the truth and that they are not simply lying or giving you a standard public relations line?' This common type of question has in fact been asked many times, of researchers and interviewers in general. It has been asked of me with the extra suspicion that perhaps people within the media, music and entertainment industry are particularly inclined to deception and lying.

A simple and practical response to this type of question is to argue that a researcher can draw on a repertoire of techniques which can be found explained in many interviewing textbooks: ask the same question in a different manner; be attentive to body language and signs of evasiveness; ask the same question of different people; check with other sources – try and validate what is being said by 'triangulation', that is by being aware of different perspectives on the same situation and by seeking other sources of knowledge about the topic. This is relatively straightforward and needs little elaboration here. However, further issues are raised by questions about any 'truth' that might be gained from interviewing. For posing this type of question about interviewing presupposes that there is some underlying truth about the world, and that we can gain access to this by asking people the right sort of questions in such a way so as to reveal this truth. If this truth does exist, there is an additional assumption that the person we might be interviewing will be aware of and have knowledge of this truth (hence, a further supposition is made: he or she can conceal it from us). The issues here concern philosophical problems of the nature of 'truth'; the relationship between thoughts, verbal utterances and the world they seek to explain; and the debates about whether the interviewer–interviewee relationship provides a means of *producing* information about the world or whether it can be used to *reveal* or *discover* already existing truths. To fully deal with these issues would lead me way beyond the scope of this introduction, but I wish to say something about this issue here and to clarify how I have approached interviewing and the material derived from interviews.

First, I consider interviewing to be about far more than the collection of 'data'. It is not, as far as I am concerned, about producing a series of standardized questions (in a survey type format) and asking these of a 'sample' of people. Interviews are very specific social encounters between individuals which occur at particular times and places. The relationship which is established and which develops (or does not develop) during the encounter will decisively influence any material derived from an interview. Interviews are not about 'extracting' information or truths that are waiting to be revealed. Instead, an interview is an active social encounter, through which knowledge of the world is produced via a process of exchange. This involves communication, interpretation, understanding and, occasionally perhaps, misunderstanding.

As a major part of my research for this book, I have used interviewing in an attempt to understand how individuals within the music industry perceive and imagine the world in which they are working. I have not taken this as a reality that is simply constructed (a 'reality' brought into being during an interview), any more than I have adopted a naive realist approach and presumed that what is said during an interview can be understood as a 'reflection' of reality. These meanings I have then sought, as much as possible, to place within their organizational, historical, social and geographical contexts. I have tried to locate the voices I have used in this book in such a way that the context of the interview is apparent and in order that the conditions within which such an understanding of reality is produced become clear. In this way, I do not intend that the voices simply 'speak for themselves' or provide an index of particular truths and, unlike some academic researchers, I am not seeking to develop so-called 'objective' concepts which are independent of the world views of the people I have placed within my study. For me, this can too easily result in rhetorical or cynical attempts to undermine or devalue the views of the people who have been spoken to and 'studied' (i.e. the researcher translates someone's words into a more authoritative discourse under the rhetorical umbrella of 'critical' or 'scientific' thought).

Since at least the nineteenth century, numerous sociologists and philosophers have stressed that, in producing intellectual accounts of the world, we do not simply study and observe human action and behaviour in a way comparable to the 'natural' or 'physical' sciences (focusing on the growth of plants, the movement of atoms or forces influencing the flight of a jet aircraft). Instead, we study social life in which people already have their own ideas, concepts and theories about the world. Hence, the production of theories and concepts through social scientific or humanistic research inevitably involves a process of mediation or of translation. We draw from existing frames of meaning and interpretations circulating in the world in order to produce our social theories. We seek to understand, interpret, theorize and develop concepts about a world that is already understood, interpreted and theorized through various existing concepts. Even if some of these ideas may strike us as rather basic or as a form of everyday common sense, we cannot go through them and find some fundamental truth on the other side.

Yet, if the researcher draws upon interpretations and meanings that are already in the world, so the people who we might be studying are drawing upon the ideas and interpretations developed and circulated by social scientists. There is an interaction and lack of separation. We cannot bracket, or separate off, social scientific interpretation from the meanings that people give to the situations within which they live. This idea, discussed as the double hermeneutic in the work of Anthony Giddens and traceable back to the writings of Wilhelm Dilthey in the nineteenth century, is very much an attempt to stress the connections between the vernacular, everyday way in which people interpret and understand their lives and the more technical and formal interpretations and theories developed by social scientists or philosophers. The point is that the two are not separate. One cannot be detached from the other and elevated to a more authoritative position simply because it has been produced through a scholarly, academic or 'scientific' method.

When conducting my own research, for this and previous books, it has been very apparent to me that people in the music industry draw upon ideas from cultural studies, sociology, musicology, linguistics, semiotics (often mediated through journalism or courses in media and cultural studies) when speaking about artists, recordings, videos and aspects of production and distribution, as much as academic writers draw on the everyday theories that are circulated by staff within the music industry. It is this that makes arguments about corporate strategies, creative activities, independent record labels, subcultures and company cultures, identity, globalization and commodification, more than simply the concern of 'academic' debate. And it is this which, ultimately, leads me to come out against experiential confusion and in favour of some order that can be explained, understood and acted upon. This book has been written with an academic reader in mind, but it is informed by the type of interactions I have been signalling – between scholarly, academic theorizing and more vernacular, everyday 'practical knowledge'. I hope that what I have written will contribute to both sides of this often fraught divide and also to the interpretative links between the two.

In terms of the book's structure, I have arranged the following chapters so as to build up an account of the recording industry and production of popular music based on the way in which specific cultural practices are produced through the interaction between corporate strategies and musical genre formations. The first chapter provides a frame, an outline of the explicit theoretical ideas that have informed my thinking and which are woven throughout the later discussion. Chapter 2 explains the reasons why corporate strategies are introduced and what these strategies involve, and considers some of their main consequences. Chapter 3 focuses critically on how companies which adopt similar strategies also attempt to differentiate themselves according to ideas about company culture and corporate identity. These first three chapters provide a context for the profiles of rap, country and salsa which follow in Chapters 4 to 6, and for Chapter 7, in which I place musical production within a more international setting. My aim in these chapters is to introduce a number of themes and issues through a discussion of different types of music, rather than to engage in a type of 'comparison' of the same aspects (for example, comparing the role of distribution, radio or geographical identities in each case). I wish to highlight the *specific* ways in which musical production is shaped by *particular* genre cultures and to highlight the broader historical and social context within which production takes place. So, for example, when thinking about the production of rap, salsa and country, we could superficially note that all are manufactured and distributed by recorded music companies which carry the same corporate logos, use the same office arrangements, accord their staff similar basic occupational titles and promote through the same media formats. However, the way in which these genres have come to be produced and circulated is very different – too often the study of pop or rock has been generalized, as if indicative of all industrialized musical production in general. The formal organizational similarities often conceal important cultural differences. Musical sounds and meanings are not only dependent upon the way an industry is producing culture, but are also shaped by the way in which culture is producing an industry. This thematic phrase leads me directly to my first chapter and to a more detailed discussion of the conceptual ideas which frame the rest of the book.

Chapter 1

Culture, industry, genre: conditions of musical creativity

A central theme of this book is the idea that *an industry produces culture* and *culture produces an industry*. This motif frames my account of the music business and production of different genres, and is used to propose a particular way of thinking about those activities and spheres of life which are often artificially separated according to the categories of 'economics' and 'culture'. In this opening chapter I wish to explain in more detail why I am adopting this approach, what I mean by using these terms and to acknowledge my debts to other writers. In doing this I will introduce some of the main themes which will feature throughout this book and which I shall illustrate in more detail in later chapters. In providing a brief and schematic outline of the theoretical ideas that have guided my thinking and that are embedded in the remainder of this book, I shall be untangling some intellectual threads that in practice are often tangled – whether during everyday arguments about music at a concert, or in the theoretical reflections and empirical studies of various writers. Indeed, this will be a temporary explanatory strategy, as I shall weave them back together in later chapters of this book.

FROM THE PRODUCTION OF CULTURE TO THE CULTURE OF PRODUCTION

By using the term *industry produces culture* I am referring to how entertainment corporations set up structures of organization and institute distinct working practices to produce identifiable products, commodities and 'intellectual properties'. This approach draws ideas from political economy and organization studies and uses these to interrogate the various corporate strategies and business practices of music and media companies. Writers who have followed this broad line of reasoning have tended to narrate a tale of the 'production of culture' during which the practices, form and content of popular music (and other cultural forms) are influenced in various ways by a range of organizational constraints and commercial criteria.

political economy perspectives
write out agency
of musicians & consumers
Culture, industry, genre   15

Many studies of cultural production in general and the music business in particular are informed by the assumptions of political economy, or what is sometimes prefixed 'critical' political economy, a label used by writers who wish to stress that they are concerned not simply with technical problems or issues of business administration but also with normative judgements concerning 'justice, equality and public good' (Golding and Murdock, 1996).[1] A central issue for those engaged in this tradition of enquiry can be summed up in the following question: How do owners exercise and maintain control within corporations and what are the consequences of this for workers and public life in general? With regard to the music business, this raises questions about the impact of patterns of capitalist ownership on the creative work of artists and the options available to consumers.

Political economy has provided many insights into the various ways that corporate ownership impinges upon cultural practices, highlighting how production occurs within a series of unequal power relations, how commercial pressures can limit the circulation of unorthodox or oppositional ideas and how the control of production by a few corporations can contribute to broader social divisions and inequalities of information, not only within nations but across the world.[2] That the major entertainment–arts corporations are continually seeking to control and thus maximize their profits from cultural production is a point that has been repeatedly emphasized by political economists. One of the key ways that modern corporations have attempted to maintain control is through the adoption of various corporate strategies (Fligstein, 1990) and I shall focus on these and their consequences in Chapter 2.

Despite its insights, however, the conclusions reached from the perspective of political economy are often predictable, portraying corporate ownership leading to rigid forms of social control and having a detrimental impact upon the creative activities of musicians, the workers employed within the corporations and the audiences for recordings. According to Steve Chapple and Reebee Garofalo (1977) in a comprehensive historical account of the recording industry in the United States, the commodification of music and the control of its production by a few major corporations also has a detrimental impact on the sounds we get to hear, leading to the erosion of oppositional or 'anti-materialist' performances as musicians and music business personnel are co-opted into an entertainment business which is 'firmly part of the American corporate structure' (*ibid.*, p. 300). Similar conclusions have been reached by other writers who have followed political economy in seeking to understand the music industries.[3]

The pessimistic conclusions reached by much political economy leave us with an image of powerful owners exercising an almost omnipotent control over the practices of musicians and choices of consumers. This immediately rubs up against the moving and enjoyable experiences that many of us gain through the products that have come to us from the music industry. I've always found political economy to be attractive when thinking about my own angst-ridden moments while a member of bands signed to record labels, but less convincing when thinking about the composition and performance of songs and the many activities that are involved in musical consumption.

One of the problems here is what Peter Golding and Graham Murdock (1996) have referred to as 'structuralism'. The term 'structure' is used in everyday discussions and in the disciplines of social science as a metaphor to explain how specific social relationships and activities seem to acquire a solid characteristic – structures of society, power structures, corporate structures within the music business, for example. This gives the impression of imposing, constraining, building-like edifices that are static, permanent and unchanging – easy to assume if you visit some of the corporate blocks in Manhattan. Yet Golding and Murdock remind us that such 'structures' are produced through everyday human activities which are dynamic, change over time and contribute to the maintenance of such 'structures'. These human activities involve musicians as much as audiences and staff working within a corporation and for its various subcontracted labels, affiliates and companies.

A related problem, again identified by Golding and Murdock, is that of 'instrumentalism': the observation that capitalist corporations have specific interests (accumulation of capital, pursuit of profits, particular way of organizing production) does not inevitably mean that the work of musicians and workers within the media industry in general can simply be reduced to and explained according to one instrumental logic. As Garofalo (1986) later acknowledged when reassessing the critique of the music industry that he had written with Chapple, 'there is no point-to-point correlation between controlling the marketplace economically and controlling the form, content and meaning of music' (p. 83). The industry cannot simply set up structures of control and operate these in such an instrumental manner. Those who focus on ownership and control through the prism of political economy often forget the less orderly organizational life within the companies; the human beings who inhabit the corporate structures. An instrumentalist approach neglects the many human mediations which come in between the corporate structures and the practices and sounds of musicians, most notably the work of the intermediaries of the music and media industries.

For many years the activities of these workers within music business organizations, and of those engaged in commercial cultural production more generally, were explained through analogies with an 'assembly line' or 'production line'. The production of hit songs, along with Hollywood movies and novels, was observed to resemble industrial manufacturing.

Critical observers conjured up an image of bureaucratic 'song factories' engaged in the routine bolting together of standardized and interchangeable melodies, lyrics and rhythms, or proposed an analytic model of anonymous administrators mechanically shifting products sequentially from artists to the public.[4]

Such mechanistic models have often been uncritically incorporated into claims that the music business was, like other industries, organized in 'Fordist' terms, utilizing mass production techniques similar to those developed by Henry Ford and selling its wares to an undifferentiated mass market (Lash and Urry, 1994). This argument may conveniently fit with a general theory about the universal emergence of a type of flexible 'post-Fordism', but it ignores the historical specificities of how the recorded music industry has developed. Since its emergence at the end of the nineteenth century, the recorded music business (and indeed the sheet-music publishing industry from which many working practices were drawn) has been organized according to small-scale productions and selling to changing niche markets alongside the creation of big hits and blockbusters (most of the recordings issued throughout the twentieth century were never simply marketed to or purchased by a 'mass' audience). In addition, since its earliest days the recording industry has employed various legal and illegal, small-scale and team-based, marketing and promotional activities as a way of approaching consumers – practices which might well be labelled 'flexible'.[5] The point, therefore, is not that the music industry has undergone a profound change – from the assembly line to a more chaotic 'flexible disintegration' (Lash and Urry, 1994). It is that the recording industry has been misleadingly characterized as mechanical and factory-like in the first place.

Long before debates about 'post-Fordism', Richard Peterson (1976) had sought to challenge superficial parallels with bureaucratic manufacturing industries, calling for a 'production of culture perspective' which he also advocated in opposition to the idea that cultural artefacts are simply the work of individual artists (from whom they are then filtered to the public). Drawing on Howard Becker's (1974, 1976) ideas about the collaborative 'art worlds' within which culture is created, Peterson (1976) wished to stress how culture is 'fabricated' by a range of occupational groups and within specific social milieus. This he illustrated with a series of increasingly detailed studies of the 'organizational structures' and 'production systems' within which country music has been manufactured, culminating in his historical study of the 'institutionalization' of country music as a process involving a complex of people in an ironically knowing task of 'fabricating authenticity' (Peterson, 1997).

Peterson's 'production of culture' perspective is a deliberate challenge to those writers who attempt to understand creative work according to what he calls the 'rare genius of a few select people'. Instead, he stresses 'the structural arrangements within which innovators work' (Peterson, 1997, p. 10). Rather than accept the partial perspective provided by individual biographies, Peterson argues that we should pay attention to the specific conditions which have shaped the way that talent has been able to emerge and be recognized in the first place. In his own writings Peterson has shown how particular types of singers were privileged as 'country' (white performers adopting specific rustic styles) and how a range of artists, managers, broadcasters, producers, musicians, songwriters and publishers played a part in systematically selecting and shaping what came to be known as 'authentic' country music. I follow Peterson's emphasis on understanding the conditions within which great individuals will be able to realize their talent, and will explicitly follow up some of his work on country music in Chapter 6.

While Peterson was writing in the United States, Antoine Hennion (1982, 1983, 1989), was researching musical production in France and reaching similar conclusions about 'collective creation', adding that music industry personnel act as mediators, continually connecting artists and audiences. Hennion observed that music business staff work as 'intermediaries', not only during the most obvious marketing and promotion activities, but also when 'introducing' the idea of an imagined audience into the writing, producing and recording of songs in the studio. Stressing how this involves a large degree of human empathy and intuition rather than organizational formulae, assembly lines and corporate structures, Hennion argued that record business staff do not 'manipulate the public so much as feel its pulse' (1983, p. 191).

The work of mediators has also been pursued by Pierre Bourdieu, who has adopted the concept of the 'cultural intermediary' to refer to those occupations engaged in 'presentation and representation…providing symbolic goods and services' (1986, p. 359). Like Hennion, Bourdieu has stressed how these workers occupy a position *between* producer and consumer, or artist and audience. Unlike Hennion, however, Bourdieu has stressed the importance of various social divisions according to shared lifestyles, class backgrounds and ways of living (or habitus) rather than the intuitive feeling of audience pulses. Bourdieu has argued that the cultural intermediaries who work in artistic production do not gain their positions as a result of formal qualifications, nor are they promoted through a bureaucratic occupational meritocracy. Instead, admission and advancement is acquired by exerting influence within class-divided networks of connections gained through shared life experiences formed among members of distinct social groups.

Bourdieu (1993, 1996) has also highlighted how artistic work is realized across a broad series of intersecting social 'fields' and not simply within an organization. He has emphasized the broader social, economic and political contexts within which aesthetic judgements are made, cultural hierarchies established and within which artists have to struggle for position. Such an idea can clearly be extended to consider the broader contexts within which musicians have to struggle to be recognized and rewarded and how this occurs across the social activities which are conventionally designated as 'production' and 'consumption'. Despite such insights, however, Bourdieu neglects to consider how such struggles are part of the formal working world of cultural organizations and commercial corporations, and how members of organizations operate across and contribute to the formation of various 'fields' as part of their daily routine.[6]

In this book I shall also be thinking about the mediations and connections between production and consumption and considering how a broader series of social divisions and ways of living intersect with the corporate organization. Rather than intuitive understanding or a sense of affiliation through shared habitus, I will be highlighting the more formal ways in which knowledge about consumers is collected, produced and circulated and how this informs strategic decision-making and repertoire policies. One of the issues I wish to stress in later chapters is how staff within the music industry seek to understand the world of musical production and consumption by constructing knowledge about it (through various forms of research and information-gathering), and then by deploying this knowledge as a 'reality' that guides the activities of corporate personnel. In economic terms this refers to the production, circulation and use of various forms of market data or 'consumer intelligence'. However, there is an additional 'anthropological' aspect to the way in which knowledge is produced within the music industry. By this I mean the construction of a type of knowledge through which production is understood by those involved in it via a series of apparently intuitive, obvious and common-sense categories which do not so much involve an understanding of 'reality' as a construction and intervention into reality (most notably through ideas about distinct 'markets' – r 'n' b market, country market, Latin market). The way this comes about and its consequences will be discussed throughout this book, and lead me to the second phrase of my central theme, the way the 'industry' intersects with the broader 'culture' within which the corporate office is located.

To pursue this issue I have adopted the term *culture produces an industry* to stress that production does not take place simply 'within' a corporate environment structured according to the requirements of capitalist production or organizational formulae, but in relation to broader culture formations and practices that are within neither the control nor the understanding of the company. This idea acknowledges the critique of production put by those who argue that the industry and media cannot simply determine the meaning of musical products, and assumes that these may be used and appropriated in various ways by musicians and groups of consumers.[7] More specifically, in adopting this perspective I am drawing insights from cultural studies, and in particular from the trajectory of thinking initiated by Raymond Williams' (1961, 1965) conception of culture as a 'whole way of life' and the writings of Stuart Hall (1997; Morley and Chen, 1996) in which he has placed an emphasis on culture as the practices through which people create meaningful worlds in which to live.

The implications of drawing on this type of approach are twofold, and also follow from Bourdieu's approach to cultural production. First, the activities of those within record companies should be thought of as part of a 'whole way of life'; one that is not confined to the formal occupational tasks within a corporate world, but stretched across a range of activities that blur such conventional distinctions as public/private, professional judgement/personal preference and work/leisure time. Second, it is misleading to view practices within music companies as primarily economic or governed by an organizational logic or structure. Instead, work and the activities involved in producing popular music should be thought of as meaningful practices which are interpreted and understood in different ways (often within the same office) and given various meanings in specific social situations. This is one of the insights provided by some of the writings within the huge body of work on the culture of organizations, an integral part of 'production', but often neglected by political economists and those studying the formal aspects of occupational activities.[8] As George E. Marcus and Michael Fischer have also pointed out; 'not only is the cultural construction of meaning and symbols inherently a matter of political and economic interests, but the reverse also holds – the concerns of political economy are inherently about conflicts over meanings and symbols' (1986, p. 85).

Hence, my point is that any attempt to study the 'production of culture' needs to do more than understand culture as a 'product' that is created through technical and routine processes and institutionalized practices. We need to do more than simply read off or assume the characteristics of sounds and images from patterns of ownership or the way commodity production is organized. We need to understand the meanings that are given to both the 'product' and the practices through which the product is made. Culture, thought of more broadly as a way of life and as the actions through which people create meaningful worlds in which to live, needs to be understood as the constitutive context within and out of which the sounds, words and images of popular music are made and given meaning. Hence, while seeking to understand corporate attempts to manage and manipulate the working life of a music company and its artists, I also wish to incorporate thinking about the broader cultural patterns within which a company is situated. This might include, for example, the experiences of class, ethnicity, gender and geographical location and borders that have an

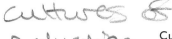

impact on how music is made by recording companies. This issue will be pursued further in Chapter 3 when I consider the culture of organizations, and it will thread throughout the book as I consider the broader ways in which the cultural worlds of rap, country and salsa intersect with and contribute to the production of a particular type of music business.

In pursuing this theme through the idea of the 'culture of production' I also wish to build on my previous work on the music industry in Britain (Negus, 1992). In focusing on the acquisition, development and promotion of artists I highlighted how the 'intuitive' assumptions that staff make when acquiring the most suitable new artists and pieces of music are based on beliefs informed by a series of gender, class and racialized divisions. These not only influence aesthetic judgements and commercial decisions, but in turn also play a significant part in shaping the 'cultural world' of record company departments.[9] Hence, I am concerned with how actions at work are interpreted in quite distinct ways, and how specific meanings guide people's understanding of their day-to-day working life. Together with Paul du Gay (ed.) (1997) I have adopted the concept of 'cultures of production' to refer to how processes and practices within production are simultaneously cultural phenomena understood through distinct meaningful practices and integrally connected to broader habits and actions occurring outside the specific place of work. This approach, signalled through the twisting of a phrase (production of culture to culture of production), not only has implications for how we might think about the relationship *between* culture and industry; it also raises questions about the idea of *a* culture industry.

THE CULTURE/INDUSTRY PROBLEM

The idea of a 'culture industry' was first used by Theodor Adorno and Max Horkheimer (1979) in work first published in German during the 1940s, although their writings were not widely read in translation until the 1960s. Drawing on contemporary approaches to political economy and business organizations, and writing explicitly against those who believed that the arts were independent of industry and commerce, Adorno and Horkheimer (see also Adorno, 1991) adopted the term 'culture industry' to argue that cultural items were being produced in a way that had become analogous to how other industries were involved in manufacturing vast quantities of consumer goods. Employing the familiar metaphor of the 'assembly line' they argued that all products were being produced with the aim of profit-making uppermost and according to the same rationalized organizational procedures. This, they concluded, resulted in a standardized 'mass culture' lacking individuality and originality.[10]

The idea of a culture industry implied two distinct but interrelated processes. First, it suggested the application of industrial manufacturing processes to a previously independent realm of cultural activity which was assumed to have been separate from business and commercial interests. Second, it proposed that the form and content of all cultural products had become basically similar, standardized by a unified industry. As Bernard Miège (1989) has argued, despite its insights and influence, one of the problems with this theory is the assumption that all 'culture' is produced in a similar way within a unified field and as a result of a single process. The production of music, radio programmes, novels, painting, films, theatre and television is assumed to manifest the same basic features and processes. In addition, there is no acknowledgement of the residual 'non-capitalist' orientation of some artisanal work or state-supported creative practices which are not guided by a strictly commercial logic.

Highlighting various differences of technological mediation, capital concentration and labour organization across a range of cultural productions, Miège, among others (see for example, UNESCO, 1982) proposed a plural notion of cultural industries, and suggested that we cannot simply generalize from one to another. This is an important point and I agree with the suggestion that we cannot transpose our theories from one type of 'cultural production' to another without sustained and detailed comparative research which is reflexively aware of whether particular creative practices, geographical locations and historical actions can be reasonably compared. We cannot assume, as Adorno and Horkheimer did and their followers have, that there are simple correspondences between media or 'cultural industries' such as film, television, recorded music or book publishing. As Miège (1989) has pointed out, there are many differences between and within industries and these can vary according to aesthetic form, content, working practices, means of financing and modes of reception and consumption.

To point to one example, an obvious difference between film and music production is the cost and human investment involved in making the product, and its manner of circulation and reception. While recording technologies, electronic instruments and samplers have increasingly reduced the cost of creating music, film production costs have escalated as ever more realistic and fantastic images have come to be aimed for and expected. While portable CD players, Walkmans and car stereos have made recorded music increasingly mobile, the products of the film industry must still be watched in the cinema or at home on a video machine. To ignore such differences and claim that music, film and book production is similarly standardized, dependent upon genre formulas, mass marketed and niche marketed, or involves a unified group of cultural gatekeepers, is to gloss over a series of significant differences of form, content, production, consumption and social mediation.

If I am wary about generalizing from the music industry to other cultural industries, it is also because I wish to raise an additional question about the very concept of the 'culture industries'. For it is not simply that the culture industries are plural (from industry to industries), it is that *all industries are cultural*. As anthropological approaches to organizations have continually highlighted, all industries are constituted within a specific cultural context which shapes the way that people think, feel and act in organizations.[11] And all are producing products or services which carry cultural meanings, and which do not speak for themselves as products but which continually require interpretation. This is why companies spend vast sums of money using advertising to encourage us not only to buy, but also to interpret, understand and grasp the meaning of products in a certain way (whether a toothbrush, pension plan, training shoe, mobile phone, food mixer, hamburger or breakfast cereal).[12]

If all industries are constituted within specific cultural contexts, and if all work activities are understood through particular beliefs and ideas, and if all products are producing cultural meanings as they circulate through public life, then it seems misleading to limit or attempt to draw a boundary around the 'culture industries' as a media–arts entity artificially separated from some, usually unstated, non-culture industries (those that can only be deduced from the presence and absence of the particular 'culture industries' which are cited when this term is used). There may be more interesting comparisons to be made by adopting a broader and less exclusive approach to the industries of culture. Perhaps it is more useful to compare institutionalized music-making (recreating the same recorded, notated or remembered sounds on different occasions and with degrees of improvisation) to commodified cooking (making the same meal, from the same menu, again with certain elements of improvisation), rather than to compare musical practice to the production of a paperback book. Certainly, I would like to open a door to this possibility and see where such a path might lead.

It is in terms of these ideas and issues that this book may have a relevance for wider discussions of the culture–industry issue. The chapters which follow are specific to the recording industry, but I would like to hope that they may be of broader relevance, not through the way that the production of music can be generalized or contrasted with film or book publishing, but through the way it might be relevant for considering the broader cultures of production through which other industries are organized and constituted, whether those industries are producing clothing, cigarettes, farm implements, restaurant food, religious artefacts or condoms. I now want to conclude this chapter by connecting these problems of cultural production to the other motifs that thread throughout the following chapters, those of genre and creativity.

CREATIVITY, GENRE AND MUSICAL PRODUCTION

As a number of writers have observed (Garnham, 1990; Frith, 1996), one of the weaknesses of industry-oriented approaches to cultural activity is that the form, content and meaning of texts are often neglected or assumed from patterns of ownership or structures of organization. One of my aims in what follows is to address this problem in broad terms by considering how the industry begins shaping the conditions within which particular genre practices and creative techniques come to be adopted. This is intended as a small step towards integrating, or at least connecting, the texts (sounds, words, images) more directly to production contexts. My concern is not with the detailed ways in which music corporations might directly shape the codes and conventions of particular styles of music (although this is clearly important). My aim, at this stage, is more general. I wish to outline how corporations shape the conditions within which particular practices can be realized and contested *as* 'creative' while also containing genre categories that might otherwise be far more unstable and dynamic.

In pursuing ideas about 'creativity' I also wish to move away from an argument, appearing in many discussions of popular music, whereby cultural production is characterized in terms of a conflict between commerce (industry) and creativity (the artists). This is a distinction that also informs the claim that subcultures and active audiences (creative) can appropriate and hence transform the products that are disseminated by the industry (again, commerce). In writing elsewhere (Negus, 1995) I have reviewed a range of claims about this issue, suggesting that creativity is often treated in a vague and mystical manner, with many writers assuming that we all know and recognize 'creativity' when we meet it.[13]

Drawing on Raymond Williams' (1983) brief discussion of the etymology of the term 'creative' and reflecting upon academic and everyday uses of this term, I want to think about this further by identifying two broad approaches to what creativity is and what it might involve. The first is an exclusivist approach, the second inclusivist. According to the exclusivist approach (from the original reference to divine creation), creativity is associated with human capacity for 'originality' and 'innovation' (Williams, 1983). Hence, it is often argued that record companies cannot find it: creativity is outside the corporate machine and dependent upon inspired musicians, writers, entrepreneurs, subcultures and small record labels. In contrast, the inclusivist approach can be found in numerous places, used to refer to conventional and routine activities such as 'creative' writing or 'creative' accounting. Here, as Williams (1983) notes, 'creative' has become something of a 'cant word' used to label all manner of audio-visual practices, from hairdressing to the production of advertising slogans and screenwriting. The first meaning retains residues of an elitist approach to culture and social life, whereby certain gifted or mystically inspired individuals have creative abilities. The other imbues the most banal of habitual working practices with an aura of artistic inspiration and humanistic worth. Both can be detected in the routine celebrations of musical performers and fans.

Any attempt to approach the issue of creativity from a sociological perspective is not only hampered by this type of everyday usage. We also have to navigate the way in which research into this area has been unduly colonized by behaviourist and cognitive psychologists searching for character traits, individual dispositions or chemical changes in the brain as a means of explaining creative behaviour.[14] Closely related are educational researchers wishing to find ways of encouraging creativity among children, and business consultants seeking to understand how to manage or promote creative thinking at work.[15] Much of the work from these perspectives takes the actual creative process for granted and has little to say about the historically formed social conditions within which creativity might or might not be realized and recognized in the first place.

I want to suggest one way out from the dichotomy of populism/elitism and a route away from individual psychological explanations by following those writers who have argued that creative practices should be understood through the notion of genre. I then wish to rethink genre in terms of a broader series of social divisions and to attempt to relate these to the culture–industry dynamics of musical production. I will outline these ideas schematically here and then develop them through detailed illustrative examples in the rest of this book.

It can be reasonably argued that the vast majority of musical production at any one time involves musicians working within relatively stable 'genre worlds' (Frith, 1996) within which ongoing creative practice is not so much about sudden bursts of innovation but the continual production of familiarity. This point has been well made by Franco Fabbri (1982, 1985, 1989) in insightful but overtly deterministic work in which he has sought to identify and delineate the semiotic rules, behavioural rules, economic rules and social rules which produce the codes and conventions that guide the activity of musicians and their audiences. Such rules may guide the notes a guitarist may select to play (whether playing jazz, rock or folk, for example), the way a star may conduct themselves in public or during an interview (aloof rock detachment or ingratiating country familiarity), the way in which audiences behave (dancing in couples, pogoing individually or sitting politely applauding) and how journalists may aesthetically evaluate a musical performance (poor musicianship or a new noise aesthetic).

Fabbri's work is important for raising questions about the creative activities of unique artists – why does inspiration conveniently fit the codes and conventions of particular musical genres? Fabbri's work also raises questions about the responses and expectations of audiences and poses a challenge to the romantic voluntarism and implied spontaneity of much active audience theory. For all its insights, however, his approach implies a very restricted, rule-bound and regulated process. Although Fabbri acknowledges that changes can occur, the picture he presents is rather static: the constraints rather than the possibilities are emphasized, and this seems to rub up against our experiences as consumers and musicians. For those actively involved in day-to-day musical activity, genres are often experienced as dynamic and changing rather than rule-bound and static. Yes, we know the genre rules – but there always seems to be something more. This point became even more apparent to me during the research for this book. For example, when I began talking to people about rap I was told that rap was 'dead', 'going nowhere' and 'repeating itself'. Indeed, at about the same time an article by respected commentator Greg Tate (1996) appeared, proclaiming that rap was indeed 'dead'. Yet I also spoke to fans and record company staff whose response to such claims was that these were the opinions of people who were 'paying too much attention to MTV and the Top 40' and who were not looking and listening where things were 'happening'.[16] Very similar parallels could be found, of course, in comments that have been made about the death of country and salsa – and indeed, about the death of nearly every genre you might be able to think of, whether rock, soul, jazz and rhythm and blues or death metal, dengue bop and techno.

These disputes raise a number of questions about how genre sounds are heard and interpreted and about the relationship of genre codes to newness. Should judgements about the characteristics of a genre be made according to those sounds heard coming from the music industry and media, or do we need to listen more carefully in the (other) right places? While musical newness is usually identified when an overt border crossing, dissolving or synthesis leads to the transformation of genre boundaries into new styles (which soon establish their own rules), an equally interesting issue concerns the more common, routine and gradually changing life of existing genres, i.e. the fact that rap (or salsa or rock) is heard as dynamic, changing and continually transforming itself despite laments of its death. It seems that what from one perspective are perceived as codes, rules and conventions are from another point of view heard as dynamic and changing musical characteristics.

Unlike the stress on genre rules, there is perhaps no developed theoretical approach to genre as transformative.[17] Although there is a range of studies focusing on the more dramatic moments of transformation and synthesis (the appearance of rock 'n' roll, in particular) and claims about the role of independent labels and subcultures in this process, there is little thinking available about the more mundane ongoing life of genres. However, some steps in this direction can be taken by following the obser-

[handwritten annotations: "Frith + Fabbri : rules → each has other as blindspot / Quintero : agency"]

vations of Angel Quintero Rivera in his work on salsa. Quintero has used a particular idea of 'practice' to oppose the notion that salsa can simply be understood formally according to a series of codes, conventions or rules.[18] Quintero (1998) writes of salsa as a 'manner of making music' that involves the 'free combination of rhythms, forms and traditional Afro-Caribbean genres'. It is this free combination which enables salsa to continually provide possibilities as a 'dynamic open form of expression' and which enables it to 'avoid and evade its possible fossilization into formulas'.[19]

Adopting this approach, Quintero is able to show how salsa has emerged historically from a number of geographic sources and how salsa practices have been both incorporated into other styles and drawn from other genres – whether this has involved the practices of bomba, rock or hip hop moving 'into' salsa, or salsa practices moving into classical, disco or rap. In each case salsa's fluidity enables the creation of a briefly realized synthesis. In this way, Quintero portrays salsa as a fluid, flexible and changing creative practice and provides one way of considering how this might easily be incorporated to and draw from other genre practices – a contrast from viewing musical creativity according to rule-bound processes, codes and conventions. Quintero's work is important for high-lighting the active reproduction and ongoing life of genres, the pleasures of familiarity and their importance for cultural identities, and the continual possibility for social and aesthetic transformation. Even if much musical activity involves musicians in putting together various audio and visual components in a recognizably familiar but only slightly different way, it always provides the possibility for newness and the crossing of bridges into other genre worlds.[20]

However, if Frith and Fabbri dwell on the codes, rules and constraints, Quintero privileges voluntary creative practice in a way that neglects how salsa, and any other genre for that matter, can easily be reduced to a few routinely reproduced musical phrases, rhythmic patterns, bodily gestures and audience responses, whether on recordings or as performed locally at *fiestas patronales* or in cabarets throughout the world. In short, the 'manner of making music' can easily be reduced to a series of mannerisms. The desire for free combination and a fluid crossing of boundaries confronts the very way in which such genre practices *are* constrained and how 'musicians, producers, and consumers are already ensnared in a web of genre expectation' (Frith, 1996, p. 94).

This web is most obviously woven by the spiders of the music industry; *[handwritten: "ew!"]* any musician will confront these generic expectations as soon as they are subject to the attentions of music business personnel and, certainly, when within sight of a recording contract. As Frith has also astutely observed, genres are used by record companies as a way of integrating a conception of music (what does it sound like?) with a notion of the market (who will buy it?). Musician and audience are considered simultaneously, as a way of 'defining music in its market' and 'the market in its music' (Frith, 1996, p. 76). In this way the desire for transformative creative practice confronts routinization and institutionalization; the potentially dynamic and provisional is made static and permanent. It is one of my assumptions that a focus on the social organization of genres can provide insights into the dynamics of this transformative/routine tension.

Hence, to briefly recap, I am not approaching creative work as inspirational and radically new, nor as something that everybody does in a kind of everyday creative way. Instead, I am trying to think about how ongoing dynamic genre practices continually confront their translation into codified rules, conventions and expectations, not only as melodies, timbres and rhythms but also in terms of audience expectations, market categories and habits of consumption. Here, I wish to clearly situate any possibilities for routinization or transformation within the context of practices of the music industry.

Musical genres are formally codified into specific organizational departments, narrow assumptions about markets, and 'targeted' promotional practices, and this is strategically managed by recorded entertainment companies. In the process, resources are allocated to some types of music and not others; certain types of deals are done with some acts and not others. Greater investment is accorded to certain types of familiarity and newness and not others. It is part of my argument that we cannot fully explore the details of the conventions, codes or rules of genres through textual analysis, nor can we begin to explain how some (and not other) genre transformations might occur without fully understanding how corporate organization actively intervenes in the production, reproduction, circulation and interpretation of genres.

Hence, in pursuing the interplay (or mutual constitution) of industry and culture I am not proposing a simple conflict *between* commerce and creativity. I am also rejecting other dichotomous models of the music industry, whether independents (creative, art, democratic) versus majors (commerce, conservatism, oligarchic); Machiavellian individuals (cynical exploiters) versus struggling musicians (innocent talent); subcultures (innovative, rebellious) versus mainstream (predictable, unchallenging).[21] Instead, I will be highlighting how the recording industry has a direct impact on how creativity can be realized, given meaning and contested at any one time. However, I also wish to take a few further steps and situate music industry practices within a broader context of different genre cultures.

In using the term 'genre culture' I am drawing on Steve Neale's use of genre as a sociological rather than formal concept, 'not...as forms of textual codifications, but as systems of orientations, expectations and conventions that circulate between industry, text and subject' (Neale,

1980, p. 19). One of the most obvious ways that these expectations may circulate is through the institutionalized system of media, particularly radio and video, and the way this contributes to the definition and boundaries of what falls within and without a genre of music. This in turn can shape what is produced and consumed, providing incentives and imposing constraints upon musicians, as well as contributing to the continual arguments about what is and is not a particular type of music (is country radio playing *real* country music or might this be heard elsewhere?).

However, the genre boundaries associated with commercial 'markets', radio or media formats and wider cultural formations do not coincide in any straightforward way. The media or music industry cannot simply 'construct' a market, 'produce' a type of consumer, nor determine an artist's meaning (as implied in some of the more media-centric approaches to musical activity) and try as they might they continually fail in any attempts to do this. The manipulations of marketing and influence of the media have been extensively discussed – and often exaggerated – elsewhere and although I shall refer to these at different points throughout this book I do not wish to overemphasize the role of the media and promotional practices. In contrast I want to place an emphasis upon the wider sociological and cultural context within which sounds, images and words are given meaning. As Frith has perceptively written on this point:

> A new 'genre world'...is first constructed and then articulated through a complex interplay of musicians, listeners, and mediating ideologues, and this process is much more confused than the marketing process that follows, as the wider industry begins to make sense of the new sounds and markets and to exploit both genre worlds and genre discourses in the orderly routines of mass marketing..
>
> (1996, p. 88)

I shall not be discussing *new* genres – this would require the lucky researcher to be in the right time and place to chart their emergence. Instead I will be concentrating on established genres and considering how the music industry orders any potential confusion through techniques of strategic management. I will be highlighting how the music industry shapes the possibilities for creative practice and how this intersects with broader historical, social and cultural processes. In this way I will be thinking about 'genre cultures' as involving far more than aesthetic debates within the 'genre worlds' of musicians, fans and critics. I shall be highlighting how genres operate as social categories; how rap cannot be separated from the politics of blackness, nor salsa from Latinness, nor country from whiteness and the enigma of the 'South'. I will be thinking of genre cultures as arising from the complex intersection and interplay between commercial organizational structures and promotional labels; the activities

of fans, listeners and audiences; networks of musicians; and historical lega-
cies that come to us within broader social formations. In developing these
themes through the substantive discussion in this book, I shall be arguing
that the social tensions and divisions formed in relation to these broader
genre cultures are shaping the music business as much as the music business is shaping the meanings of genres: in short, how an industry is
producing culture and how culture is producing an industry.

IE 'New' Forms of Music (one at the very least new
Interpretations of old 'genre rules') are not created
by some form of strategic management plan by
record companies to exploit the public, but culture in
itself is producing an industry

Chapter 2

Corporate strategy: applying order and enforcing accountability

Corporate strategy aims to control and order the unpredictable social processes and diversity of human behaviours which are condensed into notions of production and consumption and which riddle the music business with uncertainties. These include anxieties about whether existing and new artists will continue to produce and deliver what is anticipated, and questions about whether consumers will purchase their recordings and, if so, for how much longer. At the same time, strategies seek to organize, allocate and account for the equally unpredictable activities of personnel who may spend days within and travelling between different corporate buildings and who conduct their business in a relatively unsupervised manner in studios, theatres, stadiums, clubs, bars and other sites of sound. Hence, strategy provides a way of monitoring and accounting for the activities of producers, artists and recording industry personnel. It also provides a means of rationalizing and ordering the activities of consumers and audiences.

The rationale for introducing corporate strategies in the music industry is no different to the reason corporate strategy has become popular among senior business executives more generally: strategic calculation provides a means (or so it is assumed) of applying order, increasing predictability and enforcing accountability. Strategy is central to the way that modern companies organize their operations, and whether this issue has been discussed by critical political economists (concerned with how capitalist control is exerted, maintained and reproduced) or by management consultants (seeking to advise corporations how they can exercise control more effectively), writers from differing perspectives agree that strategy is one of the key ways that corporations seek to maintain control and deal with the uncertainties generated during processes of production and acts of consumption (Fligstein, 1990). As the 'problem of uncertainty' underlies the formulation and implementation of strategy, I shall start this chapter by considering this issue further before I move on to outline the main corporate strategies adopted by record companies.

THE UNCERTAINTIES AND ANXIETIES OF
COMMERCIAL MUSIC PRODUCTION

The artists signed by record companies and the repertoire prioritized for recording and release are not in any straightforward way a reflection of the talent that is available. It is a selection made according to a whole series of commercial judgements and cultural assumptions. The acquisition of artists, and the concomitant investment required, poses a number of recurring dilemmas and questions: Which artists will be successful and will they sustain their success? Which genres are worth investing in for the long term (or for a short period)? What are the up-coming future musical trends likely to be – and does the company have the skills (artists, staff) and structures (distribution and promotional) to be able to deal with them?

Existing contracted artists generate as many anxieties as potential new acquisitions: Will performers who are signed to the label continue to deliver what is expected? If a declining artist is released from a contract, will they go elsewhere and make a best-seller with another company? Although a company will have a schedule of planned releases, there is no way of knowing if an artist is going to continue producing similar music, lose their touch or simply decide to change direction. The company has a contract for a product, but it is a human product that is often temperamental and unpredictable.

The activities of audiences, understood as 'markets', pose further dilemmas as the industry attempts to grapple with the complexities of consumption. Markets are not simply out there in the world, forming as members of the public gravitate towards certain recordings and not others. Markets have to be carefully constructed and maintained; a process requiring investment in staff and systems for monitoring and researching the purchase and use of recordings. Record companies face considerable uncertainty about the success of the products that they distribute. For many years, despite numerous changes of organization and corporate ownership, the same statistic has circulated within the music industry: a claim that only one in eight of the artists acquired by a record company will sell enough recordings to recoup their initial investment and be considered a financial success. This is an elusive figure, hard to verify and as mythical as it is statistical. Yet it is an indication of how staff within the music industry perceive their daily plight. A desire to reduce this ratio of failure has motivated the continual attempts to restructure companies, the appointment and then dismissal of highly paid senior executives, and the cyclical acquisition and then 'dropping' of artists. This figure is usually cited when staff wish to highlight how their commercial success is dependent upon changing preferences and fashions among audiences and the fact that these are difficult to predict. Although companies continually engage in market research, and seek to persuade and manipulate public behaviour, they find it difficult to predict which new artists are going to succeed and how successful they are likely to be. Attempts are made to factor these dilemmas into contracts, with distinctions made between artists aimed at relatively short-term success and artists that it may be worth sticking with and investing in over a longer period. But the companies continue to get it wrong.

Technology produces another anxiety. The struggles through which new technologies are produced and introduced can have a considerable impact on how contracts are drawn up and how the 'product' of popular music is conceptualized. Artists are now acquired for much more than their ability to perform as musicians, and contracts allow for movements and cross-collatoralization into related media – meaning that recording contracts have been modified to enable companies to claw back money from an artist's earnings through films, books or games to cover any lost investment from musical recordings. Contracts also incorporate assessments of rights income that may be derived from any new sound carriers. One of the most recent anxieties has concerned the spread of cable and digital transmission. Are home computers transforming the way music is purchased, used and received? Are technologies changing performance practices and musical skills, facilitating the development of new types of artists and making some older performers irrelevant (i.e. non-profitable)? At the same time, is owning the distribution conduit and hence investing in these technologies more significant than owning the rights to the products that will pass along it? These questions may be debated at a higher corporate level, but can result in key strategic decisions about resources which can affect the entire company. For example, this can impact upon record company rosters if companies act, as Time-Warner were reported to be doing during the early 1990s, by divesting themselves of repertoire catalogues (dumping artists and songs) and using the money to buy into new distribution networks (the routes along which the artists and songs will travel).

RESPONSES TO UNCERTAINTY: THE CYNICAL AND MYSTICAL

Arguments about how the music business deals with such uncertainties tend to swing between those that emphasize a more cynical corporate response and others that propose more mystical explanations of how staff in the industry cope with these anxieties. These are not simply 'academic' theories, but explanations that are also offered by people working within music and media companies.

There are two common arguments that identify a cynical corporate response. First, there is the suggestion that the only way the industry can cope is to adopt a policy of overproduction, covering as many different genres as possible, and to engage in a strategy that is likened to throwing mud against a wall. Unable to predict what will become successful or where it will come from, record companies buy up as much repertoire and sign as many artists as possible, in as many areas as they can, and throw it all out in the hope that some of it will stick. If it sticks then the companies will pour in further investment; if it falls then they will ignore it.

The second theoretical account of industry cynicism is that which posits the industry continually holding back from involvement and waiting until some inspirational entrepreneur finds something which can then be acquired. Incapable of comprehending where new trends are occurring, cumbersome and unable to manoeuvre quickly enough to attract fresh talent, the major labels wait and then rush after the repertoires of small independent companies who have already 'tested' the commercial potential of their new talent. This is the well-recounted tale of the major companies continually co-opting or swallowing the small 'indie' companies.[1]

There are also two regularly narrated mystical arguments. First is the idea that great music 'will out' or will always 'rise to the surface', and connected to this is the idea that inspirational, idiosyncratic 'music men' (although there are and have been a significant number of 'music women') will locate, support and 'nurture' such talent, despite the odds stacked against them by the obstructive 'suits' and mean-spirited accountants.[2] This is a theory frequently posited in the United States where the charisma and mystical powers of great individuals are perceived not only as a source of new musical changes, but as the driving force that directs the fortunes and failures of large and small companies in the economy at large.[3]

If this belief at least has its source in boardroom anecdote and the myths of rugged individualism, more mystical still is the idea that there is some inexplicable developmental or cyclical logic driving the history of popular music. From this perspective, all a record company needs to do is wait for the next turn of the wheel or spontaneous change of zeitgeist to throw up the new talent and be there to make the most of it. Although such a tendency can be found in some academic writing,[4] it is more usually articulated to justify the inertia and incomprehension of those executives who can only speak of their own and other companies' success according to notions of 'luck', 'good fortune' and 'being in the right place at the right time'.

While these theories may offer a convincing explanation of some specific experiences and events, they are partial perceptions and inadequate for understanding the highly corporate musical entertainment business that enters the twenty-first century. Although the 'mud against the wall' approach has clearly been utilized by various record companies (independent and major alike), it has become increasingly wasteful as the recording and marketing of music has increased, as costs have risen (partly due to video) and as companies are able to engage in more expensive 'targeted' marketing across different media rather than aimless mud-hurling. While independent companies may occasionally and momentarily offer alternative and 'democratic' possibilities (Hesmondhalgh, 1998), the absorption of independent labels has been a feature of the music business throughout the twentieth century and has become increasingly institution-alized through a series of joint ventures, production, licensing, marketing and distribution deals which have led to the blurring of 'indie'/'major' organizational distinctions and belief systems. The great individuals may provide inspiration and a human face, but their death, retirement or dismissal is usually inconsequential in the long term and often results in no noticeable change to the life of individual companies. When Mo Ostin was forced out of Warner Brothers in 1994 it was clearly upsetting for many of his colleagues, but the company continued to enjoy success, and major artists, such as REM and Madonna, did not suddenly leave the label, as had been predicted by some commentators at the time.[5] Great individuals are only one small part of an increasingly complex system which is sustained by the combined actions of many different people and organiza-tions. As for luck, chance and other such happy accidents at work, record companies, like most of us, have to create their own fortunes within specific social, historical and political conditions and within the context of very particular corporate policies, strategies and working practices.

CORPORATE CONNECTIONS: THE MAJOR RECORD LABELS

I have already mentioned the major companies at various points in this book and I shall be referring to them in general and to specific companies in later chapters. At this point, therefore, I think it is useful to provide a brief outline of the key features of the major record label groups which have, since the end of the 1980s, accounted for the production and distri-bution of approximately 80 per cent (or more) of the recorded popular music that has been legally sold throughout the world.[6] Of course, any attempt to profile the major labels like this is dogged by the problem that no sooner has it been completed than a company division may be sold or restructured, or an entire company acquired. Indeed, PolyGram was acquired by Seagram almost immediately after I had completed the first 'final' draft of this book. It is inevitable that by the time you are reading this some of the factual details may need updating. For this reason I wish to preface these profiles by stressing three issues relevant to a broader consideration of strategy and the context within which major and minor music companies are working, over and above the individual details.

The first observation I wish to make about the following profiles is that the music industry has been characterized by a continual series of crises related to broader economic booms and slumps and influenced by various aesthetic and technological changes. As a consequence, parent corporations have continually bought and then sold record labels, restructured the organization within divisions, appointed and then sacked highly paid senior executives and laid off and occasionally redeployed staff (in addition to the continual acquisition and then 'dropping' of artists and the buying and selling of catalogues). The changes detailed below are merely the latest in a long history of organizational disruptions, acquisitions and cuts. This lack of continuity, instability and frequent crisis management creates a particularly volatile working environment and contributes to the mixture of nervous caution and reckless speculation which is such a feature of the music industry.[7]

A second point about the following profiles concerns the relative importance of the music division within the overall corporate group. All music divisions provide differential sources of revenue and profits for corporate head office, owners and shareholders. For example, PolyGram's music label was contributing more to overall corporate profitability at Philips than Sony's music division. It may be assumed, then, that Philips would more closely monitor the day-to-day actions of its management at PolyGram than Sony had been doing with its music division. This assumption seemed to be borne out by the evidence (see below), until Sony's music and film divisions presented the world with such well-publicized examples of bad management that head office in Tokyo intervened and removed senior US executives. This was not only an attempt to halt the loss of revenue but also an effort to save the reputation of the company.[8]

This leads me to my third point, the issue of intervention, the potential of corporate office to interfere in the everyday operations of the music and entertainment company. The everyday practices of music production and promotion are often experienced and frequently explained as involving a large degree of 'autonomy' and 'independence', with divisional executives saying that as long as they hit their goals they are given a 'free rein'. Yet in practice these divisions are continually accountable (just as the music division is accountable within an entertainment group and the individual labels or rock, Latin and country divisions are accountable within the music group). Intervention may involve minor restructuring, may involve the removing of senior executives or it may entail the closing down of offices. Alternatively, intervention could entail the selling of the entire music company, which is why Sony Music was once CBS Records and may, in the future, no longer be named Sony.

So, while the names and fine details in the following profiles may change, these basic structures and arrangements have become well established. There is unlikely to be a sudden growth in the number of major companies who are distributing most of the music-related products that are sold in the United States and throughout the world. Equally, it is unlikely that the music industry will suddenly become a stable place to work or record companies be managed by non-interventionist parent corporations.

EMI

The British-based EMI group can trace its history back to the end of the nineteenth century, although the modern company dates from 1931 when it was formed following a series of mergers between recorded sound and electrical goods companies. The acronym EMI – Electric and Musical Industries – already indicated, at this early date, that this was more than a music-producing firm. Significant for EMI's more recent fortunes was the merger in 1979 with Thorn Electric Industries. The resulting corporation, Thorn-EMI, then operated for a number of years as a diversified company with interests in firms producing defence and medical equipment, lighting, electronic technology and the rental of domestic appliances, and in retail outlets selling computers and household furniture.

However, the profile of the EMI music division has been decisively shaped by a process of reorganization which began in the early 1990s under the direction of President and CEO Jim Fifield. Thorn-EMI restructured into sections, disposed of unrelated businesses and focused on a 'portfolio' of three 'strategic business units': EMI Music, the Thorn Group and the HMV retail chain. As this process was under way, EMI Music increased its profits and turnover through a series of acquisitions, including the purchase of the SBK and Filmtrax music publishing catalogues, Chrysalis Records and, most significantly, Virgin Records in 1992. The purchase of Virgin increased EMI's international market share and profits and enabled the newly merged companies to 'rationalize' by combining their previously separate manufacturing, distribution and promotion systems. In practice, this immediately resulted in the company 'eliminating' a thousand jobs world-wide and reducing Virgin's artist roster by 65 per cent.[9]

One immediate consequence of Thorn-EMI's divestments, acquisitions and 'refocusing' was that the music division's contribution to the turnover and operating profits of the parent company 'increased markedly'.[10] With few significant interests in other forms of entertainment, music became Thorn-EMI's key entertainment resource. This process culminated in the separation of EMI Music from the corporate group and speculation that the company's long-term aim was to sell the music division, with British Telecom, Paramount, Walt Disney, Viacom and Dreamworks all named in the press as potential purchasers of EMI Music[11] – speculation that continued through 1996 to the summer of 1998 when I was finishing the writing of this book.

Despite such possibilities, there was widespread acknowledgement, both within and without the company, that EMI's performance in the United States had not been as successful as it might have been. Although introducing various management changes and restructurings throughout the early 1990s, EMI-Capitol regularly attained the lowest or second lowest market share of all the major companies in the United States. Quite regardless of the company's considerable catalogue (including Queen, Tina Turner, Diana Ross, The Beatles, Garth Brooks, Janet Jackson and Smashing Pumpkins) and despite being represented across genres, EMI was judged to be poor at breaking new acts. This was one of the reasons why a further restructuring led the company to sack thirty-five of its senior US executives and close the New York office of its EMI Music label in May 1997.[12]

BMG

Like EMI, the home base of the Bertelsmann Music Group has historically been in Europe, as a subsidiary of the Bertelsmann Media Group whose origins go back to a business which began publishing hymn books in 1835. Although often maintaining a low profile and operating subsidiaries under a variety of local names, the company grew by establishing printing operations, publishing magazines and developing mail-order book clubs, and was the largest media conglomerate in the world prior to the Time-Warner merger in 1988.

Also like EMI and other major corporations, Bertelsmann was 'focusing' its interests during the 1990s and reorganized into four divisions: BMG Entertainment, Books, Gruner and Jahr (magazines) and Bertelsmann Industry. This restructuring was an attempt to foster more 'American' entrepreneurial flair without sacrificing 'German fiscal prudence', according to a rather sceptical report in *The Economist*.[13] In practical terms this was an attempt to introduce a less bureaucratic reporting structure and to deal with some of the geographical problems of running an operation in the United States from Germany.

The BMG music division had been set up following the acquisition of RCA (Radio Corporation of America) Records in 1986. This was the company that had recorded the tenor Enrico Caruso back in 1904 and that possessed the lucrative Elvis Presley back catalogue. Although music had been the 'core' of the entertainment division (Dane, 1995), the company also began making cautious moves into video and film distribution and multi-media entertainment. During this period the entertainment division had been the fastest growing part of the corporation, yet figures suggested that it was contributing less than 10 per cent of overall group profits, while accounting for about 30 per cent of overheads due to investment in artists and repertoire and the cost of launching new products.[14]

Again like EMI, BMG's music labels were thought to be 'under-performing' in the United States and costs were clearly on the mind of Strauss Zelnick, who was hired as the Director of Corporate Development and given the task of diversifying entertainment interests and 'turning around' the company's RCA label, an entity which had acquired a reputation for inertia and which was routinely referred to as 'Record Cemetery of America'. As in other restructurings, one of Zelnick's immediate actions involved cutting fifty staff at RCA and its 'boutique' Zoo label.[15]

Unlike RCA, BMG's other key label, Arista, has achieved considerable commercial and critical success. Formed in 1975 by entrepreneurial 'music man' Clive Davis and sold to BMG in 1979, Arista has had success with Whitney Houston and Ace of Base and has benefited from joint ventures with LaFace Records run by LA (Antonio Reid) and Babyface (Kenny Edmonds), who have produced Toni Braxton, R. Kelly and TLC. The label has also achieved a high profile via a similar arrangement with Bad Boy Records, run by Sean 'Puff Daddy' Combs who has produced his own music, remixed artists such as Mariah Carey and recorded the late Notorious B.I.G. Arista has also been successful in country music (in particular with Alan Jackson) and in 1995 announced that the repertoire would be expanded by 're-establishing the rock history of Arista'.[16]

BMG Entertainment has attempted to differentiate its strategy from that of the other major labels by promoting itself as self-consciously 'disciplined' and, in the words of Michael Dornemann, Chairman and CEO, by approaching 'work at all levels with an eye toward thoughtful and considered judgement before acting'.[17] This has meant that funds have not been made available for expansion and speculative investment in the acquisition of labels. Instead, senior executives have been encouraged to operate with a small artist roster, maximizing the potential of performers such as Annie Lennox rather than signing new artists.[18]

Warner Music Group

The Warner Music Group can trace its label origins back to the 1920s when Warner Brothers Pictures purchased the Brunswick record label, and more recently to the late 1960s, when the Atlantic, Elektra and Asylum labels were brought together through a series of acquisitions and mergers and named WEA, an acronym that endures in parts of the company. Warner's more recent fortunes have been shaped by Time-Warner Inc., the corporation formed in 1988 when Warner Communications and Time Incorporated merged to form what was then the world's largest entertainment and media conglomerate. This merger dramatically increased the new company's combined debts to commercial banks and brought together within one corporation a wide range of entertainment media and communication interests, including magazine and book publishing, a film studio, television networks and various cable networks.

The company's business strategies, which have had a direct impact on the music division, have involved simultaneously finding ways of reducing the debt burden and most coherently managing the different interrelated entertainment interests. Like other corporations, Time-Warner has attempted to cut costs and generate revenue to pay off debts: this has been done through financial restructuring methods but also by allowing partners (such as US West and Toshiba) to take a minority limited stake in the company and by selling a stake in various assets.[19]

Time-Warner's senior executives have also publicly stated that future profitability resides in ownership of the distribution networks rather than controlling the rights to the content, a judgement supported by figures showing that the corporation's most profitable part had been its cable division.[20] As a result, investment in 'software' became secondary to the pursuit of telecommunications, cable and distribution networks. The corporation then divided the company through a distinct separation of content (music, films, television – basically software) and cable and telecommunications (the conduits – cable, telecom). In 1994, the company created a new corporate body, Warner-US, with the aim of more closely monitoring and controlling the activities of the three music labels which had previously operated with a large degree of independence. Doug Morris, who was appointed as President and CEO, indicated that his intention was to directly intervene in the running of each label. The result was a series of highly publicized clashes, both within the music group and between the music group and other parts of the conglomerate, and frequent changes of management which resulted in some of the most respected executives leaving the company (Zimmerman, 1995).

Despite all this and the accompanying speculation about its potential disastrous consequences, Warner continued to achieve the biggest US market share of any major company, and maintained this throughout the mid-1990s. One reason for the company's dominance was that the US was their 'home' market, and as with EMI, BMG and PolyGram in Europe, companies have tended to perform most successfully in their 'home' territories. In the United States, Warner's labels had established a strong presence across most genres, particularly alternative and hard rock, country and r 'n' b, and their roster has included stars such as Madonna, Eric Clapton, REM and Prince.

Sony Music Entertainment

Sony Music Entertainment is a division of the Japanese Sony Corporation, a company formed originally as Tokyo Telecommunication Engineering in war-scarred Tokyo in 1946. For many years, Sony was known as an innovative hardware company (introducing the first transistor radio and personal stereo) and became involved in software through the acquisition of two previously US-owned companies – CBS Records (purchased in 1988) and Columbia/Tri-Star Pictures (purchased in 1989).[21] These purchases were heralded with announcements that Sony would be pursuing new 'synergies' between hardware and software; they would not simply operate vertical integration (signing, producing, manufacturing and distributing music and films) and horizontal connections (the possibility for promoting music in films) but would attempt to bring the hardware and software together by using software on new hardware technologies and selling hardware to the consumers of software.

However, rather than synergies, Sony found that the acquisition of a film and music company brought a series of management problems as personnel in Hollywood, in particular, proved costly and difficult to manage from Tokyo. Sony had initially given the film and music divisions a large degree of formal autonomy. However, by 1995 business analysts were pointing to a 'loss of direction' and poor management as the film division incurred considerable losses and lost market share, and a highly publicized court case eventually resulted in George Michael leaving the company.[22]

Mr Nobuyuki Idei was appointed Chair in Japan in 1995 and immediately intervened by forcing the resignation of the head of Sony Entertainment US, Michael Schulhof. He also cut a layer of management and introduced a more direct reporting line to Tokyo. As within other companies, the degree of financial and budgetary autonomy previously enjoyed by both music and film divisions was being structurally curtailed. Despite success with films such as *Terminator 2: Judgement Day*, and *Basic Instinct* and although operating a successful music division, there were signs that Sony was recognizing its 'core interest' to be in consumer electronics which regularly accounted for about 80 per cent of turnover throughout the early 1990s; estimates suggested that the music division was accounting for about 11 per cent and the film division about 9 per cent.[23] There were also signs that Sony's interests were shifting away from music and film production and more towards the possibilities of distribution and computer networking.[24]

Despite all this, the music division had the second highest US market share and has achieved success with artists including Michael Jackson, Mariah Carey, Gloria Estefan and Pearl Jam. While having numerous label deals, Sony has operated a relatively straightforward label structure made up of two main labels: Epic, a label first launched by CBS in 1953, initially for jazz and classical releases, which in recent years has mainly had alternative rock and r 'n' b (Babyface, Spin Doctors); and Columbia, a label that can trace its historical lineage back to the American Graphophone Company which was formed in 1887 and which has tended to have more established and 'middle of the road' artists (Bob Dylan, Tony Bennett, Barbara Streisand). Other key labels are Sony Classical and Sony Discos, one of the most prominent labels in Latin America and for sales of Latin music in North America.

Universal/PolyGram

In May 1998 it was announced that the other two major recording groups would be combining – Universal/PolyGram would become the world's biggest music company. The PolyGram part of this new conglomerate traced its historical roots back to the Deutsche Grammophon Gesellschaft (formed in 1898), although the modern company began when it became part of a venture initiated by Philips Electronics and Siemens of Germany (who were later bought out) in 1962. The Dutch-based parent corporation bought 100 per cent of PolyGram (although later floated 25 per cent on the Amsterdam and New York stock markets to help finance the purchase of record labels) and lined it up alongside companies manufacturing a range of electronic consumer and industrial products, from vacuum cleaners through medical equipment to security systems.

Like the other parent companies, Philips underwent a wave of restructuring in the 1990s. In the late 1980s Philips was in a very poor financial state and by 1990 was incurring losses of 4.1 billion guilders ($2.3 billion). Management changes led to Jan Timmer being promoted from President of PolyGram to Chairman of Philips; he immediately introduced what he labelled 'Operation Centurion' and what a writer for *The Economist* called a 'brutal restructuring plan'. This involved closing factories, transferring production plants from Europe to Asia (where labour costs were cheaper) and cutting about one-fifth of the corporation's workforce over a period of three years. As a result of this 'remorseless pruning and restructuring'[25] the company announced increasing profits and an ongoing rise in share prices from 1993.

At the same time Philips judged that consumer electronics was becoming an increasingly low-profit business, with hardware becoming a vehicle for the delivery of the software which could generate far greater margins of profit. Hence, the company divested many hardware facilities and began taking an interest in media such as cable, TV, film and computer software, with the aim of increasing revenues generated from these areas.[26]

As a result of this 'focusing', the PolyGram group became increasingly important for Philips as a whole. In the past PolyGram and Philips had tended to operate at a slight distance and the relationship between the two companies had often been 'strained' (Olivier, 1995). However, during the early 1990s they were brought closer through the intermixing of personnel on the different corporate boards. The President of PolyGram was placed on the board of Philips and two Philips executives were allocated to the board of PolyGram. As Charles Olivier (1995) concluded, having mapped out these connections in detail, while PolyGram was an 'independent' company it was Philips who ultimately vetoed or gave the go-ahead on any major acquisition.

Alain Levy, as PolyGram President and CEO between 1988 and 1998, expanded the company's international operations, moved into the area of film and significantly increased the music profile via the acquisitions of Island, A & M, Motown and a 50 per cent stake in Def Jam. As with the changes occurring at other labels, (this) increased PolyGram's market share and profits and enabled cost-cutting through the combining of these labels' previously distinct promotional and distribution systems.

PolyGram also developed an interest in other areas of media production and entertainment and lined up the music business in parallel with the film division. Hence, while PolyGram's music division was 'vertically' integrated through the ownership of manufacturing and distribution systems, music publishing and mail-order music clubs, it was also 'horizontally' connected to other entertainment media and distribution systems. In terms of repertoire, PolyGram had been most represented in rock/pop (with artists such as Sting, Bon Jovi, Elton John) and classical (particularly through the catalogue of Philips, Deutsche Grammophon and Decca). It also maintained a high profile within rhythm and blues (mainly through Motown and Def Jam).

Despite its high profile and growth, and although providing a significant portion of corporate profits, Philips disposed of PolyGram to Seagram for $10.6 billion. For a number of observers this was somewhat surprising, less an example of any coherent corporate strategy and more an indication that Philips was desperately raising funds to keep investors happy. According to announcements made by senior executives at Philips, however, this sale was the ultimate 'logical' step in the company's restructuring operation. It was a firm declaration of the corporation's desire to concentrate more narrowly on its 'core business' of digital electronic technologies and to leave to others the speculative schemes of the entertainment industry and the dreams of any possible 'synergies'. For PolyGram staff, this meant a process of amalgamation with people from the Universal Music Group, a company that had itself already been undergoing considerable changes just prior to this merger.

The beginnings of the Universal Music Group can be traced to 1924, although Universal Studios (which produced *Jaws*, *ET* and *Jurassic Park*) was created in 1912. In 1990, Universal (then operating as MCA) was acquired by the Japanese Matsushita company, who, like Sony, had made many pronouncements about the forging of hardware–software synergies. Matsushita were, again like Sony, a hardware company and the corporation which developed and introduced the VHS video recorder, also owning companies manufacturing electronic goods ranging from household appliances to industrial robots. Matsushita maintained tight control of finances and gave no money for investment or acquisition; the relationship between the Japanese owners and MCA's long-standing Chairman, Lou Wasserman, and President, Sidney Sheinberg, came to a well-publicized conflict when the two threatened to resign if they were not allowed the independence to spend money as they saw fit. Partly as a result of these conflicts, which were symptomatic of a general management breakdown, in 1995 Matsushita sold 80 per cent of MCA to the Canadian Seagram Company, the world's largest drinks company, manufacturing brands such as Martell cognac, Absolut vodka and Mum champagne.

The Seagram acquisition of MCA was judged to be unusual by commentators, who assumed that old-style diversification into unrelated product lines had been superseded by more 'synergistic' or 'focused' connections to related industries. In addition, the new company had little experience in the entertainment industry. However, once in post as new President and CEO at the beginning of 1996, Edgar Bronfman Jr called a meeting of the eighty top executives from the company and informed them that he wished to cut costs, increase profits and 'redesign MCA from top to bottom' (Fabrikant and Weinraub, 1996). The management of MCA/Universal in the 1990s therefore should be understood in relation to first Matsushita's failed attempt to manage and then Seagram's acquisition and the resulting changes they have attempted to introduce. Both give a highly tangible indication of relations between parent and entertainment corporation and the place of the music division within this.

Unlike Sony, who gained a reputation during the 1970s and 1980s for being 'un-Japanese' and adventurous, Matsushita were judged a conservative, traditional and highly bureaucratic company. In theory, they had been matching their hardware expertise with MCA's knowledge of music and film. In practice, Matsushita were judged to be detached and inflexible. Most frustrating to MCA executives was the fact that they placed immediate economic caution above speculative long-term planning and would not approve bids that would have enabled the company to acquire both television and music catalogue.[27]

Seagram immediately sought to change things in four key ways. First, they promised an investment to enable the company to expand through establishing international subsidiaries and the acquisition of catalogue and major artists. Second, the company cut costs, overheads and staff by integrating various Seagram and MCA finance, legal and personnel functions. Third, they mixed staff from MCA and Seagram in establishing a steering group to point the new company in a clear direction. Fourth, they renamed the recording division the Universal Music Group, thus giving the unit a higher profile by using the more familiar 'brand name' associated with movies and the film studio.

Having relabelled the music group, Seagram's new management sought to increase the company's roster of artists and broaden its range of genres. In the past, MCA was judged to be over-reliant on revenue from its country division through artists such as The Mavericks, Trisha Yearwood, Reba McEntire and Vince Gill.[28] The new plan was to increase its interest in the other two genres that were hottest at the time, most notably r 'n' b/black music and 'alternative' rock. To do this, the company recruited Doug Morris, from Warner Music, and Jay Boberg, who had previously worked with The Police and REM. MCA/Universal also purchased a 50 per cent stake in Interscope Records with an option to buy outright in three to five years. With its critically recognized catalogue of rock and rap music, the Interscope deal immediately increased the group's share of the US music market by about 2 per cent.[29]

The acquisition and subsequent merger with PolyGram built upon the logic of these changes and followed many of the same patterns that I have been highlighting in this chapter.[30] First, it increased the share of the market enjoyed by the new conglomerate. Second, it enabled the combining or 'consolidation' of previously separate label structures, sales and distribution systems. CEO Bronfman Jr predicted that this would cut costs and generate savings of $275 million to $300 million.[31] As with other mergers and acquisitions, many staff lost their jobs and numerous artists did not have their contracts renewed. Third, this acquisition broadened the range of artists and genres within the company's 'portfolio'. Finally, it created a conglomerate with considerable resources and the potential to attract established and new artists.

The Universal/PolyGram deal, and the historical tensions between MCA/Matsushita which preceded it, provide one of the most recent and visible examples of some of the minutiae of corporate strategies in practice. With this background information in place, I now wish to move on from some of these details and to consider the aims, practices and consequences of strategy in more depth.

GROWTH AND EXPANSION: THE OBSESSION WITH MARKET SHARE

As the major entertainment corporations compete with each other (and attempt to acquire each other), their strategic intentions are usually expressed in a desire to increase market share, either through so-called gradual 'organic growth' or through the purchase of labels, catalogues and companies. Market share is not simply an end in itself, but is an indicator which represents a broader series of preoccupations and intentions. For those wishing to invest in or acquire a company, for artists considering offers from different record labels, and for people who may have no detailed knowledge about what is actually going on within a company on a day-to-day basis, the market share figures provide an indication of profitability and expertise. Companies with a high share of a particular market (whether the US recorded music market in general or the market for a specific genre in a given region) will tend to attract investment and artists. Trade magazine *Music and Copyright* suggested that the difference between a 12 per cent and a 17 per cent share of the US music market is the difference between small profits and high profitability:

> Whether a company's revenues are $700m or $1,000m, the cost of maintaining a national production and distribution system are the same. The high revenues, however, provide a company with the cash flow to finance a high level of A and R spending. Conversely, the status of a 12 per cent market share company is unlikely to attract managers of the best unsigned acts.[32]

Market share figures are also thought to provide an indication of the skills and quality of staff within a particular organization. As John Purcell has observed of business management in general, 'in theory the company with the highest market share will have the greatest accumulated experience and the lowest costs and therefore generate the most profit' (1989, p. 74). However, the applicability of this to the music industry is disputed, particularly by those who point out that the delivery of a good album from a major artist can significantly affect a company's market share. Here, theories of 'luck' are often touted – or did the company have the accumulated skills that enabled the artists to deliver the great album in the first place?

At certain moments some companies will play down the issue of market share and stress that this is not the same as profitability, an attitude most commonly associated with the 'disciplined' BMG, whose executives often point out that speculative acquisitions may raise market share but may reduce profits and produce large debts.[33] Executives in other companies will retort that market share is a more useful long-term indicator than short-term profits, and point out that the companies with the lowest market share (or the labels and divisions with it) are those that are more usually prone to restructuring, cutting costs and regularly laying off staff and artists.

In addition to purely economic judgements, market share figures can play a significant morale-boosting function within record labels, their publication being viewed in a similar way to the sports tables or Top 40 charts. It is also worth noting that the bonuses of individual executives and managing directors are heavily dependent upon increasing market share. Furthermore, market share figures are important for persuading retailers to make space to stock the products of a particular company. If one company has a 22 per cent share of the market, and another has 9 per cent (the difference between the Warner Music Group and BMG in the early 1990s), the retailers will judge how much stock to take from each company according to this type of knowledge.

CORPORATE STRATEGY, MUSICAL GENRES AND PORTFOLIO MANAGEMENT

Bearing in mind the uncertainties I referred to in the first part of this chapter, it is not surprising that formal corporate strategies have become popular within the music industry as strategic management in general has been developed as a technique which attempts to 'cope with uncertainty, to integrate management activity in various fields that are concerned with change' (Purcell, 1989, p. 71). At the same time, strategy has been formu- lated and pursued in an attempt to manage the connection between the 'internal' (production) and 'external' (consumption).

This latter aspect is important because the music industry is not simply a site of production. It is a corporate space within which various people attempt to manage the often fragmentary social relationships through which music is produced, consumed and given meaning. In the process corporate strategies attempt to connect the 'inside' of production (which is increasingly outside a company, with artists, producers and arrangers) to the 'outside' of consumption (which is increasingly brought into the company through various techniques of monitoring and information production). Corporate strategy is central to any consideration of musical mediation as it entails an explicit attempt to manage the production–consumption relationship. Like other industries, music busi- ness strategies are the result of deliberate, conscious formulation combined with a certain amount of improvisation and a degree of compromise between different parties (De Wit and Meyer, 1994).[34]

One of the most obvious ways in which record company strategy attempts to resolve the problem of production and consumption is through the organization of catalogues, departments and promotional systems according to genre categories. As I discussed in Chapter 1, drawing on the observations of Simon Frith (1996), genre provides a way of linking the question of music (what does it sound like?) to the question of its market (who will buy it?). Portfolio management provides a way of viewing the company's labels, genres and artists by dividing them into discrete units (strategic business units). This makes visible the performance, profile and contribution of each. In many ways this is part of a strategy of diversifica- tion; the company spreading its risks across various musical genres and potential sources of income. As one senior executive remarked: 'It's like a diversified portfolio. It makes business sense and also it makes a statement to the industry that we're competitive in any realm.'[35] But it is more than diversification. Portfolio management provides a way of managing the company's diverse range of interests, as each unit can be assessed and categorized according to its performance and level of investment required.

The terminology developed by the Boston Consulting Group in 1970 as a way of categorizing business units has become routinely used by senior personnel in numerous industries, and record companies are no exception. It is adopted by staff when referring to different departments, artists and genres. Terms such as 'stars', 'cash cows', 'dogs' and, less frequently 'wild cats' (or a synonym) are used to refer to artists, labels or genres. These categories provide a way of assessing and characterizing the performance of each division.[36]

Stars require substantial investment but their profile and market dominance enables the production of profits to finance further acquisitions and expansion. The delivery of albums from star artists can significantly affect a company's turnover and market share. But stars need sophisticated management, experienced staff and personal attention (as Warner's dispute with Prince and Sony's court case with George Michael would seem to confirm). Such arrangements can be costly, as can the financial terms under which a star is kept under contract. Although stars may not necessarily provide the best cash flow, particularly when between albums, they may attract further investment and prestige, and can draw other artists to a company.

Cash cows can produce sizeable profits, and with minor modifications and modest ongoing investment this category can bring in regular revenue and maintain the company's market share. Cash cows can be managed with a fairly straightforward administrative structure and standard promotional system. When I interviewed one senior record company executive in London during November 1995, he remarked that for his company, 'Techno is really a cash cow.' Likewise, when speaking to staff in the United States during 1996, I routinely heard the category of 'alternative rock' spoken of as a cash cow.

Wild cat or *question mark* refers, in the music business, to a new genre (or, in certain cases, an artist) that the company may wish to become involved with so as to increase market interests and to broaden experience and expertise. Any potential commercial success may be difficult to predict, and the company will probably need to invest in staff, artists, offices and equipment, and catalogue before obtaining a significant return.

Dogs produce little, if any, profit and are usually considered a bad investment. A company may wish to divest itself of a genre or artist defined as a dog. However, record companies may retain a dog for reasons other than immediate financial gain. This has sometimes been the case with more experimental or avant garde performers and with classical music and jazz. This practice can benefit a company, both internally and externally. Such a strategy can impress and attract other artists and it can boost the morale of personnel within the company. It can be used to justify the claim that the company is interested in 'art' as much as profits (although such a strategy can also have indirect commercial benefits).

The practice of portfolio management enables the company to assess and divide up different genre divisions, labels or those working specific artists. It allows for particular techniques of monitoring which operate to enforce a high degree of accountability within the operating units. Each unit has to report regularly to corporate headquarters; it has sales targets to hit, budgets to work within, is rewarded for good performance and can be punished for poor performance. The company can reward for contributions to profile and profitability by allocating finance for expansion and by giving performance-related bonuses. At the same time, the company can deploy sanctions for poor performances. Punishment can involve the sacking of individual senior executives and bringing in new presidents, or it can involve the closing down of entire divisions and their removal from the company's portfolio. For example, in February 1996 Capitol Records closed its urban division, dropping most of its artists and laying off eighteen members of staff. Capitol-EMI publicly announced that the company had done this in order to concentrate resources on 'stars' such as Bonnie Raitt, Bob Seger and Richard Marx, and 'modern rock' artists such as Foo Fighters, Everclear and Radiohead. This was a clear example of portfolio management in practice (and where investment priorities lie). A category of 'stars' were named as a priority and the genre of modern rock was identified as a 'cash cow'. It seemed that the company had decided that the urban division was a 'dog', a judgement that involves more than just a 'business' decision alone and which I will discuss in more depth in Chapter 4.

Hence, record companies are not unified businesses, but collections of units organized according to musical genre. Someone who works for Sony, for example, may experience the corporation in a completely different way depending on whether she or he is working alternative rock in New York City, Latin catalogue in Miami or country music in Nashville. Just as different genres do not exist in isolation but in direct relation to one another within systems of genres (Neale, 1990), so genres assume a position within a company's portfolio, with different departments continually struggling for greater recognition and further resources. I will elaborate on the character of these different units in more depth in later chapters concentrating on specific genres.

The increasing use of portfolio management techniques has exposed certain genres of music and artists that were previously less conspicuously subject to monitoring. Notable here is the fate of classical (and in some companies the same applies to jazz). For many years, within most major companies, the classical division was allowed to run at a loss, supported with revenues generated from the sales of pop and rock. The introduction of separate budgets and the redefinition of classical as a separate 'profit centre' have placed pressure on the classical division to follow other departments by balancing (or concealing) an investment in long-term acts with short-term revenues gained from the likes of Christmas albums, composer 'greatest hits' packages, collaborations between pop and classical performers (Dionne Warwick singing with Placido Domingo, for example) and the marketing of classical performers using pop promotional techniques (Nigel Kennedy and Vanessa Mae, for example).

Classical has become an integral genre within a company's portfolio, and those companies that were lacking this in their mix have sought to introduce a label, just as other companies have acquired or started labels to make up for their lack of rap or country. As an example, in 1989 Warner Music decided to set up a new classical division. To do this the company established offices, recruited staff and acquired the necessary repertoire that would enable them to present a full catalogue to the industry; most notably the company purchased the Tulda label in Germany and Erato in France. Warner then 'rationalized' the new repertoire, dropping certain 'dogs', and followed this by signing the 'star' José Carreras to a long-term contract, thus increasing the profile of the label and its credibility with other musicians and star artists. At the same time, the company allocated a budget to the division and established clear goals, defining the turnover and market share that would be expected in key territories over a five- to ten-year period.[37] This is no different to the way a company might set up a jazz department, dance section or Latin label.

THE CERTAINTIES OF ACCOUNTING: GETTING THE FIGURES RIGHT

The use of portfolio management as a way of managing record companies is sometimes referred to as a 'loose–tight' approach (i.e. tight financial control, loose regulation of day-to-day working style, dress codes and little intervention into values and ethical decisions). In practice, monitoring can involve consideration of the entire plans of each division, down to the individual release schedules of specific artists.[38] The loose–tight approach is tight enough to close down or restaff an entire division.

Unlike the owner who is present down the corridor (as happens in smaller and less multi-divisional companies), the corporation employs techniques of remote judging, for which it uses more detached indicators rather than relying on day-to-day human interaction.[39] The managers within the division have less opportunity to explain their everyday problems and to elaborate on the more 'qualitative' rather than quantitative aspects of management (how to persuade temperamental artists to deliver recordings on time or to participate in specific activities, and dealing with staff problems). Instead, getting the figures right becomes a preoccupation.

Yet, during press interviews, in annual reports and interim statements, senior corporate executives make much of their desire to locate (and indeed, their success in finding) managers with the ability to combine conventional business acumen with creative insights. When I interviewed Joe Galante, Chairman of RCA Nashville, I raised this issue by remarking that I had read articles in which senior corporate staff had said that they were seeking managers who could balance musical judgements with business skills. He responded:

> They're trying to find those, but the problem is that sometimes the people picking them don't have a clue what the person on their music is supposed to be doing. If you haven't done it, how do you find somebody? 'I think this is the right guy.' 'And what's your background?' 'I'm a consultant.' 'So you know a lot about picking artists and what people should be looking for and the right way to approach –'
> How will this person respond when the artist comes in and is furious? Does this person know how to really nurture this artist and lead a company and develop it and manage a business where you're not going to go broke backing this person's taste?...their taste in executives and their taste in music.[40]

Here, accountants come into their own as key intermediaries at the very point where uncertainty is pervasive and when senior executives are unclear how to judge the creative abilities of the managers they have appointed. Yet accounting is by no means as objective and straightforward as is sometimes assumed. Geert Hofstede, following his experience of working in various industries and from years of research, reached the conclusion that accounting systems are little more than 'uncertainty-reducing rituals'. Accountants fulfil 'a cultural need for certainty, simplicity and truth in a confusing world, regardless of whether this truth has any objective base' (Hofstede, 1991, p. 151). Certain actions are reduced to figures, and these are then abstracted out of the social context within which they were created and which they seek to explain. Hofstede argues that corporate budget practices are often little more than a 'game' driven less by any clear financial logic than by an attempt to maintain morale in the face of uncertainty.

Accounting knowledge has emerged as a particular way of ordering and assessing the actions of individuals within multi-divisional corporations. It provides a way of privileging 'hard' data (facts, figures, statistics) over 'soft' explanations (human foibles, intuitive hunches and 'belief in an artist').[41] It is, as a number of senior executives explained to me during interviews, easier to stand up at a corporate meeting and present the figures than to try explaining how artists are being developed, or why a major artist has not delivered a recording or has sold less than their last album. For Galante this sort of pressure was reducing the complex skills of managing a record company to little more than a 'lottery' based on viewing the winning financial indicators:

> At some point people are going to have to realize that you can't hit the lottery every time. There is a point at which it doesn't mean that you are a bad manager. Some people that are really good record executives have a slow season. The slow season can be two years before you get it right: 'What am I doing wrong? What am I doing wrong? I've tried this, I've tried this, I've tried that.' And then, bingo! Something happens and it changes and it doesn't mean that you were a bad guy. It means that you made some bad choices or the market-place changed – I mean any wrong song choices or whatever. But if you've done it once, and it was not a fluke, you can do it again and there are very few people – you look at a company like BMG, and I've said this to our management before; out of 5,000 people there are probably twenty, maybe twenty-five guys in the company, guys that can actually start a company from scratch and know what to do to find the people and grow the acts – and it's not the guy in Switzerland, you know, they can't really generate a business.[42]

One immediate consequence of these types of control is a straightforward reluctance to experiment, a reduction in risk-taking and a propensity towards a partial view of the world. As Neil Fligstein (1990) has noted, control strategies operate according to a type of analysis whereby the world is simplified. As accounting knowledge provides the principal means through which strategy is assessed and enforced, so such financial control encourages equally simplified aesthetic judgements, contradictory management and anxiety or confusion in the face of musical changes.

Popular music history is a testament to the way in which genres are far from static and constantly change as interacting musicians move across aesthetic and geographical borders. Yet strategic calculation is built on a desire for stability, predictability and containment. Musicians confront a continual pressure for stasis, but are required by contract to deliver 'new' albums. Staff within corporate office seek the predictable 'sure-fire hits' while being aware that the success of their company depends upon continual changes and fighting against any possible inertia by finding the 'unknown' – new genres, artists and audiences. Here an understanding of 'the market' provides the strategic link between artist and audience and produces further sources of inertia and anxiety.

MARKET INTELLIGENCE: <u>IMAGINING THE</u>
<u>CONSUMER</u>   *artist research & polling, etc.*

For many years staff in record companies judged their day-to-day sales performance and ability to reach the purchasers of their products through inspired guesswork, hunches and intuition. Now companies have numerous sources of data, including electronic monitoring of sales in retail outlets (Soundscan), ongoing researched profiles of consumers which provide a wealth of qualitative information with weekly artist popularity ratings (Soundata) and various broadcast data systems (BDS) which electronically record transmissions from radio stations and provide up-to-the-minute national and regional airplay figures. In addition, companies use information systematically gathered and collated from night clubs, record pools and a range of public places, along with routine market research produced about the lifestyles of consumers.

Some companies have sophisticated market research departments which continually monitor consumer panels and focus groups and which have accumulated mountains of material about different groups of people and detailed profiles of individual artists.[43] There are two interrelated issues which are continually researched and monitored weekly: purchase and consumption. Who buys what, when and where, with what kind of frequency, and what influences their purchase (price, visual image, radio, video, hearing music in a store or in a club – if so, which club and who was the DJ)? Why do people *not* purchase? Why do they purchase certain products and not others? What specific songs made someone buy an album? Why did they buy the single and not the album? How do people consume – how does music-buying fit into a lifestyle or particular way of living? Where do people listen, who with, at what time of day and for how long? What other activities accompany music-listening and are engaged in alongside it – which magazines are read, food eaten, television programmes preferred, clothes purchased and films viewed?

The Soundata system (available on subscription) provides information derived from a panel of about 1,200 people who have made two to three purchases in the previous six months. To take some random examples of the type of information collected: in August 1995, Soundata reported that '85 per cent of active music consumers expressed an interest in purchasing both CD and cassette versions of an album if they were packaged together at a discount'. It also reported that 'about one-third of single buyers also own the full-length album that contains the last single they bought'. It reported the continual rise in listening figures for alternative/modern rock radio stations and included percentages for the number of people changing their radio station listening habits every three months. Every month Soundata was producing artist polls which provided popularity ratings for a range of performers, broken down according to age, sex and other social characteristics. So, for example, for Portishead's first poll they gained an overall popularity rating of 6.1 per cent and their strongest following was among twelve- to twenty-year-olds. Anything over 40 per cent is considered a good rating; in September 1995, John Lennon received a 49 per cent popularity rating, which increased to 68 per cent for the thirty-five to forty-four year age group.

Further information is gained from market data collated, verified and published by the Recording Industry Association of America (RIAA), from demographic profiles produced by subcontracted research companies and from telephone surveys, mail surveys and from the use of 'bounce back cards' – the business reply postcards often included with CDs whereby the purchaser can request additional information (and instantly enter a computer file as part of 'the developed fan base'). Additional knowledge is gained from employing people to conduct polls of those attending concerts and from responses to the company's Internet site.[44]

The figures and data generated by these methods can be very influential when prioritizing artists for promotion and even when making judgements about whether to retain an artist under contract or drop them from a roster, as can detailed studies of artists. However, it would be misleading to imply that all artists are researched in such a systematic and detailed manner. As Linda Greenberg, Senior Director of Market Research at Sony Distribution explained when I had specifically mentioned Bob Dylan (who is signed to the company):

> There are many artists that we just don't bother doing research on because it's not really going to have any effect. You're usually doing research if there's a question in your mind, and it can be anything from 'There are twelve songs on this new record and five of them are so different, let's play those five songs for consumers and get their reactions' to 'The artist's first record sold half a million, the next record sold one million and the third record sold three and this last one only sold one – why? Let's find out why, if we can.' We talk to buyers, non-buyers, and get some reactions on that and see: was it just that there weren't as many singles, the songs weren't as upbeat, it was a very different feel? 'Let's find out because there'll be another record in a year and let's try to help with that.' Can we? Sometimes we can't, sometimes the artist has really made a big shift in how he or she feels about life and how they're going to write their music. Then the decision becomes: do you stick with the artist, or is this an artist that, long term, you feel is going back and forth between a variety of styles? There's a whole lot going on.[45]

Due to the apparent 'sensitivity' of certain types of research information, particularly studies of individual artists, it's quite common for the information to be closely guarded and circulated among only a few people. On many occasions not even the artist is told that they are being researched – particularly if it is likely to result in key judgements which might affect their career.

The increasing production and use of this type of 'market intelligence' has come about as part of a wider shift in the operation of business in general, whereby various technologies and techniques of surveillance and data gathering, facilitated by information technologies, have enabled those at the retail, distribution and sales side (and at the corporate overseeing division) to gain greater knowledge and act upon it. This information has been central to the growth of portfolio planning approaches, dealing with music production in terms of a series of genre divisions. 'Consumer intelligence' has thus been integral to the gradual fragmentation of markets and the separation of working practices into various sub-units defined by genre.

This type of information has also had an impact on the struggles and tensions between artist and repertoire staff (oriented to finding performers and making the music) and marketing personnel (concerned with selling and promotion), particularly when each division has based its actions on a series of separate and undiscussed hunches or assumptions about what the audience might purchase.[46] One of the key problems that strategic management attempts to resolve is this 'fit' between production and consumption, and the way that this pervades the workings of the company. While genre-based practices attempt to connect an assessment of the music with a judgement about the audience, they cannot resolve the occupational division and tensions which have historically emerged between A and R and marketing. Here the distribution division has come to play a central job in managing this tension.[47]

DISTRIBUTION: CONTROLLING THE CONNECTION BETWEEN PRODUCTION AND CONSUMPTION

The distribution divisions of the major record labels occupy a position of strategic importance within the music industry, playing a significant part in the struggle to maintain control of production and consumption. Staff in the distribution division of the major labels work at the 'interface' between record company and retailer, and include market researchers, sales staff and business analysts. Their task is to monitor stock movements within the company's warehouses and among different retail outlets, and to ensure that the company is not pressing too many recordings (and wasting valuable storage space) or making too few recordings (and losing money by failing to respond to public demand). In doing this the distribution division operates as an intermediary between the different labels and the retailers.

The initial task of the distribution division, their first reason for existing, is to get a company's products into the stores. Their more visible public face is that of the field sales staff who visit the buyers for individual stores and retail chains and attempt to persuade them to stock recordings, display them prominently and play them in-store. In attempting to do this the issue of pricing is usually more significant than any judgements about great music. Retail profit margins on T-shirts and greetings cards are usually higher than those on musical recordings. Hence, a store will take more of those products on which they can make higher profits. For this reason, the major record labels do not ship all recordings at the same trade price. Instead, certain ranges of recordings are regularly shipped at a discount and special prices are negotiated for bulk shipments.[48]

Competition between US retailers increased considerably during the early 1990s, particularly with various stores selling music as a 'loss leader' i.e. cutting the price of compact discs, and their profits, to attract consumers into a store in the hope that once inside members of the public may also purchase electronic equipment and other entertainment products with higher profit margins. As a consequence, retailer strategies became firmly based on the 'tight control of inventory' and this was viewed as the key way in which a company could maintain a 'competitive edge'.[49] Retailers did not wish to have excess product sitting on their shelves. At the same time they wanted to obtain recordings quickly if they sold out of a particular disc. Record companies responded to this. Utilizing what have become known as JIT ('just in time') methods, record company distribution systems were decentralized into a series of regional 'hits warehouses' that could deliver recordings in response to a telephoned order on the same day or within twenty-four hours.

Whoa, weird.

Following additional pressure from stores, record companies made a further concession to retailers by allowing them the opportunity to return unsold recordings. This not only cut back on the record store 'bargain bin', it also gave record companies a more realistic figure of what their artists were actually selling (many previous publicly quoted sales figures concealed the quantities being disposed of at a loss in the bargain bin). Needless to say, record companies do not want unsold recordings to be returned to their warehouses any more than retailers want them sitting on the shelf. So the distribution division began to assume the further task of making sure that the corporation's internal individual labels do not manufacture and ship too many recordings in the first place.

The decision about how many albums of any artist to press and ship is, in theory, the result of a dialogue between various departments within a record company, notably A and R, marketing and distribution. For any record company, this is not a straightforward administrative procedure but a major decision. The discrepancy between a decision to manufacture 100,000 albums and resulting sales of 20,000 is not only bad for individual reputations, it is costly. Companies attempt to resolve this through a system of internal 'inventory management' whereby the liability for such a decision is placed firmly within an individual label or business unit. It is controlled by the distribution division through a fairly straightforward system whereby individual labels are charged a distribution fee and a price for the use of warehouse space. This makes individual labels within the corporate group liable for any excess recordings that are not shipped or sold (i.e. it eats into their own unit budgets). To quote from one senior executive within the distribution division of a major music group, who I spoke to in 1996 and who preferred to be cited anonymously:

> The label owns that inventory, so if they paid for that and they paid for the warehouse space, the only exposure we have is that there's only so much space and you want to have a product that's moving at all times. You don't want dead weight in the warehouse, but it's really the label's liability. And then the fee structure also helps the process, in that the distribution company charges a distribution fee to its labels. There are various elements to that fee – percentage of sales, percentage of returns. We also have an inventory charge…the distribution company charges the label for the number of SKUs [stock-keeping units]. The label is charged for each SKU in inventory at the end of each month and then they are also charged for excess inventory. So we define excess inventory as everything in excess of, say, the last twelve months' sales. Then anything beyond that is considered excess and the distribution company assesses the label a higher fee. So there's not only the common sense of 'we don't want to over-manufacture', there is also a financial implication of over-manufacturing.…That has evolved over the years because some labels are more responsive to inventory levels, and so this is a way of making everybody more aware. Of course, there's no better way than the financial implication, you know, if you're paying more for it.

The distribution division thus assumes an important role in influencing how many recordings may be manufactured and shipped by any label division within the company. If a label decides to manufacture too many, it will end up losing money that could have been invested in artists and production. Hence, in making these decisions, individual labels become increasingly dependent upon sales intelligence and market data produced and held by the research department of the distribution division.

As the distribution division can exert this type of pressure on internal labels within a corporate group, it is not surprising that it can also maintain control of the recordings manufactured and shipped by any independent labels which may have deals with the major corporation. Although small minor or independent labels have clearly established business and repertoire plans and usually operate coherent commercial strategies, they face the continual problem of finding adequate distribution.[50] Affecting all minor companies, despite differing sizes of operation, is the problem of distribution. As Herman Gray (1988) found when studying the production of jazz at Theresa Records, the label's 'internal' problems of cash flow, organizational stability and scheduling were directly related to issues of distribution. The multi-divisional major companies do not attract the owners of small independent labels by being knowledgeable about music, funky, cool, street-wise or artist-friendly. The major corporation attracts the indie because it can distribute recordings. Here the tensions between indie and major do not so much involve conflicts of art versus commerce or democracy versus oligopoly (as sometimes portrayed) as distribution struggles – battles to get recordings to the public.

As an example of these tensions I shall cite a view of such struggles from the perspective of Nelson Rodríguez, who was the National Director of Promotion at RMM Records when I spoke to him in 1996. Formed initially as an artist management company in the early 1970s, Ralph Mercado Music (RMM) was established as a record label in 1987 and quickly signed up some of the leading salsa, merengue and Latin jazz musicians (including La India, Marc Anthony, Manny Manuel and Tito Puente). For five years they held a distribution deal with Sony Discos, a separate distribution division of the Sony Corporation. I spoke with Nelson a short time after the company had signed a new deal with UNI, the distribution division of Universal. The problems RMM encountered at Sony were similar to those within a major label group – disagreements about the numbers that should be manufactured and shipped. But RMM's plight, like that of the jazz company studied by Gray (1988), also highlights how genres are purchased in different ways and hence require a distribution system that is sensitive to this. As Rodríguez explained:

> Jazz music is very similar to salsa music in that it's a mom and pop type of music. If you're listening to a jazz station and you want to pick up a record you could go to the chains – Tower Records, the Whiz – but if you're in a local area in Detroit or Alabama or Illinois or Missouri there may not be a chain store there, so you go to a local jazz store. They couldn't find our products because Sony would not give credit to those little stores…Sony likes to do credit accounts with people who are going to be spending $10,000 per month or $3,000 a month. That's when they open up a credit line. They didn't want to open up little credits for little stores. So all of a sudden we found out that we couldn't sell a certain amount of records because we couldn't get into these stores. So our independents would call us and say, 'Look, these guys say they can't get the product.' So we started making the phone calls. We called Sony and they said, 'Yeah, yeah, that's

great, send us the names, we'll work something out with them.' Then
it turns out that they said, 'No, we called the guys up and all they
want is three Tito Puente CDs and three cassettes. We're not going to
give them a credit line for six pieces. You're talking about maybe $40
or $50, we're not going to do that.' So we started losing in that sense
and it never got any better.[51]

Not only were the potential sales too low for Sony's operation, there
were disputes between the two companies about the number of recordings
Sony would distribute:

We had an artist and they said, 'Well, what do you guys want to do
with this artist?' 'Well, we think we should press 25,000 units because
this kid is gonna be hot'.

They would go and press ten, so we would be short by fifteen. All of a
sudden there would be a boom and we don't have the product....We
would say, 'We believe in this, we're gonna do a, b and c in our
marketing strategy, we should be able to sell 40,000 of this easily.' But
what would they do? The guy would go over there and say, 'Press ten,
they're not going to do more. They'll be happy when they find that we
did ten and they could only sell eight.' All of a sudden we did twenty
with a refill for eleven, which is thirty-one – and we only had ten.
We're, like, 'Who gave you the power to decide that?' 'Well we didn't
think you guys were going to be able to do it. But don't worry, we'll
have the product prepared in three weeks.' I mean, we're going to lose
sales for three weeks? You guys don't have the right to do that!

While the distribution divisions of the major companies can penalize
their own labels through economic charges to budgets, as Rodríguez'
narration suggests, they can constrain the independents by not pressing
enough recordings. There is no doubt that signing a distribution deal with
a major company can dramatically increase the number of recordings that
a minor company can sell, improve the label's ability to get recordings into
the major stores and get them into the stores quicker. But, as Victor Gallo,
who was working as General Manager of the Fania catalogue, remarked
when I asked about the significance of the distribution divisions of the
major labels: 'They can put you out of business.'[52]
It is within these tensions, arguments and conflicts, which are increasingly distribution struggles rather than straightforward repertoire versus
markets disputes (or indie commitment to art versus cynical major
commercialism), that knowledge of the consumer plays a key role. It
informs intra-departmental rivalry to the extent that knowledge of what
consumers are doing – and legitimating that knowledge through 'hard'

information and verifiable data rather than 'hunches' or 'intuition' – is deployed in struggles for influence and position within the organization. It also plays a part in attempts to maintain accountability and control: What or who is signed? How many recordings are made and shipped? What verifiable information informs such judgements (sales figures or 'hunches')? The market data, produced and circulated within the companies, is used during the struggles between major company labels and the distribution division, and in a similar manner it mediates the arguments between the major distributor and independent labels ('We believe we can sell 50,000.' 'Sorry, our analysis suggests you will sell 10,000.'). Here, the plight of the 'external' independent and the 'internal' label unit are remarkably similar.

BALL OF CONFUSION: STRATEGY, MARKET INTELLIGENCE AND THE REAL WORLD

All of the disputes and struggles in record labels, and all the obsessive accumulating of data are attempts to understand how an artist connects with the public. Yet just how useful all this research and information-gathering might be is open to question, and this is frequently acknowledged within the music industry. On many occasions I have heard the remark that much research tends to 'confirm what you may have intuitively felt', to which someone also added, 'and if it doesn't, you find a way of making it'.

The explicit economic value of research can be addressed by posing the question: is there a relationship between successful companies and the use of research? As Linda Greenberg of Sony responded when I asked this question: 'Well, last year was not great, we had a problem market-share-wise, and I know that if anybody had said, "Well, gee, there's a relationship between research and market share", then we would have probably lost our whole department.'[53]

As Greenberg also acknowledged, research often has a symbolic value in providing a sense of direction, but may have little to do with what makes a successful company. With these doubts in mind, a further question concerns the extent to which it has anything to do with the real world that it attempts to explain. Although it assists the formulation of strategy and decision-making, and while market research gives people within the corporation a sense of certainty and security, in the process it does not so much understand the world of musical culture and consumption but invents one. As Paul du Gay has observed when writing of similar processes of information-gathering in retailing,

> The power of strategic calculation lies in its ability to divide, collate and classify. However, it is precisely through this analytic fragmenta-

tion that it loses sight of what it claims to represent. In seeking to grasp the 'Real', strategy manages instead to construct a 'reality'.

(1996, p. 90)

This constructed reality then has a further social-psychological impact within the corporation. Instead of rather casually and hopefully throwing mud against unknown targets the companies are, in theory, following a limited number of known researched targets, with specific divisions of skilled staff carefully aiming at these particular targets. Yet the real world continually thwarts the constructed reality. While strategic calculation, marketing intelligence and artist profiles enable the music corporation to adopt an approach that is more transparently logical and rational than simply throwing out a load of recordings and seeing which ones stick, it does not seem to be any more effective.

Indeed, the impact of various corporate strategies and the obsessive monitoring and information-gathering not only reduce risk-taking (a risk-taking that could at least be partially concealed within the less rational, less calculated, mud-against-the-wall approach); they can also contribute to an environment whereby a type of anxiety and existential angst is attached to what the next figures reveal or what they cannot reveal, an ironic situation whereby the very security provided by the 'data' generates insecurity and anxiety due to the way in which it does *not* provide the answers.

I will conclude this chapter by quoting once more from the perceptive reflections of Joe Galante, the Chairman of RCA in Nashville. He was one of a number of people to talk about these types of issue, and explained that the day before speaking with me he had attended a meeting at which all of the company's senior executives had been trying to figure out why there had been a drop in the label's sales, and within the music business in general. His comments provide an insight into the social-psychological impact of continually having to deal with more and more consumer information:

It just gets more confusing, it really does. I said that yesterday in a meeting. Our business was down overall as an industry last week, probably 25 per cent. Why? It was down at the mass merchandisers, but it was up at the retailers. So then you start going 'Well, was the weather good?' It was Memorial Day weekend – did people not go to malls and just go to strip centres? I don't know, I don't know. But I know it was down. We have all these spins. Why were the spins down? I don't know. We know that there's a problem, we know we're successful. Why is it happening? I'm not sure. I'm not sure which is better sometimes; I mean, before, we were successful and we didn't even know it, but we were happy. Now we're in trouble all the time.

Seriously. You come in on a Monday, our airplay is in front of us on BDS [Broadcast Data Systems] and we know what's going on immediately. Tuesday is *R and R* [*Radio and Records*], Wednesday is Soundscan. By the end of the week you're just – one week you're up and the next week you're down. Whereas before, you felt like you were building something over the course of time.[54]

The work of record companies is now based far more on strategic calculation, data management, monitoring and measuring techniques and the explicit application of forms of management theory. It is based less on gut feeling, hunches, intuition and inspired guesswork. There is more knowledge of a very instrumental and rational type available, and, as a consequence, less will to act on more speculative types of knowledge.

The methods have changed, but the consequences do not seem to have changed. Record companies do not seem to be able to manage talent more effectively and still produce far more failures than successes. Galante's comments may be, in part, a manifestation of nostalgia for a time when things seemed simpler and when the buck took longer to stop. But they are also an indication of a changing world within the music company, a world of strategies without vision, order without insight: strategies which operate to reduce risk-taking, increase anxiety and curb spontaneity.

Chapter 3

Record company cultures and the jargon of corporate identity

For many executives in record companies the issue of 'culture' is important, not only in terms of the sounds, words and images associated with their artists, but as a way of understanding the day-to-day working world or way of life within the organization. Numerous senior personnel have been influenced by the prescriptive literature which suggests that a company's distinctiveness and economic competitiveness is dependent upon its 'corporate culture'. Hence, the perceptions and practices of many people within the music industry are informed by assumptions about the culture of organizations. In the first part of this chapter I shall draw extensively on the voices of recording industry staff to give a sense of what corporate culture means in the music business, and to indicate how and when this idea is used. I shall then introduce some critical reflections and argue that, while the issue of culture within the music business is important, we should not simply confine our discussions of this issue to the boundaries of the organization. Instead, I shall argue for a focus on the broader cultures of production which intersect with the corporate world.

Those music business personnel who profess a belief in the importance of company culture usually do so for two main reasons. First, although monitored as part of a portfolio of assets, individual operating units and company divisions have a degree of independence to establish their own ways of working in terms of office environment, staff characteristics, dress codes, working hours and habits of daily interaction. Second, when seeking to attract artists and senior executives most companies can match each other's financial offers, so an additional appeal is made based on claims about how a company can provide the most sympathetic conditions and supportive environment for creative work. These aspects are often alluded to when executives are recounting anecdotes about how they did or did not manage to sign a particular artist. For example, Don Ienner, when reflecting on his inability to attract Green Day to Sony, remarked:

> We were the first major label that was out to sign Green Day. They
> walked into the Warner Brothers building in Burbank, which is a

beautiful wooden building, three floors, very homey. They're California kids. And after spending a couple of days in our marble and stone building here in New York, they decided to go with Warner Brothers.

(Zimmerman, 1995, p. 19)

Whether or not the 'homey' building was the sole factor in such a decision, it was considered to have an important influence on the company's ability to attract artists. Another non-economic factor considered crucial for attracting performers is the roster of other artists signed to a label. It is something of a music business cliché, repeated to me on many occasions, that 'Neil Young attracted more bands to Reprise than anything',[1] as are other anecdotes about the way in which, at certain moments, stars such as The Beatles, David Bowie and Aretha Franklin have attracted artists to their respective labels.

However, it is often not the stars but those artists who might be considered a poor investment in economic terms who can contribute to a company's ability to attract performers to a 'creative' environment. As Bob Merlis reflected from his years at Warner Brothers, speaking in the same building that Green Day had found so attractive,

> There is something to be said for the profile of the company. We've had artists here who have not really sold a lot of albums but who have been kind of touchstones for other artists. I know that REM have always been impressed with the fact that this was the company that for ever maintained Van Dyke Parkes, Ry Cooder and Randy Newman, despite the fact that they basically didn't sell a whole lot of records.[2]

Such assumptions about the way in which a company's artists are perceived connects with another belief – that a company '*is* its artists'; the artists on the roster provide an index of the entire organization and its culture.

CORPORATE CULTURE FROM INSIDE AND OUTSIDE: PEOPLE AND NATIONS

So, what is this entity labelled and spoken of as company culture? There are many books and articles which attempt to provide an answer to this question, and a huge amount of literature devoted to identifying, analysing and providing ways of modifying the constituent parts of any 'company culture'. Despite the numerous writings on the subject and the various industries that have been studied, this aspect of the music business has received little, if any attention.[3] In attempting to contribute to this neglect here I should acknowledge that I am not approaching the 'culture' of the recording industry from an immersion in debates about organizations. Rather, I have been led *to* this issue from researching music production, as it has arisen during interviews with recording industry personnel. I shall be referring to some of the writings that address the issue of company culture in a more general and critical way later in this chapter. However, my main aim is to set out what culture and corporate identity mean for those within the recording industry, as part of my attempt to understand how cultures of production are experienced, understood and contribute to the environment within which music production takes place.

The first problem I confronted in thinking about and trying to research this question further was the simple fact that the very staff who, in one breath, claimed that company culture was important (and thus directed me to this issue) then found it very difficult to identify the characteristics that distinguished their company from their competitors, or which united their different offices in, say, London, New York or Los Angeles. When I responded to pronouncements about company culture by posing such a question to various personnel in both Britain and the United States, most found it very difficult to respond, perhaps not surprisingly as I was asking about something that is taken for granted as part of the routines and habits of the working day.

However, as I visited various companies and spoke informally to people outside their workplace, and as I trawled through ever more trade articles, I began to accumulate a series of descriptions, observations and characteristics that had become identified with specific companies. These are admittedly impressionistic, and I present them here with the intention that this be taken as an outline sketch which might hopefully inspire some further research. In addition, at this point in the book I have decided to present these perceptions anonymously, mainly because a number of people would begin freely pontificating about their own workplace, and even more readily about the 'culture' of other companies, and would often suddenly pause after a certain remark and prefer that their comments were taken 'off the record'. For this reason I shall not unfairly attribute many of the comments in this section, as I discuss perceptions of the major companies.

There are three points I wish to draw out from the following brief profiles. First, the differential way in which companies are perceived from the outside and the inside, whether or not an individual has or has not previously worked for the label being referred to. Second, the way in which 'culture' is often reduced to or explained as a consequence of the activities of gifted or charismatic individuals. Third, the way in which the identity of the major record labels is perceived to be refracted through the prism of national identity. Following the profiles presented in the last chapter, you should remember that companies are not static and that this is another historical 'snapshot' of a changing industry.

Sony Music Entertainment was, for those in other companies and for ex-staff members who wished to distance themselves from their previous employer, a record company that maintains 'a culture of control' and 'order' and a highly bureaucratic corporation – 'even press releases have to be signed by about seven people'. Sony was described as 'inflexible', a company in which 'people know their place'. It was frequently asserted that staff were motivated to work through 'fear' and 'paranoia'. For a number of observers this was perceived as an environment that had been deliberately fostered by President Tommy Mottola who, in the words of one person, 'instituted a reign of terror and really bootstrapped that company. It worked.' In a profile of how Mottola had 'rebuilt' the corporation, the *Los Angeles Times* preferred the adjectives 'aggressive', 'abrasive' and 'brash', an approach reflected upon by Mottola himself in his remark that when he was appointed, the corporation was 'a stodgy monolith full of complacent yes-men who wondered why no band would sign with us' (Philips, 1996, p. D4).

The Japanese influence was also seen to be pervasive. Here is a typical comment made by one music journalist:

> Sony has changed and the people over there very much know that they work for Sony and they're in the Sony building and the Sony super-store is downstairs and there's a huge restaurant at the top with a privately maintained sushi bar that flies in fish from Japan daily or something – it's quite something to behold.

A similar remark was made by an executive who had been employed in various positions within the industry:

> In a thousand years from now if someone's digging through the ruins of New York City and they find fifty tons of white marble, they'll know that was the Sony Club....This is the white marble sushi bar and the waterfalls and elaborate dining rooms; excesses.

The sushi bar seemed to be a symbol, perched on the top floor of a 'cold' granite corporate block which housed a tightly controlled corporation – the sort of place that put off Green Day.

However, perceptions inside the company turned out to be more complex. Perhaps the only characteristic that was acknowledged from all of the above was the bureaucracy – 'the number of signatures required before I can get things done' – but this might apply to all of the major labels. Internally staff argued that Sony was not simply one Japanese-owned corporation, but a company of distinct parts that maintains what are perceived to be the historical traditions of the Epic and Columbia labels (Columbia tracing its origins back to the end of the nineteenth century):

Sony is really still the old CBS records, it still has a very American flavour....You really have to remove the name Sony, it really is a record company with two major labels and a lot of sub-labels, headquartered in New York.

And as one member of staff also reflected when talking about different parts of the company:

Oh, the Columbia people, it doesn't say Sony Music on their business cards. They work for Columbia Records, they work for Epic Records...all the people who work for the different labels know that the food chain leads them back up to Sony Music, but when they say who they work for they work for Columbia Records...I mean, at conventions I've been with people from the labels and they don't ever say that they're at Sony Music, they're at Epic...there is a difference and there is a different culture for each label....The Columbia people are different from the Epic people.

I have included this unattributed quote at length to highlight how a company that has often been judged to be monolithic and orderly is also perceived and experienced internally as diverse and composed of distinct elements and different cultures, a contrasting set of views that raise questions about whether this type of talk about 'culture' tells us very much about Sony Music as a corporate entity.

In contrast to external views of Sony, those outside the PolyGram Music Group (prior to its merger with Universal) perceived the corporation as a 'mixture' of different cultures or 'labels with their own culture' such as A & M, Island, Mercury, Motown and Def Jam. This view was acknowledged and shared internally, where staff would speak of the company as composed of 'different entities' and praised what they perceive to be the 'entrepreneurial' culture that has been created by having a diversity of distinct labels within the same corporation. However, for Edgar Bronfman Jr, CEO of Seagram, who acquired the group for their Universal operation, PolyGram had been guilty of contributing to the 'confusion' arising from 'too many labels' operating in the US music business.[4] Universal planned to reduce the number of distinct label identities producing similar music and to simplify the portfolio.

For its US critics, the PolyGram Music Group had also suffered from being 'too European', its staff being 'more reserved' than those from the United States. This was judged to affect the company's ability to sell recordings and acquire artists in the United States. Alain Levy, who was appointed as CEO in 1988, is French and was described as 'cold', with the *Wall Street Journal* reporting that he was 'infamous for ignoring subordinates in elevators'. The same article quoted EMI's President Davitt Sigerson, an ex-PolyGram employee, remarking of French executives:

> It may take years for them to address you by your first name, but that doesn't mean that they are distant...it's a sociological trait. If you talk to any Europeans about Mr Levy, they will find comments about his remoteness to be absurd.[5]

Opinions like these have also been used to support the belief of many within the industry that the reason European-based companies (such as PolyGram, EMI and BMG) have been unable to succeed in the USA is their failure to understand how to work with 'American executives'.

While staff within the company referred to the environment in PolyGram's New York corporate building as 'friendly' and 'informal' (and not 'cold' or 'distant'), such outside judgements about remoteness led to a direct response that was sensitive to such criticisms. In 1996 PolyGram appointed UK-based, West Indian-born Roger Ames as President of the music group, and in doing so Alain Levy stressed that 'Roger is not a foreigner that we are sending to the US to find out how the market works. He values my label presidents there, and is totally acceptable to them, which is important to me' (quoted in Clark-Meads and White, 1996, p. 6).

Like PolyGram, the culture of the BMG Music Group has been described as 'European' and more particularly as 'German'. National origins were frequently alluded to in response to my questions about BMG's culture and identity. One person recalled that when BMG acquired RCA in the middle of the 1980s, the phrase 'Big Mean Germans' was circulating as an explanation of the BMG acronym. Someone else who had 'spent a lot of time there' remarked that it was run by 'Germans with a very organized approach. You can see it in the way they operate. Very organized; it's a generalization about Germans but it certainly holds true at BMG.' One journalist observed: 'They are managed from Germany and you go around the top floor and all their secretaries speak a little "like zis".' Such perceptions also framed a profile of Michael Dornemann, then head of BMG Entertainment, which appeared in *Music Business International* where the reader was informed that his voice 'still has a noticeable German accent' and that, although international, BMG is 'German at its very heart' (Scott, 1994).

Such views not only support arguments about why BMG has not been able to succeed in the US, they feed into judgements about its inability to revive the fortunes of one of its key labels: the once US-owned RCA (originally the Radio Corporation of America) which, as I mentioned in the last chapter, was being routinely referred to as 'Record Cemetery of America'. RCA was also judged to be 'always a mess', 'moribund', 'sleeping and passive' and 'anonymous'. Internally, staff were aware of these perceptions and argued that it was due to RCA's inability to establish a strong back catalogue in the US. Internally, however, people would also stress RCA's connections to smaller, more 'street-wise' labels, such as Talking Loud, the home of the Wu-Tang Clan.

For many years, internal staff and external observers have made clear distinctions between RCA and BMG's other major label, Arista, a company run by legendary 'music man' Clive Davis and strongly associated with this individual personality. Executives in other companies speak highly of Davis, crediting him with the ability to pick hits and persuade artists to go back into the studio and record extra tracks, and praising his negotiating skills in establishing successful working relationships with small r 'n' b labels (LaFace and Bad Boy, for example). Davis also projects the image of being involved in every aspect of the record company operation, and in the opinion of Dave Laing, observer and analyst of the industry for many years, is 'one of the last examples of a "one-man" company'. While RCA is housed in BMG's US headquarters in an ostentatious and imposing building that dominates Manhattan's Times Square, Arista is physically separate and tucked away in a more modest terraced building down a side street some twenty minutes' walk away.

Unlike some of the remarks about 'cold' Europeans, the US-owned Warner Music Group was usually described as a 'warm and friendly' place to work. However, the mid-1990s marked a moment of crisis when the company's culture and years of 'stability' were perceived to be dramatically changing. One senior executive, who had spent many years working in different locations for the company, nostalgically portrayed an almost mythical working environment, described as a 'warm, caring human way as opposed to a dictatorial, domineering, by-the-book corporate, conglomerate sort of way...ever since I was in the music business, people wanted to work for Warner Brothers'.

Known for being 'artist-friendly', for inspiring 'loyalty' in its staff and for its 'unbureaucratic' atmosphere in which there was 'a lot of autonomy', the Warner group was, by the middle of the 1990s, well on the way to becoming what Adam White of *Billboard* described as a 'post-character corporation'.[6] A similar judgement was made by one senior executive with over ten years' experience within the company, who remarked:

> We were very loose, easy and freewheeling, but it's not the same any more. The company is encumbered by a large debt and we are no longer Warner Communications, we are Time-Warner and you have two very different corporate cultures here.

The Time-Warner merger in 1988 was judged to have set in motion a process that had resulted in a poorly managed attempt at centralizing Warner's three key labels (Warner, Elektra and Atlantic). One consequence was the departure of key senior 'music men' whom many had considered to be 'untouchable', notably Mo Ostin, Lenny Waronker and Bob Krasnow. For those within the company and for many external observers, these individuals had been integral to the 'culture' of the company and it was believed that an environment fostered by these idiosyncratic personalities had been destroyed and transformed into a more 'anonymous corporate culture'.

Understandings of the strategies and cultures of record labels are peculiarly prone to this type of explanation. The success, identity and direction of a label is explained as a consequence of the extraordinary insights and abilities of charismatic leaders, people perceived to have the ability to motivate staff and inspire loyalty, commitment and a sense of duty in a way that new corporate owners are incapable of doing.[7] From one perspective, figures such as Mo Ostin or Clive Davis may well have stamped their mark on specific labels and given the impression of being 'untouchable' – but they still had to get the figures right, Ostin to his bosses at Warner Music and Davis at BMG. As such, the great individuals also employ routine management and accounting skills and are continually collaborating with a range of junior and senior colleagues.

If Warner was judged to be a company that had established itself through the contributions of individual personalities, for many US-born staff it was also important that the Warner Group was not 'foreign-owned'. While I was informally socializing with one junior employee the conversation was brought around to this issue with the remark, 'You know, we are the only US-owned record company – it makes you think.' Elsewhere, during an interview, an executive remarked, 'I never forget that we are the only US-owned company.'

National identity and perceived national characteristics or continental traits are integral to the way in which many executives in the United States judge the different companies they work for. It provides a way of marking out differences between companies that are, in most respects, very similar. The 'Americans' are 'direct' and 'warm', the 'Europeans' have a tendency to be 'distant' and 'aloof', the Japanese can be 'cold' and 'inscrutable' (a stereotype, a cliché, but a word actually used by one executive). Staff in Britain tended not to perceive individual companies within the UK in such national terms, but often and without prompting would make observations about the characteristics of staff in the US music business. When I was talking to people in the music business in London prior to my research trip to the United States, I was occasionally advised to be prepared to find people in the US divisions of the companies who would be 'loud' 'aggressive' 'egotistical' and 'always shouting at each other'.

These examples provide an indication of how music companies and individual executives are frequently judged through the discourse of national identity – the idea that, collectively, individuals from different parts of the world possess certain particular, idiosyncratic qualities and characteristics. This is frequently assumed to explain the 'culture clashes' which might occur – whether between European and US executives at a record label or Japanese managers and Hollywood producers in the film industry.[8] Nationalism may be a very recent way of drawing boundaries around human groups and may involve a sense of belonging to an 'imagined community' (Anderson, 1983) but it produces strong feelings of psychological attachment which frequently manifest themselves, in this everyday routine way, in the most narrow stereotypical attribution of characteristics to different music companies. Although companies like to be known as 'global' and despite the similar dress codes and jargon found in the executive suite and the recording studio in London, Tokyo and New York, the competitive struggles and working practices within the music industry are frequently perceived through the prism of national identity. As Michael Billig has observed in his study of 'banal nationalism', the idea of nationhood is always 'near the surface of contemporary life', operating through 'unmemorable clichés' that should be taken seriously 'because of, not despite, their rhetorical dullness' (1995, p. 93).

SUITS, JEANS, SNEAKERS AND MUSICAL CHAIRS: 'CULTURAL CHANGE' IN THE MUSIC BUSINESS

In much of the above discussion I have presented executives within the music industry speaking about the 'culture' of their companies as if it is shaped rather spontaneously and mysteriously by the wills of charismatic individuals and whims of national differences. However, companies have also been engaging in more down-to-earth and calculated attempts to 'engineer' their cultures. The two major companies that I have not yet profiled here, EMI and Universal, had both been through various unstable periods and by the middle of the 1990s were making explicit attempts to 'change' their culture. In each case, culture was understood in terms of individuals and perceptions about national differences. A focus on the specific ways in which these two labels were attempting to make organizational changes provides a further insight into what company culture means in the music industry, and how senior executives think they can go about changing it.

I have already mentioned some of the corporate restructuring that occurred within the EMI Music Group in the previous chapter. While much of this activity was motivated by financial concerns, a number of organizational changes were introduced in an attempt to acknowledge negative judgements that were being made about the company's identity. For many years, the British-owned company had been perceived as 'stuffy', 'bureaucratic' and 'lacking in identity' (whether or not that latter phrase is a contradiction in terms). The purchase of Virgin Records in 1992 and the influx of senior Virgin staff into the organization was thought to have significantly changed things. According to one executive with many years of experience within the company, a process of 'Virginification' had occurred and this had resulted in a shift towards a less formal atmosphere, characterized by more 'jeans and T-shirts' and fewer 'suits and ties'. This was perhaps more apparent in the UK than the US, where EMI was a less-known entity, had not really developed this type of identity, and relied largely on the profile of Capitol Records, an 'American' label established during the 1940s which made use of the logo of the Capitol building in Washington and which initially released recordings by artists such as Nat King Cole and Frank Sinatra and later, during the 1960s, by The Beatles.

Despite having these successful artists within the historical archive, the contemporary company was consistently judged to be under-performing. In an attempt to deal with continual poor economic performances, EMI's CEO Jim Fifield had responded to the 'national issue' by initiating what trade magazine *Music and Copyright* judged to be a total break with 'its traditions' and described as 'the most thorough-going process of Americanization' – appointing various US-born executives to run divisions.[9] However, the US executives who were initially appointed, such as Daniel Glass at EMI Records and Jim Bowen at Nashville, were very soon replaced by other executives who were explicitly briefed to 'change the culture'. Here I will focus on the changes at EMI New York as an example of one of the many attempts to reorganize a music label.

Davitt Sigerson was appointed as President and CEO of EMI Records in September 1994 and brought with him twenty years of experience as a singer, songwriter (for artists such as The Motels and Graham Nash), producer (including David & David and Olivia Newton John), journalist (*Melody Maker, Rolling Stone, Village Voice*) and executive at PolyGram. Although born in the US, he had lived in the UK since he was thirteen, and only returned to the US at the end of the 1970s after receiving a master's degree from Oxford University. Sigerson's appointment was thus hardly an example of straightforward 'Americanization', and he came with a broad range of experiences and the potential to understand the problems that a British music label might have working in the United States.

Prior to his formal appointment as President, he had spent three months working in a management position which, as he recalled, had given him the opportunity to 'observe the company and people in it and talk to people and form some conclusions'. Sigerson's immediate boss in the US, EMI Group North American Chairman Charles Koppelman, had briefed him to make substantial changes to the label. Davitt thought that it needed it. As he recalled:

lol

It needed a culture. I needed to do it very dramatically and the way to do it was by bringing in a lot of different people. Some of it was also re-tooling the company for what we were trying to do with it. But it was to get people in here who were passionate about music and who had something to contribute – not just people who were sort of obsessed with success, which is a kind of hollow vibe to worship, but people who have personal experience of what it's like to covet a pop record. You have to know what that feels like. You have to have gone to the store yourself at midnight to buy the record because you can't wait for tomorrow. You have to take it home and have it.[10]

In his own words, Sigerson wanted to 'change the culture', again by removing and bringing in people, and in doing this he wished to transform the perception of EMI within the industry:

I mean, EMI was the last place that someone would have thought of to bring a quality artist. We were known for the fast buck and the quick fix and the pop sensation and the one-hit wonder....It was very important to me to eradicate what had been the very unhealthy old culture, which was a place that was obsessed with success and making money and having a certain style and profile, and turn it into a place which was really passionate about music.

Honourable aims, and ones which might be expected from Sigerson's musical background. But how do you do it? What does it practically involve? In response to my question, he replied:

Well, I fired eighteen senior executives in my first afternoon here on the job....I said, 'You know, it's much better because we don't know each other. This doesn't reflect on your performance. It couldn't, because I have no opinion. I'm doing something differently, I'm configuring the place in a different way, and I have to judge you as the senior management of this whole company by the choices that you made, and they're not the choices that I would have made.' In some cases, having been around them and sat in meetings and had some conversations, I was able to have some real concrete evidence as well. One senior executive said, 'Well, why are you doing this?' and I said, 'Well, I've heard your views on a number of subjects, and frankly I've never agreed with anything you've said. That doesn't mean that I'm right, but you can't really be a senior executive in a place where nothing you say is going to get acted upon. We view the stuff differently.' So it was not a hard thing to do on that level, and it was a tremendously liberating thing for the artists who had been signed here, almost all of whom were miserable, and for the junior people here, who felt that

whoa

they were working in a place that didn't have a soul and that didn't care about the music. It created a tremendous initial burst of high spirits for everybody.

Sigerson estimated that between September 1994, when he took over, and March 1996, when I spoke to him, 70 per cent of the people who had been working at the company when he took over were no longer employed. Other members of staff I spoke with acknowledged the impact of these changes. Publicist Ricardo Howell, for example, considered that the working atmosphere had become 'more relaxed' and 'less manic', recalling that prior to this new management; 'you'd come in in the morning and turn on your screen and there's the boss sort of looking at you'.[11] Sigerson observed the change to be apparent in attitudes, values and dress codes:

> They were all known for wearing their Armani suits and suspenders and they sort of tore around the place and all had limos. It was very much about 'what table are you getting at the restaurant?'. The first day I left the office here as the President of the company I walked out with a bunch of the remaining senior people, and there was a whole line of town cars outside and I went out to hail a taxi cab and they all looked at each other. The next day I walked out and there were no town cars waiting outside.

Sigerson not only cut the staff working for the company, he cut the artist roster. In his first year the label released twenty-four recordings as opposed to sixty-four the previous year. He also brought in staff who were committed to the philosophy of developing artists for the long term rather than simply having short-term successes. When I spoke to Davitt in March 1996 he was building on these initial changes and putting in place a label he believed would be able to attract talented artists who would wish to stay with the company for the long term. He was seeking artists who would build catalogue and grow as 'career acts' by creating 'a body of work' over a long period. One artist who was being treated in this way at the time was D'Angelo.

Sigerson's 'culture' changes, his 'retooling' and reconfiguration of the company and his belief in a long-term and committed approach requiring some degree of patience was ultimately to be thwarted by movements at a higher corporate level. Just over one year later, in May 1997, in yet another exhibition of cost-cutting and crisis management and in a further attempt to restructure the organization, EMI corporate headquarters sacked Sigerson, along with thirty-four other senior executives, and closed down the EMI New York office (Buckingham, 1997). Sigerson was not without a senior position for too long, however. In January 1998 he was appointed Chairman of Island Records, part of the PolyGram group of labels whose head was the 'very French' Alain Levy, whom Sigerson had been asked to comment upon by the *Washington Post*. Whether or not Davitt judged that the culture of Island was in need of change, he might perhaps have reflected on the irony of becoming Chairman of the same company he was signed to as an artist. It was while at Island that he had, in his own words, 'all the bad experiences on the receiving end of one of these big machines rolling over you that it's possible to have'.

While these changes were being introduced at EMI, similar attempts were being made to transform company culture at MCA Records (shortly to be renamed Universal). In Chapter 2 I referred to some of the corporate strategies introduced by Seagram, notably making cash available for acquisitions and investment, and to new President Edgar Bronfman's publicly stated desire to 'redesign' and 'transform' the corporation (Fabrikant and Weinraub, 1996). Here I want to provide more details of how this was connected to attempts to bring about organizational rearrangements that were understood as 'cultural change'.

The changes introduced at MCA/Universal also highlight the connections and interactions that occur between a music label, an entertainment group and their corporate owners, in this case between MCA Records, MCA's headquarters at Universal City in California and Matsushita's headquarters on the sprawling outskirts of Osaka in Japan. I have already referred in the previous chapter to the tensions between MCA's management of Lew Wasserman and Sidney Sheinberg, and Matsushita. From the perspective of those in the music company this posed a double burden. First, many were bewildered as to why Matsushita had purchased a major (80 per cent) stake in MCA in the first place. 'Synergy' was the publicly touted idea (the connections between hardware and software), but nothing seemed to be happening. Michael Rosenblatt, Senior VP of A and R, recalled:

> You know the old bosses, the Japanese, were just not receptive. Nobody understood why they bought us, because they weren't doing anything. They weren't investing, they wouldn't let us grow. Nobody could figure out why we were there; what did they want with us?[12]

The hard-to-fathom 'Japanese' were judged to be one problem contributing to MCA's stasis. A further problem was seen to reside with the management of the entertainment group itself. The *New York Times* described the 'old MCA' in the following terms:

> Under the 50-year reign of its 82-year-old patriarch, Lew R. Wasserman, MCA had gained a reputation as the austere antithesis of Hollywood glitz. Run by men in conservative suits, it was known for

its rigid chain of command, its competing fiefs, its intimidating corporate culture and a cost-consciousness so deeply embedded that Mr
Wasserman himself regularly checked overtime claims.

(Fabrikant and Weinraub, 1996, p. 3)

Seagram's acquisition led to the appointment of Edgar Bronfman Jr as
Chairman and CEO (Seagram being a Bronfman family-owned corporation). Along with Ron Meyer, who he appointed as President of MCA, he
aimed to change the company, making claims that both film studio and
record company would become 'talent-friendly' and 'exciting' places to
work. One of his first changes at the music group involved appointing
Doug Morris as Chairman. Morris had previously been at Warner, which,
as noted earlier in this chapter, had gained a reputation for being artist-
friendly, and Morris (although perceived by some people to be one of the
reasons why it was losing this image) immediately recruited a number of
his former colleagues to MCA. As Michael Rosenblatt observed with
obvious enthusiasm, making the connections between the Seagram acquisition and changes occurring in the record label,

> The new guy and the Seagrams people, Bronfman – he's bringing in all
> these new people. If you look at all the people that are here now and
> running all the labels, we have the best. I mean, all the people who
> were running the Warner companies are here now....It is helping to
> change the culture of the company. The people that were here before,
> you know, the guys who were running it before – Sid Sheinberg and
> Lou Wasserman – they were brilliant at what they were doing but
> didn't really get what *we* were doing. Because the numbers were good
> they said OK, we're fine, let's keep it going. But it wasn't. It was
> deceptive. It wasn't fine and we weren't one of the happening cutting-
> edge labels, and now we're turning into that.

As in other interviews I tried to get a clearer idea of what this change of
culture actually involved. Rosenblatt explained:

> We have about 300 employees – it's all about people. People posi-
> tioned properly in a company can really change the culture of a
> company. Well, you can't do that at TWA or American Express, you
> change two people there and it's not going to change anything. But at
> MCA Records you change a couple of key people and it's a different
> company....You know, the guys that were here before used to wear
> suits and ties to work. The guy now – I usually dress casually, and I
> went into my first meeting with him and he was dressed in sneakers
> and a baseball shirt. And that sends a message to the artist that this
> guy is not a suit. He's not a suit and he gets the music, which he does.

Rosenblatt's observations here are similar to those of Sigerson in two specific ways. First, 'culture' is collapsed to 'people', and second, these people are judged according to what they wear and a pejorative judgement is made of people who wear (and thus are) 'suits'. This is common in the music industry. There is a belief, held more among A and R staff than elsewhere, that 'creative' people dress casually and that the wearing of a suit is a sure sign that someone does not understand the music. On three different occasions it was pointed out to me that the major labels organized their US corporate blocks in such a way that 'the suits' did not have to travel in the same elevator as the creative types with their baseball caps, jeans, trainers and Walkmans. A caricature, perhaps, but one that is based on a certain reality if you stand and observe those waiting to catch elevators in the lobbies of Sony, BMG, Warner and PolyGram in New York City. Most elevator systems travel to a limited number of floors (from ground to 2–24, or from ground to 28–45). One accepted logic is that the higher you rise, the more senior or 'corporate' it becomes.

The assertion of difference from those caricatured as 'the suits' is one way in which artist and repertoire staff assert their identity, establish their closeness to the musicians and producers and claim their distance from administrative and business affairs staff. There are arguably as many accountants grooving to their corporation's music as there are A and R staff who do not like the music they are dealing with, who are working with artists because they have been allocated a particular performer and not through any passionate commitment to the music. At the same time, accountants can retort that they are not paid to 'understand' the music in the first place. As music business accountant Eric Longley remarked: 'I say to my clients, "It doesn't matter whether I like your music. What matters is, am I providing a good accounting service?" Some of them, I do go to their gigs because I like their music.' Of his days at Manchester's Factory Records he recalled: 'When I was at Factory I used to wear my suit to work at least once a week to remind people we're in a business to make money, this is not a game.'[13]

The significance of accountants and business affairs staff is severely downplayed if they are simply reduced to 'suits' and assumed to have little understanding of and contribution towards the creative process (i.e. if we uncritically accept A and R logic). While the high-powered executives and star artists may continually move between the few major labels and while a continual stream of young staff may come and go, financial analysts, legal staff and accountants can remain with the same corporation for many years. This is where the source of a major label's stability often resides.

Although artist and repertoire staff are often thought of as the initial point of contact for any new artist who may be signing to a company, it is the business affairs people (accountants and lawyers) who will be involved in drawing up the finer details of any contract. A and R staff may provide a hip face, may hang out in the mythical 'street' and club, may discuss song arrangements with their artists and book an act into a studio. But it is business affairs staff who will approve the payments to the studio. If a band find themselves recording on a Sunday morning and suddenly decide that they require additional equipment or session musicians and that this will take them over budget, then it is more usually the signature of the head of business affairs that will release the funds to allow the creative process to continue. Hence, an artist's personal relationship with the director of business affairs is arguably more important than their repartee with the young scout who may have first seen them playing in a club, and who may be with a competing company or working in a record shop in two years' time. Business affairs staff assess the economic potential of any acquisition over both short and long term. They are then involved in continually monitoring an artist's economic performance and will judge at which point a performer, catalogue or genre is no longer commercially viable. Any artist signing to a company would do well to think less about the style of the talent scout and more about the integrity and commercial philosophy (and indeed the musical preferences) of the president of business affairs.

My earlier profiles of companies, and Sigerson's and Rosenblatt's assessments of 'cultural change', certainly provide an indication of the specific ways that staff within the music industry understand and interpret the identities of different companies. Such beliefs can also be found in annual reports and corporate advertising where appeals are made about the distinct identity of the company. Yet it can be misleading to accept self-promoted definitions of a 'unique' organizational culture, particularly in the vague terms routinely used by executives when referring to their own and their competitors' 'cultures'. An immediate challenge to such an idea can be observed in the way that personnel are continually moving between record companies, sometimes en masse. At one point at the end of 1995 and beginning of 1996, it seemed as if MCA was turning into Warner Music, with the number of ex-Warner employees who were joining the label (Zimmerman, 1995). Similar observations were made about how Jim Bowen had populated EMI's Nashville division with ex-MCA staff during the early 1990s. As Ruby Marchand, VP of A and R at Warner Music International remarked, reflecting on the crossing of staff to different companies: 'There's movement, so that people who were maybe educated in the Warner fold are now at PolyGram.'[14] These musical chairs are institutionalized in *Billboard* magazine's 'executive turntable', a weekly column that highlights the continual movements of staff between the major record labels.

Considering these movements alongside the similar organizational structures within each company and the very pragmatic concerns guiding most strategies and daily activity (budgets, sales, advances), I would conclude that claims about the distinctive 'corporate culture' of the different major labels are often decidedly mythical. Such myths are certainly held in place by assumptions about national differences, even when the same executives move between 'European', 'Japanese' or 'American' companies. The belief in cultural change is also maintained by assumptions about the abilities of charismatic individuals to provide the type of leadership that can transform an organization. Yet many of the changes introduced under the rubric of 'cultural change' might more plausibly be viewed as part of the daily micro-political manoeuvring that characterizes the industry. Clothing certainly communicates and conveys all sorts of cultural meanings. But the transition from suits to jeans and trainers may have less to do with a significant change to the 'culture' and more about the desire of the newly installed president to recruit an alliance of buddies and trusted colleagues, who just happen to wear jeans and trainers (or who pragmatically recognize that it is appropriate to dress this way in such an organization). He or she might be merely marking out their territory, creating their space, ensuring that delegated tasks will be carried out and establishing their presence and alliances within the corporation. Yet the myth of cultural change endures as a way of legitimating such organizational changes.

THE SUCCESSFUL CORPORATION AND THEORIES OF MANAGEMENT CHANGE

Despite the sentiments of staff who have worked for the Warner group for many years – the belief that one reason for the label's success over a long period was the 'stability' of the working environment – the management of music companies has involved the introduction of continual changes in personnel and organization. Why should such organizational changes be so frequent, and why should the implication that they are contributing to 'cultural change' be so attractive? The answer to this question is related to my discussion of strategy in the previous chapter, in which I highlighted how numerous management and organizational changes are introduced in a desperate attempt to make a company label or unit more successful and ultimately more profitable. In many cases, change is simply introduced for the sake of change, the rationale being 'it's not working, we must change it'. The alternative option is to cut the 'under-performing' unit or label from the portfolio. The decision to make these changes may well be irrational and have little base in any clear reason or logic, but it can be rationalized and understood through the idea of 'cultural change'. That is to say, senior executives believe that it is not a mistake to maintain a rock, jazz or country division *per se*, and that there are no problems with corporate management above this division. The problem, so it is believed, is within the division itself, and senior management assume that changing the people will lead to a change in the 'company culture'. Such is the logic of many organizational sackings and recruitments in the music business.

This type of reasoning is attractive to corporate office ('there is nothing wrong with our structures, assessment methods, accounting systems and distribution arrangements') and also appeals to the newly appointed president and staff ('we can turn this around, it's just a matter of new people changing the culture'). Such ideas are explicitly informed by beliefs about the importance of company culture, promulgated by the prescriptive literature and various 'management gurus' who champion this cause.

Notions of company culture go beyond the belief that the right environment, populated with the most suitable people, will attract artists to music companies, and embrace ideas about how business in general can be made more competitive. As Graeme Salaman has concluded from a thorough review of the writings on this subject, 'the claims made for "cultural change" are enormous' – cultural change, it is asserted, can provide the 'formula' for success, improve efficiency and increase the commitment and involvement of staff in the workplace (1997, p. 241). Perhaps more significantly, it is argued that cultural change can improve a company's economic performance, an idea that numerous books have endorsed and management theorists have propagated in business seminars.[15]

This belief has also guided various writers and researchers in their attempts to identify the 'components' or 'elements' of culture, and has informed the notion that these can be managed or 'engineered'. For example, in an influential and widely read book on *Corporate Cultures*, Terence Deal and Allen Kennedy (1988) identified 'elements of culture' such as organizational symbols, heroes, rituals and values, and suggested that these could be identified, isolated and modified for the benefit of the corporation. In opposition to this and numerous other books and articles proffering a similar prescription, Caren Siehl and Joanne Martin argued that such claims have 'not been – and may never be – empirically demonstrated' (1990, p. 242). Siehl and Martin point to a number of problems with this type of approach. First, echoing Hofstede's observations about accounting practices (see Chapter 2) they have disputed the belief that financial performance can be 'measured' in any straightforward way. Second, they have challenged the way that organizational strategists have treated 'culture' as single and unified (a homogenous company culture) and thus reduced complex cultural beliefs and activities to 'indicators' which can be isolated and measured. Against this, Siehl and Martin have argued that claims of a causal relationship between 'culture' and financial performance are profoundly misleading. While there may be a 'link', it is unlikely to be open to such a manipulative and mechanistic approach to its realization, i.e. do this with your 'culture' and your economic performance improves. For Siehl and Martin, the obsessive focus on performance has been hampering attempts to understand the broader ways in which culture is related to organizations. A similar point has been made by Hugh Willmott who has argued that the narrow focus adopted in this type of reasoning results in the 'abstraction of organizational culture and symbolism from its wider historical and politico-economic contexts as culture is dissected into rituals, myths, sagas and the like' (1993, p. 521).

With these criticisms in mind, I would argue that the problems Sigerson was attempting to resolve at EMI may have been about far more than 'cultural change' or getting the right people into a music label. This point would seem to be borne out by the way in which higher corporate office intervened and closed down his unit before he could realize the task. The 'problem' was perhaps broader and more profound, less connected to what was going on 'inside' the New York label and more about how this label was interrelating with other label groupings and units within the corporation (all competing for space and resources), and how, in turn, the corporation was connected to music cultures in a wider sense. It is my argument in this book that 'corporate cultures' and the 'cultures' that create the music industry are not simply contained 'within' organizations and their business units.

THE INDUSTRY WITHIN CULTURE

Prescriptive approaches to understanding organizations with a view to introducing management changes tend to treat 'culture' as an observable entity that is contained 'within' the organization. This, of course, makes it easy to offer ways of 'managing culture', as the corporate entity is empirically known and identifiable and not concealed within various interpretations. As Kathleen Gregory (1983) has observed, such an approach avoids and evades the research which has found that 'large, internally differentiated and rapidly changing organizations' often only 'command part-time commitment from their members' (1983, p. 365). This is very true of the music business, partly through the way in which portfolio management prioritizes financial goals without any due concern that everyone in the company should share the same values or ethical beliefs in achieving these goals. Hence, there is scope for differentiation and for staff to inscribe their own values within the practices of the company. Not only are there differences between a corporation's labels based in the same city, but the geographical dispersion of a company's offices leads to visible and audible contrasts in the working world in the major labels' offices in New York, Nashville (the country division) and Miami (the Latin division). These would extend further if we consider the international dimension (and staff's continual perception of national differences). Such differences clearly pose a challenge to any assumption that Warner or Sony or BMG may have a distinct company culture and that this can be found threading throughout the organization. As Gregory has argued, following her own research on 'technical professionals' working in Silicon Valley, there are various 'occupational communities' and these can 'provide employees with identities and significant reference groups within and outside the company' (1983, p. 370).

In Chapter 1, I stressed the importance of understanding the 'culture of production' against writers who have merely focused on the structures and organizational constraints shaping the 'production of culture'. Here I wish to extend this to move explicitly away from any assumption that the 'culture of production' can in any simple way be equated with ideas about 'company culture'. Following Gregory's suggestion, it is important that we look outside a company when considering what is going on *within* an organization. Drawing further on insights from Geert Hofstede's (1991) work on how organizational life is shaped by national, regional, ethnic, religious and linguistic affiliation, I want to approach music industry organizations as embedded in a surrounding context and always in the process of translating and mediating such cultural characteristics, giving them a specific form through particular working practices.

The following three chapters are an attempt to explain in detail how record companies are embedded within and interact across a surrounding cultural context that can have a more significant impact on the workings of a corporation than any attempts to 'engineer' corporate culture or manipulate the office environment. By arguing this, I'm suggesting a shift towards wider questions about culture. These include questions such as: To what extent are music industry practices shaped by – but at the same time an intervention into – regional, ethnic, religious or linguistic affiliation? How does gender, sexuality or class create patterns which shape the presentation of artists? And how does this inform the male/female and heterosexual/homosexual 'roles' that can be found within the music industry in general and which are acted out across particular genre cultures?

In moving in this direction (although not addressing all of these issues in detail in this book) my general point is that to understand the issue of culture and the music industry it is necessary to think away from organizational culture in a narrow sense and towards the broader cultural patterns that intersect with an organization, to think away from *culture within an industry* and towards an *industry within culture*. This is the line of thinking through which I will focus a number of the threads from these first three chapters in the following profiles of rap, country and salsa.

Chapter 4

The business of rap: between the street and the executive suite

Rap has usually been approached as an aesthetic form of African-American expression: a resistant, oppositional, counter-cultural style created via the appropriation of technology and existing musical signs and symbols (scratching, sampling, mixing), drawing on a long tradition of diasporic creativity (with varying inflections of both an essentialist and anti-essentialist argument that point both back to and away from the slave routes of the Atlantic). Although the music industry has been referred to and acknowledged by a few writers,[1] most of the writing has tended to concentrate on cultural criticism[2] and locate the 'politics' of rap within the domain of a cultural struggle conducted across the broad terrain of 'consumption' that is lived outside the world of the corporate entertainment industry.

This perspective has clearly demonstrated that rap has been made as a cultural practice that involves the quite explicit creative appropriation of existing sounds, images and technologies and their reconstitution as a new art form. The creation of rap has also highlighted the tangible connecting points that link the often inadequate concepts of 'production' and 'consumption', and has illustrated how consumption can *become* production. In the process, creative practice and aesthetic discourse have produced a particular type of cultural-political identity which can be understood in terms of a long tradition of black creative activity, not only within the United States (Fernando Jr, 1995; Vincent, 1996) but within the context of a diaspora of the black Atlantic (Gilroy, 1993).

This chapter is not a direct challenge to such an account but an attempt to add a further dimension to the arguments and knowledge through which rap is understood as both a musical genre and cultural practice. My argument is that to understand rap, both in the past and its potential in the future, then cultural explanations alone are not enough. Rap is also a very particular US business. As Kevin Powell wrote in a magazine profile of the highly successful Death Row Records, prior to the death of Tupac Shakur and the imprisonment of Suge Knight:

There is no way to truly comprehend the incredible success of Death Row Records – its estimated worth now tops $100 million – without first understanding the conditions that created the rap game in the first place: few legal economic paths in America's inner cities, stunted educational opportunities, a pervasive sense of alienation among young black males, black folk's age-old need to create music, and a typically American hunger for money and power. The Hip Hop Nation is no different than any other segment of this society in its desire to live the American dream.

(Powell, 1996, p. 46)

In the struggle against racism and economic and cultural marginaliza-tion, and in an attempt to 'live the American dream', rap has also been created as a self-conscious business activity as well as a cultural form and aesthetic practice. A skim through consumer magazines such as *The Source* or *Vibe*, publications that address both artists and fans (often at the point where the two merge), reveals frequent references to issues of 'career plan-ning' and business management, often presented as a form of educational intelligence. A typical article in *The Source* began in the following way:

We all have dreams, aspirations and goals...things that we dream of but for whatever reason don't follow through on. For many of us, that dream is getting into the recording industry. So before you just dive with reckless abandon into the murky waters of the biz, here are some steps that might make the going a bit easier.

Knowledge: Go to the library and do your homework. This will give you a basic knowledge of the day-to-day operations of an inde-pendent label. It's also very important that you do an internship at an independent label (a minimum of 6 months). Make contacts, ask ques-tions and take notes. It is important that you are able to experience, first-hand, the struggles you will inevitably face.

Business plan: As in starting any business, you must have a plan. You need a 5-year business plan that includes a projected budget. Your business plan should reflect you. You're the one who has to live by it.

(Payton, 1997, p. 96)

The article then goes on to cover other issues under the subheadings of cash, legal counsel, operating a business, communication, artist, produc-tion, manufacturing and distribution and promotion – throwing quite a different light on to the idea of rap spontaneously emerging from 'the streets' (an issue I shall come back to shortly).

In a similar way, a reading of trade magazines such as *Billboard* will turn up a number of articles in which rap artists and entrepreneurs, whether Suge Knight or Chuck D, explicitly discuss their commercial strategies and business plans or where executives such as Angelo Ellerbee, President of Double XXposure, discusses his 'charm school for rap artists' (Snyder, 1996). As Bahamadia commented during the promotion for her first album:

> You have to understand that this is a business. When you sign your name on the dotted line on your contract you are literally a walking human business as well as a human being. So you have to study this business, ask questions, educate yourself and have a plan B and a plan C.
>
> (Fitzgerald, 1996, pp. 22–3)

I hope that in some small way this chapter might educate and inform. I also wish to argue that, to understand what rap might mean and its potential as a form of cultural expression and communication, it's also necessary to understand it as a business that links – and perhaps more significantly separates – artist and audience in quite distinct ways. In very broad terms, this chapter follows the central theme set out earlier in this book by considering how the industry sets up structures of organization and working practices to produce culture and also by highlighting the way that broader culture processes and practices connect with the industry – the uneasy relationship between the genre culture of rap and the corporate cultures of the music industry.

In developing the theoretical focus I outlined earlier, I shall illustrate these dynamics by analysing how the industry organizes the production of rap in a very specific way and bases working practices on a particular construction of knowledge about the social world. The approach to the relationship between rap music and the recorded entertainment industry that I am proposing here is more complex than the often narrated tales of co-optation, exploitation and forced compromise to a commercial agenda, although these pressures are certainly not absent. At the same time, it is an attempt to avoid the celebration of black entrepreneurialism or the endorsement of rap as a type of material success-oriented 'fun capitalism'.[3]

The title of this chapter, 'Between the street and the executive suite', signals a further broad argument and general theme that weaves throughout. First, it signals the way in which rappers who have often been identified solely with 'the street' are also executives. I consider this important, for while the portrayal of rap artists as creative iconoclasts from the margins certainly reclaims a value for activities that have been devalued, it fails to adequately acknowledge that rap is, potentially, not 'outside' or bursting out from the periphery but central to the development of the practices and aesthetics of the contemporary music industry. However, this is not simply to replace rap artists and entrepreneurs at the centre of a fun type of capitalism. Instead, my aim is to raise questions about *why* and *how* rap has remained 'on the street' – materially and discursively. Here 'the street' operates as a metonym for a particular type of knowledge which is deployed by executives throughout the music industry, a type of knowledge which legitimates the belief that rap *is* and *should be* outside the corporate suite. Hence, I use the theme of the street and executive suite to signal the way in which the discourse of the street (and the mythical 'being in touch' with it) is integral to how the music industry deals with rap practices. One consequence is that this maintains a separation of experiences and contributes to the ongoing reproduction of the broader economic, cultural and racialized divisions across which r 'n' b and rap have been and continue to be made.

In approaching rap in these terms, this chapter, like those that follow, is a deliberate attempt to try and steer a course away from the dichotomy between modernist despair at the power and influence of corporate commodity production and postmodernist celebration of the possibilities provided by cultural consumption and appropriation. It is also an attempt to suggest that the politics of culture need not simply be waged on one side or the other, but during a significant series of connections and relational practices which connect production and consumption and the articulations through which the corporate organization and music industry occupations are linked to broader cultural formations.

CORPORATE DECISIONS AND CULTURAL DIVISIONS: THE MAJOR COMPANIES AND THE BLACK MUSIC DEPARTMENT

To understand how the recording industry has come to deal with black music in general and rap in particular, it's necessary to recall my earlier outline (Chapter 2) of how the industry, and specifically the US music business, deals with different genres. As I discussed, the major record companies use a technique known as portfolio management in order to divide labels, genres and artists into strategic business units, making visible the performance, profile and financial contribution of each division. Well-established genres are often referred to as 'cash cows' (see Chapter 2). A genre such as rap, however, despite the revenues it has continued to generate, may be classified as a 'wild cat' by industry analysts who are uncertain about its future aesthetic changes and nervous when trying to predict 'potential market growth', and by business personnel who are uncomfortable with the politics of black representation foregrounded by the genre and anxious about confronting political pressure from the moral opponents of rap (these issues I shall elaborate over the following pages).

It is within the context of corporate strategies of portfolio management that the major companies and their labels have come to deal with black

music in separate divisions. Historically, the contemporary management of rhythm and blues within separate formally defined corporate entities can be traced back to a reorganization of the music business that occurred during the late 1960s and early 1970s. The creation of 'black divisions' during this period was a response to commercial opportunity, social and political pressure and cultural changes. A number of factors contributed to this. One involved pressure from activists associated with the civil rights movement and the National Association for the Advancement of Colored People, who urged the major labels to give a more equitable remuneration to black artists and sought greater representation for industry personnel. Additional pressure came from the so-called Fairplay Committee. This was a group, associated with DJs and radio personnel, that managed to combine what many supported as 'commendable aims' (a fair deal for African-American artists and music industry staff) with alleged acts of intimidation and violence and a desire to extort money through being 'the prime collector of payola for all black disc jockeys' (Wade and Picardie, 1990, p. 175).[4]

A further influence came from within the major companies themselves, where senior executives were beginning to reassess how they dealt with different types of music. After commissioning research, the major companies selectively followed the key recommendations of a 1971 report for CBS by the Harvard Business School, that had advocated the formation of black music divisions.[5] This was for many executives a logical restructuring and response to promotional practices and radio broadcasting which had dealt separately with African-American recordings through a series of euphemisms which began with the term 'race music' during the 1920s (Garofalo, 1994, 1997). Reebee Garofalo (1993) has also pointed out that when the 'race music' labels of the 1920s (such as Black Swan, Merit and Black Patti) were hit by the Great Depression, they were bought up by major labels (such as OKeh and Paramount) and maintained as a distinct 'race music' series, kept separate from other parts of the catalogue. Hence, although the major labels began setting up black music divisions and departments from the early 1970s, the practices upon which this built can be traced back throughout the twentieth century.

One benefit of such a practice is that these divisions have provided a space for black staff within a company, people who may not otherwise have gained employment in the music business. These separate divisions have also ensured that musicians are managed by personnel with knowledge, skills and understanding of their music (not all of whom are black, obviously). However, staff within the black divisions have experienced an unstable and uncertain existence. One of the most significant disadvantages is that the department can easily be cut back, closed down or restructured by the corporation (whether this is due to an assessment that the genre has changed or simply because cuts have to be made). A similar fate can befall many departments when exposed as business units, from the cutting of the smallest Latin division in the 1980s to the reorganization of the largest hard rock division in the wake of the rise of post-Nirvana 'alternative rock' in the early 1990s.

However, it is often the black music division that is subject to greater cutting than others. A notorious example of this occurred in February 1996 when Capitol Records closed its urban division, cancelling the contracts of most artists and sacking eighteen members of staff (most of them black). This was yet another example of EMI's drastic restructurings, discussed in more detail in Chapters 2 and 3. On this occasion the company publicly explained that they had closed this division so as to concentrate resources on their 'stars' (such as Bonnie Raitt and Richard Marx) and their modern rock artists (Everclear and Radiohead). In the week that this occurred, I happened to have an interview arranged with Havelock Nelson, a *Billboard* writer who, over the years, has been involved in organizing various hip hop workshops and educational events. As he remarked: 'This happens so much whenever there is a budget cut to be made; it's always the black department that suffers.'[6]

For J.R. Reynolds (1996), another columnist working for *Billboard*, this event represented 'the systematic extermination of black music at Capitol Records' and 'cut the company's ties to the r 'n' b community'. As such, this was far from simply an 'economic' decision. Reynolds pointed out that it could not be justified in market terms: in 1995 r 'n' b and rap had sold 132 million albums and accounted for over 21 per cent of the music market in the US.[7]

Despite the corporate reasoning presented to the press, the 'commercial' strategies of music corporations are not simply business decisions alone, but are informed by a number of value judgements and cultural beliefs. In this instance, whatever the dynamic within the company, to many outsiders this looked suspiciously like racism and a distinct lack of commitment (in terms of staff and investment) to sustain an involvement in black music and what Nelson George (1989) has called the 'rhythm and blues world'. George has used this phrase to refer to the 'extramusical' significance of rhythm and blues as an 'integral part' and 'powerful symbol' for 'a black community forged by common political, economic and geographic conditions' (1989, p. xii).

Hence, one issue here is that of occupational insecurity. The music industry is a notoriously insecure place to work, but black music divisions can be particularly unstable. For as long as they have been in existence the variously named r 'n' b/black/urban divisions have been chopped and changed. They have been closed down and reopened as a way of dealing with financial booms and slumps, and staffed and restaffed as senior management has continually changed its thinking about how to deal with r 'n' b. Recent shifts include the transition from appointing senior staff with

backgrounds in promotion during the middle of the 1980s to heading the black divisions with attorneys, artists' managers and producers in the early 1990s, and then bringing in artists and producers in the middle of the 1990s.[8] This instability was rather ironically signalled by a panel organized for a music business convention by the coalition Sista Friends, entitled 'You're Not Really In The Record Business Until You've Been Fired'.[9]

This instability intersects with a broader issue of historical continuity. Although numerous African-American executives have contributed to the formation of the modern music industry and the history of recorded popular music, all have continued to occupy a 'precarious position' (Sanjek, 1997). The black music divisions have not been allowed the space to establish their own agenda. One conspicuous point here is that there are very few senior black executives within the corporate hierarchy who are above the black division and hence involved in the decision about closing down business units or restaffing existing departments. This is frequently acknowledged within the industry and has been emphasized by Garofalo, who has noted that 'black personnel have been systematically excluded from positions of power within the industry' (1994, p. 275). There is a strong sense, and a justifiable belief held by many in the industry, that the black divisions have not been allowed to develop a continuity and a sense of history that is consonant with the African-American contribution to US musical culture.

This issue was publicly raised by Andre Harrell, whose music industry career has seen him move from performer (in the act Dr Jekyll and Mr Hyde), to head of Uptown Records (a joint venture with MCA which broke acts such as Mary J. Blige and Heavy D and The Boyz) to President and CEO of Motown for a few years in the middle of the 1990s. While at Motown he observed:

> Black music is becoming *the* music of the popular culture. Because of that, companies are repositioning their priorities and trying to get in the game. But as black music becomes more important, there should be more black presidents and black chairmen. As soon as the black executive's artist reaches platinum, suddenly the artist and manager have to deal with the president of the corporation, because *he* controls the priorities at pop radio. The black executive becomes obsolete. As his music gets bigger, his power diminishes. He's more or less told, 'Go find the next act and establish it.'…That's why young black executives don't get to become the old chairmen – the wise men who've seen it and done it. They get to stay hot black executives so long as their instincts are hot…the black executive is not given the opportunity to become the business *and* the music. Why not? Why shouldn't he be the one that everybody reports to? When you get an act that sells 5

million – at a major company – the black executive's out of the room. But when there's some sort of problem, the major label looks at the black executive: 'Why can't you handle this act?' When the artist hires a violent manager and the violent manager is coming up to the record company the label's like: 'How did it get to this?' How? Because *they* [the white executives] couldn't see it coming. Because *they're* not sensitive to his issues. By then the relationship between the record company and the artist is dysfunctional. And the black executive gets blamed and fired. But *they* created the monster.

When I had the artist, I talked to his mother, his girlfriend, his babies' mother with the two children, dealt with his drug counsellor, and whatever other dysfunctional Generation X problems he has. He'd call me late at night.

But he feels like they're just business people. And they *don't* understand. And they *might* be racist. He's comin' with all that energy. Even if they like him as a person, he still has 400 years of issues he has to get over to accept them. And they have a lot of work to do to gain his trust and respect.

(DeCurtis, 1995, p. 94, emphasis in original)

Harrell spoke these words with considerable experience, highlighting how racial identity, racism and the history of racial antagonism inform relationships that are often blandly referred to as 'business decisions' within the corporate suite. Ironically, Harrell did not last long in his post at Motown, but his comments were publicly vindicated just under two years after the publication of this interview. It was then that PolyGram (the current owners of Motown and the corporation which had appointed Harrell) removed Eric Kronfeld, their domestic music president, from the board after he made 'several racially insulting remarks' in relation to the company's r 'n' b act Dru Hill. Alain Levy, PolyGram President, immediately appointed Clarence Avant who became the company's first African-American director (Johnson, 1997).

It is within the context of this history that the music industry began dealing with rap (or not dealing with rap) during the 1980s. At one point it seemed that the major companies had neither the inclination, the understanding nor the skills to deal with rap. It was partly anxiety, partly lack of expertise and incomprehension on the part of the majors that allowed many small companies to carve out a considerable niche during the 1980s. It's often claimed that the small companies were in touch with 'the streets'. But it is not as straightforward as this – the large companies have also allowed small labels to carve out such a niche.

INDEPENDENTS ON THE STREET: KEEPING IT OUTSIDE THE CORPORATION

If one way in which the major companies have attempted to manage African-American music has involved the continual cutting and restructuring of their r 'n' b division, the other has been based on a series of changing relationships with minor companies. There is a familiar explanation offered for why so many successful rap recordings have come from independent labels: they are 'closer to the street'. It's a view held by many observers of the music industry. As Tricia Rose has written:

> It became apparent that the independent labels had a much greater understanding of the cultural logic of hip hop and rap music, a logic that permeated decisions ranging from signing acts to promotional methods. Instead of competing with smaller, more street-savvy labels for new rap acts, the major labels developed a new strategy: buy the independent labels, allow them to function relatively autonomously, and provide them with production resources and access to major retail distribution.
>
> (1994a, p. 7)

This perspective draws on the long-running argument that changes in popular music are driven by the activities of independent companies. There is an element of truth in this claim; it is often easier to identify a new sound and participate in its circulation from outside the gatekeeper-riddled systems of the major companies. It should also be acknowledged that many black independent companies are also attempting to assert their autonomy and self-sufficiency (George, 1989). However, this is a partial and rather too neat and tidy explanation of why rap has ended up *produced* on so many small labels, even if the artists do tend to be *marketed* and *distributed* by the major companies.

There are a number of ways in which this argument has been challenged. One counter-claim has proposed that rap has been somewhat closer to the middle-class suburb than the street. According to David Samuels:

> Since the early 1980s a tightly knit group of mostly young, middle-class, black New Yorkers, in close concert with white record producers, executives and publicists, has been making rap music for an audience that industry executives concede is composed primarily of white suburban males.
>
> (1995, p. 242)

There would seem much evidence to support such a claim. Many of those involved with the influential 'street savvy' labels – such as Tom

Silverman at Tommy Boy, and Russell Simmons and David Harleston at Def Jam, were from educated and middle-class backgrounds. The backgrounds and actions of various artists, such as De La Soul or Chuck D, for example, could also be cited to support this argument.[10]

Yet, this claim is equally partial. In terms of production, rap has, since it first began to appear on recordings, been produced from multiple points of origin with distinct inflections of geographical place (Houston, Atlanta, Los Angeles, Washington, Philadelphia, Georgia), class identity (De La Soul or NWA), ethnic representation (Fugees, Tres Delinquents, Cypress Hill), urban, rural differences (Arrested Development, Smoothe Da Hustler). Not only has rap been stylistically diverse, this diversity has been created across complex identity amalgams. Hence, it is misleading and partial to collapse these variances into any straightforward model of inspiration from the streets or collusion of the black middle class with white executives.

Equally, the idea that the integrity of rap is undermined because a large part of consumption can be located within the white suburb is also simplistic. A strong case against this claim has been argued by Rose (1994a), who has pointed out that purchasing statistics do not in any straightforward way equal 'consumption'. Sales figures – such as '75 per cent of rap records are owned by white teenagers' (Whalen, 1994, p. 12) – cannot account for the complex ways in which rap is *circulated* and how recordings are appreciated, used and re-used. Young males in the white suburbs may have the disposable income to purchase a recording that will sit on a shelf looking cool, while, in contrast, black urban youth may circulate recordings and listen to them repeatedly, record them, mix them – there may be a much higher 'pass-along-rate' (Rose, 1994a).

What does seem clear is that, as rap has been and continues to be made, appreciated and circulated, it has intersected with and crossed numerous borders of class, neighbourhood, gender, ethnic label and 'national' belonging. Yet it has not been crossing many divisions *within* the music industry. There are two distinct, but interrelated, regimes of containment I want to identify here: first, organizational practices through which rap is confined to a specific 'position' within the industry and not accorded as much investment (economic, staff, time) as other types of music; and second, those through which a particular type of knowledge finds expression in a discourse of 'the street'. These simultaneously deny the complexities I have just referred to, and in doing so construct a simplistic commercial cultural 'reality' for rap production which is easily accommodated to the management practices adopted by the music industry.

MAJOR ANXIETIES: AFFILIATIONS, REPRESENTATIONS AND EXPECTATIONS

One of the characteristics of rap that initially confused the major companies was the way that rap proposed a series of working relationships across different musical entities: cliques, collectives, affiliations and group and label identities that connected together different 'bands' and individual performers. This is signified in the continual appearance of performers on each other's recordings and the way that this establishes very specific networks of affiliation and alliances, e.g. the performers who have grouped around such entities as The Dogg Pound, Dr Dre's Aftermath and Puff Daddy and The Family.

The genre culture of rap posits a different notion of musical practice, not only in the well-documented use of existing musical elements and technologies but in terms of the idea of a 'career' and sense of belonging to a musical entity. This is quite a contrast from that of the stable, bounded and predictable rock unit or pop band, the solo performer and self-sufficient singer-songwriter which the industry has become competent at producing and comfortable in dealing with. Rap posits a fluid series of affiliations and associations, alliances and rivalries – occasionally serious, and usually related to neighbourhood and representation.[11] These affiliations are lived across various group and individual identities.

This is connected to another issue which the industry has also found uncomfortable, the representation of 'the real' or what is often referred to as 'being real' and the politics of identity which has accompanied this. This aspect has often received more superficial mass media coverage than serious debate about the issue which it raises and has frequently been reduced to simple arguments about profanity and the generic imagery of violence and misogyny that has characterized so-called gangsta rap. The 'discussion' is often informed by a simple stimulus–response model of media effects and an aesthetic reductionism through which rap becomes merely lyrics. One consequence is that there have been overt political pressures put on record companies – from 'community' organizations, government and state forces – and this has further encouraged the major companies to distance themselves from the genre culture of rap.[12]

Further judgements made by staff within business affairs and international departments have also had a decisive influence on the acquisition and drawing up of contracts for rap artists. There are two 'business decisions' here which are far more than straightforward commercial judgements. First is an assessment of the ongoing revenue that can be generated from rap: what is referred to as 'catalogue value'. Rap tracks are routinely compared to conventional songs and it is asserted that they cannot be 'covered' – re-recorded, re-sung, re-performed by other artists. Hence, rap tracks are judged to have a short catalogue shelf life, in terms of their ability to bring in ongoing copyright revenue from their re-use.[13] In addition, the revenue that rap can generate during any assumed 'shelf life' is considered to be less than other types of music. In the words of one corporate attorney:

> Music publishing and rap is a nightmare because so much of it is parts of songs. You know, they have, like, one-eighth of this song and two-thirds of another song…because everything is owned by someone else that can make those deals less expensive, but also less lucrative for the publishers than otherwise….The publisher looks at how much they can collect on a particular album, and sometimes because of the number of samples on the album the amount they can collect can be pretty low.[14]

As Thomas Schumacher has observed in his discussion of sampling and copyright law, rap 'highlights the ways in which notions of authorship and originality do not necessarily apply across forms and cultural traditions' (1995, p. 265). Not only do they not apply, they pose problems for the 'universals of legal discourse' (Schumacher, 1995, p. 265). Hence, the music industry copyright system, itself established upon culturally coded assumptions about the character of a composition and performance which can be traced back to the nineteenth century (Frith, ed., 1993), is inscribed into these business relationships and informs these apparently straightforward 'commercial' decisions. One consequence is that rap is perceived to be less attractive in terms of the criteria through which long-term catalogue value is accorded. Hence, less will be paid to artists as advances and royalties, because less can be earned.[15]

A further pragmatic business judgement that affects the amount invested in rap is the assumption that it does not 'travel well'. Here a strand of racist anxiety which permeates the international music industry manages to combine with a narrow aesthetic evaluation. One senior executive in an international department remarked that he had sat in meetings and heard rap recordings being referred to as 'too black' for international promotion,[16] a broad sweeping claim that is justified specifically with the assertion that lyrically rap is 'parochial' – although the history of popular music is littered with parochial lyrics appearing in numerous places around the world. While rap does foreground poetic vocal performance, it is misleading to imply that this works simply as lyrics and not as an emotional performative sound event. This argument from within the industry, like Tony Mitchell's claim that US rap has remained 'resolutely local' (1996, p. 26), seems to reduce the genre's aesthetic complexity and rhythmic, harmonic and melodic cosmopolitanism to rap lyrics.

Hence, there are a number of ways in which the music industry seeks to contain rap within a narrow structure of expectations: through confine-ment within a black division; through arm's-length deals in an attempt to avoid dealing with various alliances and affiliations; through judgements about rap's long-term historical and geographical potential to endure. One consequence is a straightforward lack of investment, and the adoption of practices to keep investment down (it is easier to deal with production units than to invest in staff and office space within company). At the same time, rather than bringing the culture – the people, the practices – into the industry, the major companies have tended to maintain a sharp border. This can be contrasted with the treatment of rock in the late 1960s and early 1970s. During this period there was a noticeable and often commented upon movement from the rock subculture and so-called counter-culture into the music industry – a period when the 'revolution-aries' were on CBS (as one marketing slogan proclaimed at time).[17] This has continued, with a new wave of young white males recruited into the US music industry in the early 1990s following the success of Nirvana and the stabilization of grunge into modern or alternative rock. As Joe Levy, a music writer for a number of years, observed in 1996:

> I have not seen r 'n' b and hip hop have the same impact that the big boom in alternative rock had on the industry. Certainly two years ago there was this influx of young people in their twenties going to labels as A and R people and vice presidents of this or that, and these were almost uniformly young white kids who were coming into work alter-native rock in the wake of Nirvana....There's a career path in the industry that has to do with alternative rock and I don't necessarily know that it's there for rap and r 'n' b.[18]

Rap personnel have not been embraced or recruited in the same way. For example, when Capitol closed its black music division the company dropped most of its artists and moved only a few acts over to the EMI label. The company publicly announced that this was because EMI had the expertise to deal with them. Yet a few weeks later, when I interviewed Davitt Sigerson, President of EMI Records, and asked him to explain how he deals with rap, he said:

> I don't have anyone doing r 'n' b A and R. What I've adopted as a model is to have a bunch of different production deals or first-look arrangements with entrepreneurs who bring me stuff...it's a very affil-iative sort of creative community and process and I don't need to be in a camp.[19]

Earlier I referred to George's use of the term 'rhythm and blues world' to suggest that r 'n' b is more than a genre of music. Likewise, George has characterized rap culture as a 'post-civil rights, ultra-urban, unromantic,

"more than a gence of music"

hyperrealistic, neonationalistic, anti-assimilationist, aggressive Afro-centric impulse' (George, 1992, p. 93). In the above discussion I have highlighted how these genre cultures relate to the organization of the major companies and inform major–independent relationships within the music industry, suggesting that rap culture is kept at a distance from the main offices of the corporations. Despite the influence of rap and hip hop on the aesthetics of music, video, television, film, sport, fashion, dancing and advertising, the potential of this broader cultural formation to make a contribution to music industry business practices is not encouraged. Indeed, as I now want to argue, this distance is maintained by the discursive practices articulated through the myth of the street.

REBELS, INDIES AND THE STREET

I have already suggested that the major companies tend to *allow* rap to be produced at independent companies and production units, using these producers as an often optional and usually elastic repertoire source. This is not to deny the struggles of artists and entrepreneurs for both autonomy from and recognition by the major music companies. However, I am stressing the above point because I think we need to be wary of the increasingly routine rhetoric and romanticization of rap musicians as oppositional rebels 'outside' the corporate system, or as iconoclasts in revolt against 'the mainstream' – a discourse that has often been imposed upon rap and not necessarily come from participants within hip hop culture itself. In addition, it is important to remember that small companies are not spontaneously or straightforwardly inclined to be more in tune with new musical developments. That certain independent labels (such as Atlantic, Stax or Def Jam) have been so at specific historical moments is beyond dispute. But most rap labels have very soon entered into formalized and fairly standard commercial relationships characteristic of those between major and minor companies, a division of labour based on a production/distribution split. Despite such close ties, the making of rap is usually explained with numerous references to 'the street'.

In very general terms, rap is often associated with the street by senior executives when talking about different types of music. For example, Kevin Conroy, Senior VP of Marketing at BMG, remarked that, compared to other styles, rap and hip hop 'is a business that really grows from the streets'.[20] In a similar way, the corporate *Advertising Age* once informed its readers, 'The streets where a rap album begins, of course, are very far from the suburban record stores where it ends up' (Whalen, 1994, p. 12). As Michael Rosenblatt, Senior VP of Artist and Repertoire at MCA, remarked, aware that he was using a somewhat clichéd idea: 'A lot of the rap does happen on the small labels because rap is much more of a street thing, it happens on the street. I know it sounds trite, but it really does.'[21]

Apart from these very general associations of rap with the street, there are two further and more formal ways in which 'the street' is articulated. First, in terms of 'taking it to the streets' – what is often referred to as street marketing. Second, in terms of 'bringing it from the streets' – frequently referred to as 'street intelligence'. Both practices involve formalized management practices and systematic commercial procedures that are by no means peculiar to rap or r 'n' b.

TAKING IT TO THE STREETS

The promotion and marketing of rap, like other genres of music, involve the use of techniques that, elsewhere, I have characterized as 'promotional war games' due to the way that they are referred to by staff within record companies through a number of 'war-like metaphors' (Negus, 1992). So, for example, when Capitol still had a presence in black music, the label's rap promotion unit was called 'Capitol Punishment', and the head of the section was referred to as the 'chief commander and warden' (Nelson, 1994, p. 26). The term 'sniping' is routinely used to refer to fly-posting bills which make no reference to the record label involved, merely signalling the name of the act and tracks or album. The so-named 'street teams' (largely made up of college or radio DJs) have been described as 'right there in the trenches'[22] and as engaging in 'reconnaissance missions into urban enterprise zones' (Rubin, 1997, p. 99). When I spoke to David Harleston, then Senior VP of the Black Music Collective at MCA, he referred to 'the use of guerrilla marketing tactics and street promotion'. When I rather naively asked what this might involve, he explained:

> Well, it's going to places where consumers are and hitting them where they live. So we no longer just rely on radio or rely on video, which are both very important. We also promote at barber shops and swap meets and things like that and...playgrounds where folks are shooting basketball...we have street teams who hit people with singles and flyers and stickers and stuff like that....When you take a rap project to radio, radio wants to know that the street is behind it before they'll commit to it. You can't go to radio cold.[23]

The term 'street marketing' is shorthand for building an interest in a track or artists through a long process that can involve circulating recordings to influential party-givers, using word-of-mouth networks, approaching local radio mix shows and college radio and promoting through stickers and flyers placed in public places where the targeted 'demographic' will take notice. This was institutionalized by Loud Records, a label half-owned by BMG, in their promotion of a number of acts, particularly the Wu-Tang Clan. As Steve Rifkind, Chairman of Loud Records, has claimed:

> I can tell a record company in two days if they have a record or not....We know that kid from the time he steps out of his house, every step he's making, where he's going to hang out, what's the scoop on where to eat lunch at, where he's getting his hair cut, what's the cool way to get it cut, what's the cool record store to go to. We know all these things, and before we attack we get all the information from the street first.
>
> (quoted in Rubin, 1997, p. 99)

Prior to forming Loud Records, Rifkind had established his reputation by promoting recordings by acts such as Boogie Down Productions and Brand Nubian. He followed this by promoting Nike sports gear, spending some time with Nike founder Phil Knight. This gave him the experience which he drew upon when formulating a strategy for selling the Wu-Tang Clan. In his own words: 'a kid who's going to buy a pair of Nikes is the same kid who's going to buy a Wu-Tang record' (quoted in Rubin, 1997, p. 100).

The ultimate aim of street marketing is to build up such a 'buzz' that the radio stations will feel that they have to programme a recording as they themselves will want to be heard to be 'in touch with the streets'. As Marcus Morton, VP of Rap Promotion for EMI, commented:

> You have to have the DJs and the people that are the trend-setters. They kind of herd the sheep around. They have to like it. And every-body else – y'know, if you look at the people that programme the cross-over stations, nine out of ten of them think that they are the hippest thing on the planet, but in reality they're not. They listen to somebody else. Which is either their DJ – that's why you have a mix show DJ because he's supposed to be really in tune with the streets and really in tune with what's going on. And he's supposed to play it on his show and then translate it back to the people who run the stations so that they can put it into regular rotation.[24]

In practice, the activity of 'street marketing' relies upon a number of well-developed acts of persuasion that have been deployed within various industries for a number of years. This includes utilizing the 'personal influ-ence' of key opinion-formers, 'selecting target markets', using concepts of 'followers' and 'niches', and 'branding' and 'positioning' products.[25] These practices are not peculiar to rap, but are used when selling a range of products throughout the entertainment and fashion industries. As Terri Rosi, VP of Black Music Marketing for BMG Distribution, commented when I remarked that 'there's a lot of talk about "the street" ': 'I know and that's very annoying because the end result is that you talk about "the street" but you really want it on radio and you want it on MTV.'[26]

BRINGING IT FROM THE STREET

As implied in Rifkind's comments about following the movements of 'the kids', street teams are also responsible for information gathering and feeding that data back to headquarters. This is sometimes described as an informal process of intuitively hanging out in colleges, neighbourhood record stores, clubs, playgrounds and parties, an experiential process of 'developing an instinct' by keeping an ear and eye on what is going on. However, the process is also far from spontaneous and is organized in comparable ways to other types of information gathering. To quote from Terri Rosi once more, this time at length:

> It is systematized. You have a guy out there called a street promotion person who is hanging out in stores and clubs and talking to people, and he may even actually go into a college campus. He may be wherever people gather that are those people. He has to learn his market-place and know where he's supposed to go. They put up stickers in advance so when it comes two months, three months later, 'well, yes, I know the ABC band,' or whatever. So in that sense, it is a form of street intelligence and you get feedback and you learn after a while who can pick the hit, you figure that out, but it's very people-intense. You're out there, you're moving, talking and working and doing all that kinda stuff....We've got twenty of them all across the country, and there will be one person in the record company who works with the street team. So they give their reports, where it's going to work, where it's not going to work and their reputation is on the line. I can't tell you that I'm the street person in Oakland and tell you, 'Man, this is gonna jam,' and then I ship these records in there and nobody likes it at all. Because, well, 'Who did you talk to?'...You don't want to lose your job because you didn't do the right thing. So, yes, in that way it is very systematized.[27]

Street intelligence is about 'knowing markets' and 'knowing consumers' and, like street marketing, it involves employing conventional business management techniques based on monitoring, data gathering and accumulation. Yet these conventional marketing practices and business activities are elided through the discourse of the street, denying that this is similar to the other activities that are daily being conducted and initiated from the corporate suite.

MORE THAN MUSIC: RAP, FASHION AND PRODUCT ENDORSEMENT

On page 98 I referred to Steve Rifkind's association with the Nike company and highlighted how this influenced the way Loud Records presented and promoted the Wu-Tang Clan. From the days when Run DMC made reference to Adidas in their songs to the appearance of Coolio and Method Man on the catwalk to present Tommy Hilfiger's new 1996 fashions, clothing has been central to the marketing and making of rap. This has been increasingly recognized by magazines such as *The Source* (which accrue a large part of their revenue from the clothing and sports shoe manufacturers who place advertisements in their pages), performers (who have been increasingly endorsing different products and creating their own lines of clothing) and record labels. As Jim Parham, Director of Sales at Tommy Boy, remarked when explaining how the music and merchandizing were being brought closer together:

> We are gradually tying the music into the clothing. Right now the clothing is sort of an entity unto itself, but the way it originally started was that we made clothing items as promotional items for the music or the label and they were really popular, so we developed it into an actual selling line and we will hopefully be expanding that in the next couple of years.[28]

Many rap musicians have recognized such connections and formed their own successful companies. Notable here is Wu-Wear, the clothing and accessory company established by the Wu-Tang Clan. This company have stores throughout the United States where you can purchase T-shirts, socks, baggy jeans, coffee mugs and key-chains, all featuring the distinctive Wu-Bat brand logo. Like other companies, Wu-Wear have recognized the importance of music video for promoting clothing as much as for selling music. As Mike Clark, CEO of Wu-Wear, observed: 'Videos are hands down the best advertising you can have' (quoted in Edwards and Stein, 1998, p. 71). Not surprisingly, the Wu-Tang Clan themselves wear their own clothing in their videos. But, like other major clothing companies, they have sought other celebrity endorsements, and artists including Bjork and Rage Against The Machine have publicly worn Wu-Wear, as have various athletes. In 1997 the company made $10 million (Edwards and Stein, 1998) and also signed a deal with the Federated Department Store retail corporation, the owners of Macy's and Bloomingdale's (Parker,

1997). As Public Enemy's Chuck D proclaimed in an advertisement which appeared in *The Source* of September 1996 and in which he was launching his own Rap Style International: 'So You Wanna Be In The Music Business...Whatcha' Gonna Wear?'

The business of rap is about more than music and clothes and can embrace all manner of consumer products, visible and audible in the way that Queen Latifah has appeared in a box of cereal during an advertisement for Frosted Cheerios, as LL Cool J has been rapping in advertising for Major League Baseball, and as Method Man has appeared on billboards dressed in Reebok clothing while KRS-One was promoting Nike. 'Business awareness' and the range of revenue sources that can be linked to the genre have been recognized by numerous rap performers. As Allen S. Gorden 'Tha Ebony Cat' explained, discussing the range of endorsement opportunities being pursued by different artists and companies: 'In an increasingly complex, often hostile, marketplace, many rappers are refining their portfolio by pursuing endorsement opportunities' (1997, p. 98). Whether or not rap culture might enter the corporate suites and boardrooms of the major record labels, the discourse of portfolio management has certainly entered the business of rap.

CULTURE, INDUSTRY AND RAP

In this chapter I have focused on how the making of rap is managed by the music industry, and I have highlighted how various corporate strategies, which utilize the technique of portfolio management as a way of allocating staff, artists and investment, directly intersect with the deployment of a particular type of knowledge used to understand the world and to produce a 'reality' that informs the perceptions and activities of staff. It is not that there are organizational structures (such as the black music division and deals with small production companies): it is that these are operated according to a particular type of knowledge through which the world is imagined in a particular way, a knowledge that depends upon many systematic data-collecting techniques. At the same time, uncritically received cultural assumptions and common-sense ideas about the social location of rap are continually articulated to notions of the street. In many ways this situation is symptomatic of broader social relationships and beliefs about rap culture and the way in which these intersect with and become 'part' of the industry – a process that requires much more empirical and theoretical work before it can be fully understood, but which I have tried to evoke through the idea of 'culture producing an industry'. Such broader cultural political tensions are structured into what are often taken to be straightforward economic, organizational and business practices, activities that are lived by those working within the industry as if they are merely responding to 'the world out there'. One significant consequence is that the rhythm and blues world and the genre culture of rap in particular are kept at a distance from the dominant interests and agendas within the main offices of the music corporations.

Yet rap produced in the United States has managed to move out from such regimes of containment – both at home and abroad. There is a final twist. The physical and discursive borders erected by the organizational arrangements and knowledge practices of the contemporary music industry have meant that rap music and musicians have not been 'co-opted' or invited into the boardroom in quite the same way as have other types of music and their makers, most notably the way in which rock moved from the street to the executive suite.[29] Often denied direct access, offered licensing deals, lower budgets, poorer contracts or simply cut from the roster when there is a financial crisis, rap has (partly out of necessity) been able to generate alternative resources, and through these the genre has continually reinvented and redefined itself in those spaces and places designated (for want of terminology rather than as a transparent description of a 'reality') as 'underground'. That rap musicians have managed continually to redefine the style itself while crossing social and cultural barriers, both within the US and beyond, is a process which has occurred despite, rather than because of, the ways in which the recording industry has sought to organize the production of contemporary popular music.

Chapter 5

The corporation, country culture and the communities of musical production

Since early in the twentieth century the music labelled as 'country' has enjoyed a number of periods of popularity and apparent decline. This has prompted cyclical theories which seek to explain the genre's dynamic of change and aesthetic renewal as well as the business practices which contribute to this. These cyclical theories are spoken of by executives working on Music Row in Nashville and are written about by researchers who have studied the production of country music. A key reference point here is the work of sociologist Richard Peterson (1976, 1997), who for more than twenty years has systematically applied his 'production of culture' perspective to the institutionalization of country music, explaining how the various booms and busts have been accompanied by stylistic changes that, since the earliest days, have involved the quite deliberate 'fabrication of authenticity'.

In this chapter I will not be arguing with Peterson's account of the practices and organization of Nashville songwriting, production and marketing. Nor shall I spend too much time toiling over the same territory that he has carefully researched and elucidated in his writings. Instead, I wish to contribute some ideas that might puncture the boundaries of Peterson's 'production system' and open up some connections to the broader genre culture within which the country music business has been made. My route into the changing character of country culture and industry will be through a discussion of the consequences of increased corporate monitoring of and intervention in the day-to-day workings of a 'music city' that had previously enjoyed a large degree of independence from corporate HQ.

Just as rap has been associated with very specific places, so country music has become firmly linked to the town of Nashville. A central issue I shall be discussing here concerns the way in which Nashville is understood and experienced in various ways: as a geographical place, as a 'music community' and as an industry category. This theme will provide a further way of developing the culture–industry argument that runs throughout this book. This point will lead me to consider how Nashville, as a country music city, has been experienced and constituted as part of 'the South' within the context of a broader series of historically changing economic, political and cultural relationships stretched throughout the United States. This has not simply resulted in any straightforward tension between 'art' and 'commerce', but has led to a situation in which notions of 'family' and 'community' have rubbed up against a particular way of doing business and come to mediate the interactions between those creating country and corporate headquarters.

When using a term such as 'country music business' it is important to bear in mind that this could encompass a lot more than the activities associated with writing, recording and performing songs. The broader country music business includes associated theme parks, clothing businesses, tours and package holidays, museums, bars and restaurants as well as a plethora of merchandizing, media and entertainment products. In this chapter my focus is on the country music recording industry, somewhat artificially bracketed from these other commercial domains, and my aim is to provide a sense of how the production of this genre of music is organizationally and geographically located within the operations of the major entertainment companies.

A BRIEF HISTORY OF RECORDED COUNTRY MUSIC

The history of country music has been told on many occasions and in many different ways. Here I want to pick out a few events relevant to the development of country as a business and commercial genre. The roots of country are usually followed back a long way and most frequently traced to the movement of people from Ireland, Scotland and Northern England to the 'new world' and their subsequent meeting with the musical styles of African-Americans and immigrants from other parts of Europe. Various aspects of what would later be called 'country' culture and a 'hillbilly' style were developed and operating as a commercial 'business' long before the modern recording industry and radio broadcasting provided a particular channel and format for the production and distribution of the music.[1] However, what Bill Malone has called the 'the commercial exploitation of southern folk music' (1985, p. 34) was a process that decisively involved new technologies of cultural production and communication; the phonograph and radio broadcasting. These new forms of technological mediation were used together as a way of 'discovering', 'refining', 'modifying', organizing and ultimately, according to Malone, for bringing about the 'standardization of country music' (Malone, 1985, p. 34), an issue I shall return to shortly.

With the phonograph providing possibilities for the circulation of musical recordings, the first country records to be widely distributed date from the 1920s and were initially made 'on location' by executives from New York, such as Frank Walker and Ralph Peer, or produced in Atlanta by Polk Brockman (Peterson, 1997). It was Jimmie Rodgers, sometimes referred to as 'the father of country music', who is often credited as one of the first major recording artists to demonstrate that country had broad popular appeal and was more than simply an 'ethnic' regional music. Rodgers' significance was not only due to his highly distinct and influential country-blues yodel singing style, an aesthetic testament to the Anglo-Celtic-African influences on the music, or to his 'rambling man' image, which provided both an inspiration and a template for later artists. He is also important in the history of country production because of the phenomenal commercial success he achieved during a time of economic austerity, in the years leading up to and following the Depression, between 1929 and 1933. This was a visible and audible signal that country (or hill-billy) was both a creative and a commercial phenomenon.

Throughout this period, Nashville had yet to become the country music 'capital'. As Peterson (1997) has argued, during the 1920s it seemed as if that title might be fixed to Atlanta, and perhaps, during the 1930s, to Chicago. During the 1940s and early 1950s the growing country music recording industry had yet to centralize and was dispersed, as a variety of labels were recording artists cheaply using new technologies in locations including Houston (Gold Star), Beaumont (Starday), Memphis (Sun) and Cincinnati (King) (Malone, 1985). However, the consolidation of the contemporary country music industry and its association with a particular city (Nashville) was also gaining momentum and of crucial importance was the radio performance event, *The Grand Ole Opry*. This began broadcasting in 1925. It was the most popular of the radio variety shows or barn dances and directly contributed to the establishment of a link between country music and the city of Nashville. As Bill Malone has noted:

> *The Grand Ole Opry* was a catalyst which after the war had attracted a pool of talent and an expanding network of promoters, booking agents, publishers, and the like to Nashville. The proliferation of recording studios and publishing houses, which fed off each other, encouraged the coming of musicians and songwriters who would be permanently based in the city.
>
> (1985, p. 256)

Session musicians based in one location, who didn't tour but who established a reputation for being able to play together in a flexible and adaptable manner, were also an important influence which attracted writers, performers and other musicians. Once label offices, promotional teams and studios had been established in Nashville it seemed economically illogical to then move them out to another location, particularly to New York or Los Angeles where real estate and office space was more expensive. Hence, in many respects Nashville became a music city through the combined efforts of various people, organizations, producers and media systems (notably radio) rather than through any natural link between sound and city. Yet, once established, it became synonymous with the star names of country (such as Hank Williams, George Jones and Patsy Cline) who were migrating to, recording in or moving through the city.

Alongside radio, the introduction of sound into the cinema was also important, not only for the dissemination of country sounds but for the 'western' and 'cowboy' image associated with and adopted by many performers. The success of Gene Autrey and Roy Rogers was facilitated by the Hollywood film industry and the development of 'singing cowboy' movies. In contrast to radio and cinema, television did not have such an obvious impact. The influential *Grand Ole Opry* did not broadcast on TV until the 1970s and then had to follow precedents set during the 1960s, when country on television had tended to be 'overproduced, slickly professional, and only marginally "country"' (Malone, 1985, p. 272). It seems that rock 'n' roll translated to the medium of TV far better than country.

During the 1960s the entire US music industry underwent a period of corporatization involving numerous mergers, acquisitions and takeovers, a process discussed at length by Steve Chapple and Reebee Garofalo (1977). This accelerated a process of consolidation, occurring throughout the 1950s, which had already led to the integration of country production into the operations of the major record labels. By the 1970s, country production was incorporated into an expanding, and increasingly bureaucratic, conglomerate-controlled music industry. Facilitated by changes occurring in country music radio, a twin dynamic of cross-over began occurring, with artists such as John Denver, Ann Murray and Olivia Newton John moving from the country charts to the pop charts and back again, and Nashville studios beginning to adopt pop production techniques leading to the establishment of a narrowly defined 'Nashville sound' which incorporated strings, brass and background choruses. Partly in reaction to this, the 1970s witnessed a return to a more 'rootsier' music, influenced by and allied to southern rock bands such as Lynrd Skynrd and the sounds of the California country rock scene (Poco and The Eagles, for example). This trend was of both aesthetic and commercial significance, a point signalled when The Outlaws released an anthology titled *Wanted* (1976) which became the first million-selling country album. Yet the brief late 1970s boom which attracted companies such as Warner Brothers to Nashville for the first time quickly gave way to a period of aesthetic decline. For many fans and observers country music reached its nadir with the film *Urban Cowboy* (1978), featuring John Travolta. This movie, according to its critics, threatened to reduce the genre to little more than superficial pastiche.

Yet just a few years later country was booming again. This time it was due to a new generation of roots-inflected, rock-influenced and video-facilitated artists who again began gaining both commercial success and critical acclaim. A new type of country performer appeared. The male model was Garth Brooks, a modest yet flamboyant country boy with an elaborate and exaggerated stage show straight from the rock tradition. Soon after, Shania Twain appeared on the scene, utilizing a type of soft sexy pop glamour and using marketing techniques that relied on video, personal appearances in shopping malls and radio and television shows rather than traditional touring and performing before a 'live' audience. With more country music stations than any other genre of music in the United States and with the pop charts apparently declining in commercial significance, it seemed that the balance of power and influence within the music industry might be about to shift. The money appeared to speak: country music record sales had increased from $538 million in 1982 to $1,488 million in 1992. Newspaper articles began proclaiming that country was to become the 'new mainstream' and that Nashville was to be perhaps as significant as Los Angeles or New York. Yet such changes were not as dramatic as they may have initially seemed at the time. The year of 1994 began to be viewed as a 'peak', with 1995 and 1996 described as a 'levelling-off period' with sales beginning to fall by 1997 (Flippo, 1996; Peterson, 1997). The boom was, in many ways, the latest stage of a longer period during which distinct cyclical patterns of change have been identified in country music.

CYCLICAL CHANGES AND THE DIALECTIC OF HARD CORE AND SOFT SHELL

One of the most astute sociological observers of the themes and trends that I have covered briefly in the above potted history has been Peterson, who has adopted the oft-used phrase 'hard core' and contrasted this with its little-used antonym 'soft shell' as a way of understanding how aesthetic changes arise from a constant tension between two types of artist and audience (Peterson, 1995, 1997; Peterson and Kern, 1995). Peterson's work is suggestive of the tensions across which recording companies have continually sought to organize and profit from the production and distribution of country music.

In proposing an enduring 'dialectic' of hard-core and soft-shell, one of Peterson's principal aims is to challenge versions of country music history as a linear narrative that moves from rustic roots to modern pop style. This, argues Peterson, is a way of writing history which incorporates ideological assumptions about the inevitability of musical 'progress' and which connects this to a nostalgia for an imagined pure, spontaneous and immediate way of making music that has apparently been corrupted by modern technology and commercialism. In contrast, he suggests that the history of country music can be understood in terms of two kinds of performance tradition and that these, in turn, relate to audiences in different ways.

From its earliest days, the genre culture of country music has been characterized by two distinct types of performers. Peterson identifies and characterizes these as follows. The hard-core performance tradition utilizes a southern or south-western accent, freely deploys 'southernisms' and foregrounds an untrained voice with a nasal tone. Lyrically, songs tend to focus on concrete situations and personal life experiences. Instrumentally, there is an emphasis on an unelaborated 'roots' style, with artists adopting an informal 'warts and all' type of approach to stage presentation. Visually, hard-core style draws on a repertoire of 'hillbilly' and western clothing, particularly leather and denim. In contrast, the soft-shell performers have tended to sing in relatively accent-free standard American English and to foreground a trained voice with studied interpretations of songs. Lyrically, there is a preference for general situations or the evocation of specific circumstances described in a general way, with less emphasis on first-person direct experience. Instrumentally, soft-shell performers make use of contemporary pop techniques of the time when they are performing, whether brass, strings, woodwind or synthesizers, and their stage presentation tends to be more formally packaged and 'professional'. Visually, the artists tend to be tailored as mature popular singers, with men in slacks and turtleneck sweaters, and women as 'folksy but not folk' (Peterson, 1995, p. 290). These characteristics, which I have summarized briefly, can be found in two distinct traditions of artists, and Peterson's point is that the history of country can be interpreted as a series of reactions between the two, with country swinging from hard-core roots (Ernest Tubb, Hank Williams, Loretta Lynn) to soft-shell pop (Patsy Cline, Crystal Gale, Kenny Rogers). In this way, Peterson presents an argument about the ongoing musical changes within the country genre, suggesting that there is a 'dialectical' tension between these two types of performers which results in a continual pendulum swing between the two styles and series of reactions against one another, rather than any mutual synthesis.[2]

However, Peterson is not simply offering an explanation of cyclical changes in performance aesthetics; he also suggests that the 'two kinds of performers differ as much in the way they relate to audiences as in their performance styles' (1995, p. 277). From research conducted with Roger Kern (Peterson and Kern, 1995), which drew on surveys by the US Census Bureau and opinion-poll data along with information collected at concerts, Peterson produced a profile of hard-core and soft-shell country music fans, differentiating between those with a strong affiliation to country and those with only a secondary liking for the genre. Hard-core fans are more likely to live in or near the country, are more likely to be farm workers or drawn from blue-collar occupations, and in general have 'much in common with the stereotypic image of the country ethos presented in the music of, for example, Hank Williams Jr: poverty background, small town, mid-life, blue-collar and white, a survivor' (Peterson and Kern, 1995, p. 4). The soft-shell fans, in contrast, tend to be more affluent, better educated, employed in white-collar occupations and are less likely to come from a small town. Further distinctions are identified according to musical tastes and consumption habits: hard-core fans are relatively 'frugal' and prefer closely related genres such as bluegrass, religious music and rock, whereas soft-shell fans are more 'omnivorous' and like a broader range of music.

These distinctions are used to make a particular argument about the 'contribution' that fans make to the 'music's cycles of popularity'. Peterson and Kern suggest that the hard-core fans play a central role in sustaining the hard-core tradition of performance. Not only do they identify with the elements of a shared lifestyle that are constructed and communicated by the performers, through their loyalty to one type of style they 'give commercial country music its continuing credibility even as the music changes from decade to decade' (Peterson and Kern, 1995). In contrast, soft-shell fans are not so deeply involved and tend to drift in and out of country music, being attracted to the genre at different times, often coming to country through rock, pop, world beat or as a result of social activities such as line dancing.

Peterson's and Kern's argument about country fans is, in many ways, impressionistic and schematic and has little to say about any generational changes that may cut across such a recurring 'cyclical' pattern.[3] However, they do acknowledge that this is a speculative profile of fans, drawn largely from secondary survey data, and propose it as a starting point upon which future research could build rather than as a definitive theoretical model. From my perspective, their argument raises some important points about the circulation of country music. First, their research suggests that the production of country hinges on the connection between fan and performer and that, in my terms, a broader genre culture is crucial for maintaining the meanings of country styles. In terms of the industry, Peterson shows that a performer's songs, lyrics, visual identities and stage manner are produced and mediated through distinct 'systems of production', marketing outlets and promotional systems. Yet, at the same time, he also highlights how these have to connect with and be interpreted by an active audience. This is certainly something that the country music industry is very aware of: the loyalty of country fans and the importance of fan events are central to the way in which the production and distribution of country is understood by those within the industry, a point I shall return to later in this chapter.

This immediately poses a challenge to Malone's (1985) idea, cited earlier, that the industry has been capable of 'standardizing' country music and reducing the range of styles available. It could be countered, from Peterson's work, that the fans – whether hard-core loyalists or soft-shell tourists – have also been playing an important part in defining country, and hence maintaining musical performance within a narrow series of stylistic expectations. This fact perhaps has broader relevance. When people complain that a specific style of music has become predictable, the culprit is often identified as the music industry. Yet, in many cases, we should perhaps also ask how artists themselves and their fans have played a part in the process whereby styles become standardized into a few easily identifiable generic patterns and audience responses. This is not intended as a glib defence of the industry. My point is that as fans we are not separate from any perceived processes of standardization and routinization. We are not detached observers who are merely looking on or listening, but are part of this process and, as such, we might also be playing a part in the maintenance of generic codes and standard expectations. One of the most obvious forces involved in such processes is undoubtedly country music radio. If anything will provoke people in Nashville to invoke the spectre of Adornian standardization, it is the radio media.

FEAR OF RADIO: CORPORATE RESPONSE STRATEGIES AND THE NATURALIZATION OF THE COMMUNICATIONS MEDIA

When I visited Nashville during May 1996 I spoke to many people, formally during recorded interviews and informally at gigs or in bars, and asked about the importance of country music radio. The more I asked the more I found that one phrase, and a rather old cliché at that, kept recurring: 'The tail has started wagging the dog.' There was a widely held belief, constantly asserted, that radio had become so influential and powerful that it was having a direct impact on who was being signed to publishing and recording contracts and was ultimately influencing the way in which artists were recorded. It was thus crucial to the prospects for artists and the revenue for publishers and record companies.

More than any other subject, mention of radio elicited a flurry of metaphors. It was referred to as a 'great moving target, it moves slowly'.[4] It was likened to 'a four-lane highway. It handles a lot of traffic. It's very cool in terms of allowing you to get speed going and cover long distances but it's not six lanes.'[5] It was described as a 'funnel that we all have to go through'.[6]

With these perceptions shaping the realities of record company staff, I became interested in what record companies were seeking to do about it. How were they responding to the situation? Radio is often felt to be a constraint by musicians and industry staff working with various genres, but it is perhaps more acute in country – could anything be done about it? My own conclusion was that there was a fear of radio that led, initially, to a large amount of anxiety and ultimately to resignation and an attempt to naturalize the situation as something that was just 'there' and could not be changed.

In theory, at least, country radio should have been providing ample opportunities for promoting the repertoires of different types of artists. The number of stations had been increasing each year and had peaked in 1994 when the Country Music Association reported a total of 2,427 operating in the United States, more than any other musical genre format. However, most were following the programming policies and practices of the two or three leading stations, who were considered to be influential in setting the agendas for airplay. Hence, despite a large number of stations, playlists had become relatively narrow and restricted.

The only real alternative was perceived to be on AAA or Americana, a chart introduced by the *Gavin Report* in January 1995 as a reporting category for a small number of radio stations and referred to as 'an alternative, roots-based, songwriter-driven format' (*Gavin Report*, 1996, p. 29). According to advocates such as Cheryl Cline, Americana had provided a space for 'DIY country' and was a 'vital part of the alternative to Top 40 country schmaltz' (1996, p. 2). For the *Gavin Report*, however, the category was not necessarily indicative of an alternative scene, but was primarily a radio category that enabled a company to launch an artist among a few niche stations. This occurred in the case of Alison Krauss, who had achieved this in 1995, moving from 'Americana core artist' to 'mainstream country superstar'.[7] Not long after its inauguration, many working on Music Row believed such possibilities to be rare and most assumed that there were too few stations and that these were themselves fragmented and having little impact upon the major country stations.[8] However, just three years after its launch, there were signs that the category was becoming more coherent, recognized and acknowledged as a label that was useful for promoting artists, not only across the United States but also internationally.

Discussion of radio in Nashville often provoked nostalgic thoughts of the days when the music industry operated according to guesswork, hunches, intuition and personal contacts. It may be a romantic fantasy, but it is used to recall an era when there was less systematic market research and certainly no EPoS (Electronic Point of Sale) technology to bring up-to-the-hour accounts of what is selling in retail, or BDS (Broadcast Data Systems) telling anyone who cares to know what is being transmitted across the nation.

Senior executives in record companies often look back fondly to the days when personal relationships with disc jockeys at radio stations were crucial to the promotion of artists. The DJ might have been a fan who would play a record simply as a result of their enthusiasm for the music, or for the hell of it – to take a chance. Alternatively, the plugger might persuade the DJ or programme director that competitors were playing a particular song and that it was taking off across the nation (even if it wasn't, it was difficult to verify). And, of course, there are numerous old anecdotes about DJs playing recordings in return for drugs, sex or cash.

However, radio has changed. First, the activities of radio stations in the United States are more scrutinized and subject to closer regulation. Second, stations have begun employing an ever increasing variety of methods of audience measurement, feedback and research, and then using the subsequent 'data' to inform judgements when assessing the persuasions of the pluggers. In addition, radio stations have been increasingly employing consultants to assist in the formulation of playlists. Consultants have become crucial intermediaries and have been central to the way in which record companies have been losing out in their power struggle to influence radio.

Consultants act as contracted advisers to specific radio stations. Their job is to monitor musical trends, track spending on advertising and follow listener research and regional consumption patterns across the networks. They then advise individual stations of the most competitive and commercial strategies. Consultants may suggest that a station stop playing the recordings of specific artists, no matter how successful (Mary Chapin Carpenter, Garth Brooks, Emmylou Harris were all mentioned to me by frustrated record company staff). They may advocate 'narrowcasting' even further, reducing the scope and range of music that is played. In some cases a consultant may advise a station to switch 'formats' (i.e. musical genres) and go for a completely different 'demographic' (i.e. group of listeners/audience).

Rather than radio stations engaging in audience research and producing their own commercial data, the task has been passed over to consultants who have been accorded the key tasks of monitoring audience trends and assessing musical styles. This has a number of advantages for the radio station. First, staff within the radio station do not have to listen to the vast number of recordings being solicited from record companies, as they will be advised by the consultants which ones are hot and which are not. They can concentrate on their main task of generating advertising dollars. Second, individual programme controllers and radio station managers can no longer be held responsible for any bad judgements in selecting music, as they are not making assessments about which recordings to play. This leads to a third point: the radio station can effectively pass the buck and put the blame elsewhere. Radio station personnel can evade the responsibility for failures and also for any reluctance or unwillingness to play a particular recording that is being promoted by a specific company. In short, the blame can be passed to the consultant.

This situation crucially changes the personal relations that the record company pluggers attempt to establish with radio station personnel. As I have discussed in detail elsewhere (Negus, 1992), pluggers who visit radio stations have usually attempted to build strong personal relationships with DJs and radio station programme directors. The aim was always to establish a mutually 'symbiotic' relationship (Hirsch, 1972) whereby the radio station will occasionally do a favour by playing an unknown artist while the record company will provide the station with a continual supply of predictable music. In this sort of relationship it is always possible for the plugger to appeal to the personal side of the programme director or disc jockey and ask for a favour or for the station to take a risk with one song. With consultants involved, however, the radio station personnel are under no such obligation or influence. A track is not played, simply because a consultant has advised that it is unsuitable. As a result, the career paths of radio station staff, and any cash bonuses earned, can result from these rational routine procedures rather than the more risky and unpredictable methods that might have involved accepting payola, returning favours or acting on hunches.

For those in Nashville, this situation is particularly frustrating because radio is so central to the marketing of country music. Unlike other genres such as rap or rock, where a company may try to create a buzz about an artist either live, in the clubs or among an alternative network of listeners prior to contacting radio, country labels are preoccupied by radio and view this medium as their starting point. Although video is important, particularly for establishing the visual identities of artists, investment in its production and promotion tends to follow the first signs of success on radio. The preoccupation with radio can have dramatic consequences for artists. To quote Walt Wilson, Vice President and General Manager at Capitol Nashville:

> If you cut the album for mainstream radio and radio says, 'No thanks,' then you've got to go back in and recut the album, or else you've got to let the artist go. If you cut the album for the sake of music then you can market it and promote it and you just assume and accept the fact that you're not going to get radio support and that's it....But if you've signed an artist specifically hoping that you were going to get mainstream sales, based on radio success, if radio says, 'No thanks,' then you've got to go back in and redo the project.[9]

According to Wilson, this happens 'more than a lot of labels want to admit'. The rationale for such a response was also succinctly highlighted by Wilson: 'If you've already got half a million dollars invested in a project, if at that point you realize that you are not going to have a shot, you've either got to walk away from your investment or you've got to go and fix it.' Here 'redoing' the project and 'fixing it' will usually entail selecting new songs and re-recording existing songs. This may involve finding new songwriters, recruiting another producer and employing different musicians. If all this juggling, modification and rethinking does not lead to a 'radio friendly' recording then it may ultimately result in a decision to drop an artist. The company will simply not renew the contract when the 'option' clause comes up (usually once a year), and will write off the investment and consign that artist to history after only one failed attempt to gain airplay and with an unreleased album partly or completely recorded.[10]

The alternative, the possibility of building an audience through the 'grass roots', is an idea that is spoken of but rarely put into practice, for the simple reason that it requires a lot more investment and is not as straightforward as going to radio. While touring is central to the promotion of country music, artists tend to go out on the road after they have achieved a degree of radio success and record sales. The main focus, the key 'target', is radio. When radio says no, this can lead to fatalism and a pessimistic resignation that things, although once different, cannot be changed. When I was interviewing Walt Wilson, I mentioned to him that many people had been complaining to me about the state and influence of radio. He responded:

> The thing that everybody has to realize is that there have always been complaints about radio. There will always be complaints about radio, from the listeners' side and from the record label side....But if you've been in the business for a long time, like I have, it doesn't do you any good to complain about radio because it doesn't make a difference. They don't care, and the best way to deal with radio is to understand who they are, and what they're all about is that they are a business, and if you understand their business and you know how to work within their business and you do the best business plan that you can to deal with that, you either win or you lose. You can yell, you can get frustrated and try to think of all kinds of fancy ways to get around it, but the reality is – and particularly now since the Telecommunications Bill was signed [February 1996][11] – that radio has become an even bigger business....These broadcasting groups are spending literally hundreds of millions of dollars buying these stations, and they want one thing, and that is advertising dollars, and they are not going to take chances.

Here and elsewhere, I detected a sense of hopelessness – staff in the music industry portraying themselves as helpless voyeuristic victims, looking on as radio becomes an ever more powerful business shaping the way in which record companies are able to work. Tim Dubois, the

President of Arista Nashville, spoke of needing to 'work within my format' and stressed that radio provided the 'parameters...which you have to operate within'. He also went one step further and naturalized radio as part of his 'environment':

> Quite honestly, I think it's useless to sit around and whine about radio...us griping about radio is like a basketball player griping about gravity. It is the reality of the situation and you just have to work within what it gives you.[12]

Here, radio is compared to gravity. It is part of the natural working environment. A socially produced constraint is not recognized as such, and nor is it resisted. Such are the perceptions of the constraints of radio and their tangible impacts on the creative process and such is the contribution of the radio business to the constitution of country culture. However, there is more than radio shaping the way in which an artist comes to have an album in the country charts. Also important is the management of catalogues according to specific assumptions about the social and cultural characteristics of different genres.

COUNTRY DIVISIONS: RACE, GEOGRAPHY AND MONEY

Just as those involved in the production of rhythm and blues have had to deal with the historical legacy of racialized musical categories and the transposition of this into song catalogues, promotional practices and company departments, so too have the producers of country. As Reebee Garofalo has pointed out in his history of US popular music: 'The marketing categories of the music industry have often classified performers as much by race as by musical style' (1997, p. 9). This practice can be traced back to the 1920s, when the music industry allocated popular music into three distinct categories: 'race' (African-American popular music); 'hillbilly' (white, working-class rural styles); and 'popular' (the type of music produced by Tin Pan Alley) (Garofalo, 1997). I also wish to quote an anecdote at slightly longer length to give an indication of how such practices artificially separate black and white music, artists and audiences, and to build upon my discussion of rap and rhythm and blues in the last chapter:

> Were it not for this artificial separation of the races, popular music history might read quite differently. When Syd Nathan, the founder of King Records, encouraged his r & b and country and western artists to record different versions of the same songs, he understood

intuitively that pieces of music do not automatically have a genre, that they can be interpreted in many idioms. Still, in keeping with prevailing industry practices, he marketed his r & b releases only to black audiences and his country records only to white audiences. While Nathan was not limited in his choice of artists or material, he, like many others, accepted the notion that a separation of the races was 'the way things were'. These same prevailing industry practices led Leonard Chess, head of Chess Records, to inform Chuck Berry that his demo of 'Ida Red' ('Maybellene') had to be redone because it was too country sounding. In doing so, Chess was telling Berry in no uncertain terms that there was simply no way to market a black man as a country singer. Were it not for that reality, Chuck Berry might well have had a very different career trajectory.

(Garofalo, 1997, p. 11)

In his extended discussion, Garofalo notes instances when such practices were challenged and also refers to some of the confusions encountered in some early song catalogues, where 'black' or 'white' artists were not so clearly classified or were simply labelled in the wrong way. Yet these were usually exceptions, and the barriers referred to by Garofalo have endured and continue to operate just as strongly at the end of the twentieth century; a country singer is still expected to be white.[13]

The production of country music has not only been established within the context of such racialized organizational boundaries. Country music has also been instituted as a company subdivision or department (and ultimately a business unit within the corporate portfolio), which is geographically separated from the day-to-day negotiations and setting of agendas at corporate headquarters in New York City and Los Angeles. For very many years few major labels had a great presence in country music and the oldest labels with the strongest back catalogue were RCA and Columbia. For much of the genre's history, staff based at the headquarters of the major labels had little interest in what went on in Nashville; the music was 'an exotic, regional music that outsiders – those record executives in New York and L.A. – could never really understand' (Gubernick, 1993, p. 20). One Nashville executive recalled the attitude as 'let the guys out in the sticks make their "hillbilly" music – and the hillbillies were happy with this'. In addition, there were moderate economic expectations; a top-selling album was expected to sell between 200,000 and 300,000.

The corporate neglect of Nashville began to change slightly during the 1970s, particularly when The Outlaws' *Wanted* was issued by RCA and became the first million-selling country album, and when other labels, such as Warner Brothers, began to take a brief interest in the city by setting up subsidiary offices. However, it was during the latter part of the 1980s when the interest of the majors began to accelerate. The degree of involvement and movement to the city was captured in a 1995 article in trade magazine *Billboard* where it was reported that, in 1989, when Arista Nashville was set up, there were seven country labels in the city – by October 1995 there were twenty-eight (Newman, 1995).

There is one obvious reason why offices, subsidiaries and labels were being established in Nashville during this period: there was money to be made and other companies wished to follow the immediate commercial success achieved by the newly established country labels that had been set up by Arista and Atlantic. However, other reasons also influenced the movement towards country.

First was the appearance of a new type of country artist with youthful appeal, incorporating contemporary rock and pop elements of musical style and visual presentation, facilitated by the growth of video outlets such as Country Music Television and the Nashville Network. Notable here was the success of Clint Black, and following him Garth Brooks, whose album sales were certified by the Recording Industry Association of America as exceeding 60 million by May 1996. Brooks provided a kind of template, often referred to as 'hunks in hats' or 'hat acts', for other male artists such as Alan Jackson and John Michael Montgomery. Performers such as Brooks were not just presenting a new commercially successful aesthetic style: they were also adopting a more reflexive approach to their own identities as performers and were acutely aware of their constitution as a commodity within a star system, partly as a result of the introduction of various university music business programmes or courses. In her study of Trisha Yearwood, Lisa Gubernick has observed that:

> Yearwood was one of a new Nashville breed that believed in the balance sheet as much as the song. Her degree was in the music business, and she had come up behind Garth Brooks, the marketing major who became the most popular singer in country music history. 'Country music is a business,' she said. 'I'm the head of a corporation, and my name is the bottom line.'
>
> (1993, p. 64)

If this new type of artist was important in changing country music both creatively and commercially, a further important factor was the introduction of a new method of reporting the sales of recordings, the Soundscan system. Prior to the introduction of Soundscan in 1991, the retail sales figures used for chart listings had been compiled as a result of a rather ad hoc and whimsical procedure which relied upon the physical reporting of stock movements by staff within individual stores. In contrast, the new method involved the electronic monitoring and measuring of point-of-sale transactions at about 80 per cent of US retail outlets where recordings were sold.

For many years staff in Nashville had suspected, and occasionally complained, that personnel within major stores who were more predisposed to rock, r 'n' b and pop had neglected to report the sales of country recordings. The immediate impact of the new recording system was tangible and seemed to bear out this grievance. On the *Billboard* chart of 18 May 1991 there were twenty country albums, of which four were in the Top 50 and twelve were in the Top 100. One week later, with the introduction of the new Soundscan system, there were thirty-four country albums, with eight placed in the Top 50 and seventeen appearing in the Top 100. This was a visible sign of the commercial significance of country sales and sent a signal out through the networks of the entire music industry. Companies and labels were quick to begin responding.

The statistics provided by Soundscan not only indicated that the audience for country was greater than had been imagined: the figures dovetailed into a re-emerging perception that country was more stable and had greater long-term potential than other popular genres. When I was interviewing executives in Nashville during 1996, many explained to me that part of their success was due to the way in which country appealed to a large constituency of record buyers who had become alienated by both alternative rock and rap. There was a widely held belief that ageing popular music fans, themselves living a more sedate lifestyle organized around family and careers, had moved away from rock and soul as a result of their discomfort with the musical and social noise of alternative rock and rap.

Such a view was not held solely by executives in Nashville, but was part of a broader perception of changes within the United States. Bruce Feiler (1996) argued that country's 1990s boom had been directly related to the changing circumstances of the influential post-war baby boom generation, those people whose defining musical moments had been the rock 'n' roll of the late 1950s and rock of the early 1960s, and who were becoming more associated with a suburban lifestyle. Arguing that the shift from rural areas to the city, earlier in the century, had benefited jazz and r 'n' b, Feiler suggested that the movement of US citizens from the city to the suburbs had facilitated the popularity of country music, directly contributing to the 1990s boom.

Feiler was drawing on claims about major demographic shifts which have resulted in population movements from the centre of cities to the suburbs, and the creation of what has been metaphorically described as a 'doughnut – emptiness and desolation at the centre and growth on the edges' (Jackson, 1996, p. 15). This has occurred at the same time as migrations from rural areas to the suburbs, and has prompted writers such as Kenneth Jackson to argue that the United States has become the first nation 'in history to have more suburbanites than city and rural dwellers combined' (1996, p. 15).

These may be contested claims, yet, like the assumptions of those executives in the music industry who believe that country has attracted the ageing rock and soul fans, these beliefs have been used to propose a further argument about musical preference: 'As Americans aged and moved to the suburbs, they became increasingly interested in themes that have long been the mainstay of Nashville songwriters...country pounded out tales of love, heartache, family ties and middle-aged renewal' (Feiler, 1996, p. 22).

Whether there has been such a straightforward demographic change, and the extent to which a corresponding shift in musical preference can be mapped on to this, is beside the point. Such beliefs were significant in producing a particular imagined world of musical consumption, and this then guided decisions and actions taken within the corporate world of acquisition, production and marketing. These sentiments connected with and provided a particular way of interpreting the 'hard' data produced by Soundscan and other market research organizations. Producers, A and R staff, marketing people and senior management began acting *as if* country was the new mainstream pop music of the 1990s. The suburban country fan became an important component of the corporate imagination as it attempted to connect the genre to a market.

This brings me back to an issue I have referred to earlier in this book concerning the movement of record companies towards a more explicit portfolio management approach to artists and genres. Country was now not simply 'out in the sticks' or a distant division being allowed to 'do its own thing', but a key unit within a regularly monitored portfolio of assets. Companies lacking a country division or Nashville office were quick to set one up, and those with an existing operation began viewing the country division or label as a far greater source of profits than in the past. As country became more profitable and as artists regularly began to sell more recordings, so there were greater expectations of what the Nashville division might achieve and be able to contribute to company profitability. Senior managers running the divisions in Nashville also recognized this potential and appeared at the corporate bargaining table asking for more resources (in competition with the demands from the rock division and black music department). The allocation of more resources to the Nashville division then resulted in greater monitoring by accountants from the major corporations and in turn greater expectations of and pressure for immediate results.

I have already discussed some of the general consequences of this greater monitoring in Chapter 2, explaining how corporate strategy impacts on the desire for risk-taking and produces a heightened anxiety in anticipation of and in response to various sales statistics and market data. Here I want to highlight two further consequences: first, the relevance of corporate assessment to the careers of individual executives and artists;

second, the impact upon the collective sense of belonging which is a characteristic of working life in country music labels. To make my first point I want to quote from Scott Siman, who was Senior Vice President of Sony Music Nashville when I interviewed him in 1996. To put his comments in context, I should add that we had reached the end of the interview and I had asked if there were any other issues that he thought important which I had not asked about. He responded by saying that he was particularly interested in the future 'creative direction of country music'. This prompted me to ask to what extent his own future career prospects were dependent upon commercial success and to what degree they were affected by being associated with finding new aesthetic trends. After a pause for thought, he responded:

> I think it's all bottom line, truly. I really do. I think the executives that are probably the most admired are the ones that have been associated with the biggest hits. I think that's it. I look back and I'll use as an example Mary Chapin Carpenter. The person who actually signed her in this division is not even here now...you don't hear people running up and down Music Row saying, 'Larry Hanbury, now that was the guy. He signed Mary Chapin Carpenter.' You don't hear it. But, here's Tim Dubois who signed Alan Jackson and Brooks and Dunn and he's a genius....It was the turning point for both of those artists, and they're great artists but I don't think you can compare them to Mary Chapin Carpenter and the effect that she's had and has on people's lives – insofar as the people who create music, it's not even close. It's not even close. And somebody like Chapin, who is maybe the only true entertainer in our format besides Garth Brooks – she writes, she plays, she sings, she co-produces, she does it acoustically, she does it electronically, she writes her tour book, she's in soundtrack, she's in TV, she does everything, PBS special, TV specials, you name it – internationally incredibly successful. Here's the most broad-based artist I can think of in our format and she should be the entertainer of the year. But yet, you see, artists like Brooks and Dunn will win it, because they sold more records. They've had more hits on country radio. So they are perceived, within the industry, to be the bigger success. Again, I'm not knocking any of these artists, I work with these artists, they do make great country music...but what it leads back to is the executive, which is what you asked, because Tim Dubois is perceived as [adopts other voice]: 'Hey, man! [claps hands] He's wow! He had The Tractors, they sold a bunch of records and I don't even know what they're about, but, you know, they sold records, so he's really neat.' But Larry Hanbury, who signed the most influential artist to come out of Nashville in twenty years, certainly one of the top two or three most influential artists, people don't talk about.[14]

This quotation provides an insight into the sort of reality within which senior executives in Nashville are operating. Executives are not simply caught in a conflict between art versus commerce in any straightforward and dichotomous way. Instead, they are having to respond to the way in which the criteria of art and commerce are differentially established, recognized and acknowledged within the corporation. As I highlighted in Chapter 2, although major entertainment corporations state that they are seeking staff and managers with both business acumen and musical insight, they tend to assess only the business acumen and leave the musical insights unassessed, unrecognized and unrewarded. It is hardly surprising, then, that an executive who wishes to remain in the industry should seek to ensure that she or he gets the figures right.

With increasing commercial success, with more million sellers and with a 'bottom line' logic having a tangible impact on Music Row, it might be reasonable to suppose that Nashville was becoming more important within the corporate power structure of the music industry. Indeed, such a claim has been made by Don Cusic (1995), who has argued that Nashville has shifted from being an 'outpost' of New York City and Los Angeles and become a 'financial centre for the US music industry' (p. 238). However, despite their label's increased economic importance, many senior executives in Nashville were not sharing such a view. Many people I spoke with still felt that they were looked down upon by key staff in Los Angeles and New York, those in a position to shape agendas within the corporation. This was noticeable in the observation that staff from head office were often 'uncomfortable' in Nashville, thought the best hotels second rate and didn't wish to stay long when they visited.

In this respect relations between Nashville and corporate headquarters were mediated by more than the bottom line. Cusic's argument about the increasing importance of the country divisions was based on the assumption that, because it had become an important source of revenue or key budget centre, Nashville had therefore begun to occupy an equally significant cultural position, thereby achieving an equal or even superior position to New York or Los Angeles. This was and is far from the case. Indeed, in many respects, Nashville's economic success has exasperated an already existing antagonism. If the 'hillbillies' were not understood and appreciated when they were allowed to 'do their own thing', there is evidence to suggest that they have been no more appreciated as a result of success in the 1990s. In the words of Joe Galante, Chairman of the RCA Label Group in Nashville, who has worked in both Nashville and New York:

People in New York still don't understand country music and they treat it more as a business, as opposed to a community, and just don't have that sensitivity to what goes on. They try to come in with the attitude of 'we know what's happening 'cause we're on the big picture'

and they don't have the sensitivity to the music. I mean, the people
that are here, that are in this town, care about the music and they're
proud of what they do and don't like people to look down upon their
country format.[15]

Galante was not the only person to refer to those working in Nashville
as a 'community'. There was a general feeling among many observers and
participants of a tangible tension between Nashville as a 'business unit'
within a corporate portfolio and Nashville as a music-making community
with a long history.

Similar but slightly different tensions often arise between people in
Nashville and those from Los Angeles. Here the antagonism is not simply
towards those from corporate office but instead against various producers,
songwriters and musicians who have moved to Nashville without recognizing that it is a 'community' as well as a business. *Music Row Magazine*
columnist Rusty Russell had a swipe at such people in an editorial in the
summer of 1996:

> I have no problem with the transplant thing – most of us came here
> from somewhere else at some time. And most of us, I would hope,
> came here with the attitude that we had something to offer and a lot
> to learn. Great. That's what it's about. But during the last couple of
> years a cadre of buddies from out west (let's not get nasty and name
> names – we'll just say it's a place with lots of earthquakes and movie
> stars and traffic jams and palm trees) have moved into town, having
> pretty much made a mess of their own back yard, and they've brought
> along a truly annoying, insouciant vibe. Very industrious bunch,
> though, especially when it comes to schmoozing…hear this: Nashville
> didn't just pop up one morning out of nowhere like a mushroom. We
> are no bunch of poor hicks sitting around on hay bales strumming C
> chords, and we haven't been waiting for you to come along and save
> us from ourselves. The hard-won diversity, world-class recording scene
> and friendly, creative atmosphere that are today's Tune Town are the
> result of three generations of hard-working, talented and (mostly)
> giving people….Moving here, buying a pair of boots and piecing
> together bits of clichéd lyric into your 'own' songs does not make you
> a Nashville act. No doubt you brought something valuable with you.
> Please remember that you're not the first.
>
> (Russell, 1996, p. 25)

The causes and sources of the tensions present in these quotes, which in
different ways highlight the experience of and defensiveness of a Nashville
'music community', can be located in a complex of economic, political,
cultural and geographical divisions that have shaped and continue to have

a direct bearing on the way in which country is circulated. From my perspective, it is yet another example of the complex ways in which broader cultural processes and patterns intersect with and 'produce' an industry.

NASHVILLE, THE SOUTH AND COMMUNITIES OF COUNTRY PRODUCTION

The idea that those producing music in Nashville might be a 'music community' is one that immediately begs many questions. It seems clear though, quite regardless of just who might consider themselves to be within and without such a unity, that this sense of community is lived and experienced in two ways. First, as a geographical sense of community created as a result of living and working in one specific physical place and cemented through numerous lunchtime meetings, evening gigs, golf days, fan events and the socializing which occurs between peers who are employed in the same profession and share working spaces, residential neighbourhoods and leisure pursuits. In this sense, those making music in Nashville also liken themselves to a 'family'. As Eddie Reeves, Executive Vice President and General Manager of Warner Reprise, explained:

> For the most part all of our major competitors are all people that we know and we're friends with….Faith Hill's producer now runs Liberty, Jimmy Bowen who ran Liberty before that ran MCA and Bruce Hinton worked for him, and Jim Ed Norman who runs this label used to record for Jimmy Bowen's label, and Bruce Hinton and Jim Ed and I shared an office together in Los Angeles when we were in business together…Scott Hendricks was Faith Hill's producer on our label and he's Tim Dubois' good buddy, they came from the same part of Oklahoma, and Tim runs Arista and Scott now runs Liberty, so it's that kind of thing. I guess you could say it's like this group of people, and here's kind of what happens, and now the people that are running labels are people that are our friends. We're very strong competitors with each other and I guess it's like in a family.[16]

In this quote, Reeves highlights how a 'family' has been created over time as a similar group of people have gradually become closer through playing in bands, producing, collaborating and competing with one another. This has led to the formation of enduring friendships and close personal ties and these have come to shape the working world of country music production in Nashville.

In addition to this sense of a recognizable 'family', established through close personal contact over time, it also seems reasonable to think of those involved in country music production as constituting a broader 'imagined community' (Anderson, 1983) which is not necessarily confined to the geographic borders of a specific place. Although never meeting all other 'members', the sense of community is lived as a 'known' entity that is bigger, beyond and of greater significance than the commercial country category and the organizational department or record label. Hence, this broader community would take in members physically located in New York State, Texas, California and elsewhere.

This strong feeling of being part of a country community informs how staff interact with musicians and fans and also with people in other parts of the company, influencing such taken-for-granted judgements as those about the length of the working day, the most suitable leisure activities to engage in and the most desirable places to live. Beliefs which cement relationships within the 'family' and the 'community' also influence decisions about artists, feeding into assumptions about the ethnicity of country performers, and connect with particular notions of the gender roles and modes of sexual expression expected of artists.

This sentiment of belonging to a musical community also mediates the relationships between staff in Nashville and those at corporate head offices in New York and Los Angeles. In turn, these relationships and this sense of belonging are informed by a broader North–South divide and cut through with cultural–geographic divisions created as a result of the antagonisms between the urban–rural and country–city, and their resulting differences of lifestyle, cultural practices and musical preferences.

A sense of musical community, as a feeling of belonging to a genre culture, is experienced and expressed as working practices intersect with aesthetic judgements and a broader series of political, economic and social factors, and as emotional investments in music confront and uneasily mesh with social structures and corporate constraints. A country genre culture is experienced as a 'community' – as more than an organizational unit, label division or task within a unified corporation. Between the permanent and provisional, it is an impulse which articulates the experience of and desire for music-making in terms of 'family' and 'community' (and not in terms of 'art' or 'creativity') against the pressures to reduce such actions to a business unit or routine for making a quick buck. The 'country community' provides, at the same time, a refuge, a reactive defence which draws upon southern sentimentality and deploys this against perceived north-eastern and western commercial cynicism. In turn it is also a dynamic impulse for a more equal and convivial mode of music-making. It is unstable, dynamic and contradictory and not reducible to any simple or stereotype assumptions about country culture.

The distinct beliefs and sentiments that characterize country culture, and the specific conditions within which these have emerged and been maintained, are of direct relevance to the idea that Nashville might have the potential to become as important as New York or Los Angeles within the music industry: Nashville is firmly part of 'the South' – with all the burden of meanings that small geographical signifier carries. This point has been made by David Sanjek (1995), who has observed that country music has had to deal with ignorance, antipathy and uncritically received stereotypes about the music and place of the South within the United States, residues of antagonisms and prejudices which can be traced back at least to the Civil War in the middle of the nineteenth century.

As a further way of putting such optimistic dreams of Nashville's significance in a broader historical context, it is worth briefly recalling similar claims that were made some twenty to twenty-five years before. During the 1970s the southern economy began growing and much debate ensued about the possible consequences. A key theme of much of the discussion was captured in the title of Kirkpatrick Sale's book *Power Shift: The Rise of the Southern Rim and Its Challenge to the Eastern Establishment* (New York: Random House, 1975). In certain ways, Cusic's claim about the Nashville music industry during the 1990s echoes such an idea. Certainly there are parallels to be found in discussions of the growth of the South during the 1970s and speculation about the increasing significance of Nashville in the 1990s. In both cases, however, economic importance has not led to any type of 'power shift'. Indeed, later assessments of the changes that occurred during the 1970s might equally be applied to what was occurring in the music industry during the early 1990s. Southern cities have, in general, remained dependent upon economic and organizational authorities, agenda-setters and decision-makers that are headquartered outside the region. Wendell Holmes Stephenson and E. Merton Coulter (eds) have argued that, during the 1970s, 'Southern metropolitan areas became larger, more complex, and more sophisticated, but to a striking degree they remained "branch-house" cities' still managed from 'California' and the 'snowbelt cities' (1995, pp. 432–4).

It is also worth noting that the music community within Nashville is less integrated into the related media industries which have become important for the making and circulation of contemporary music. Staff based in record company head offices in New York (PolyGram, Sony, EMI, BMG) are located within a hub of national and international news, entertainment and communication industries and their networks. Meanwhile, record company headquarters in Los Angeles (Warner, Universal) are located within the entertainment complexes of Warner Brothers and Universal movie studios, with their connections to a range of entertainment media.

In contrast, the city of Nashville only temporarily enjoyed the benefits of having an 'international' airport for a few years until the middle of the 1990s, and the music industry is not so integral to the life of the city as is sometimes envisaged by outsiders. Those who work in Music Row, the modest few tree-lined suburban streets of predominately one- or two-storey buildings, also occupy an ambiguous position within the city. As Sanjek has noted, the city of Nashville 'has always been less than whole-heartedly enthusiastic about being the home of the country music industry' (1995, p. 52). Unlike the cosmopolitanism of New York City or Los Angeles, which may facilitate border crossings and interactions between different sectors of the recording, media and entertainment industry, the music community in Nashville is more insulated, often eyed with suspicion by the old landed-gentry types whose wealth and position is drawn from money handed down through generations. Most staff within the country music business share no direct affinity with the other main businesses of the town, the insurance and Bible industries (Gubernick, 1993; Sanjek, 1995). Perhaps the closest affinity is with the fans, an integral part of the community and family of country culture.

FAN CULTURE AND ARTIST–AUDIENCE RELATIONS: CONTACT, CONSTRAINT AND THE COMMON PEOPLE

As Peterson has suggested in his many writings, the 'culture' of country music cannot be understood by reference to the texts alone – the lyrics, songs or album covers. Instead, we need a more sociological understanding of how the specific characteristics of country culture are given form and meaning through a series of events and performances which link artists and audiences in quite distinct physical circumstances and imaginary forms of identification. Despite occasional attempts to interpret country culture from various songs texts and album covers (Tichi, 1994), the dynamics of country culture are best understood, not through any textual codings, but through the connections between fans and performers (Ellison, 1995; Peterson, 1997).

The relationship between fan and performer is central to how staff in the country music business understand what they are doing, and this rela-tionship is a key dynamic through which a sense of community is made tangible and present. It is also commercially important, being integral to the marketing and circulation of country music. Central to country culture is the interaction between fans and performers through the traditional live performance and tour, and as a result of various associated events during which fans and artists meet. Country artists are required and obliged to be accessible and available to their fans in ways that perhaps have no parallel in other genres of music. The annual Fan Fair is perhaps the epitome. Each year in June over 20,000 people from all over the United States and abroad converge on Nashville and queue for hours to be photographed with and receive the signature of their favourite artist, and to collect all sorts of memorabilia available from stalls and exhibitors during and after hours of musical performances. The Fan Fair provides a tangible, audible and visible sense of the bond that connects performers to their fans, particularly in those instances when the artists have become familiar enough with members of an audience to refer to them by their names.

Fans are central to the production, reproduction and circulation of numerous genres of music and for this reason a number of writers have developed or employed theories of the active audience, as a challenge to assumptions about passive consumption or against crude models suggesting the manipulation of behaviour by the entertainment industry.[17] When thinking about active audiences it is also important to remember that fans and their activities are not simply located 'outside' the world of production and the corporate office. Not only do fans visit, and hang around outside, record company offices, they also bombard record companies with letters, requests and complaints – actions that are often utilized by music industry staff when recruiting for consumer panels or creating databases of an artist's 'fan base', and which have become increasingly formalized through Internet access and company websites.

An artist's potential relationship to their audience and fans is crucial to their ability to gain and maintain a recording contract. When the significance of fans is considered by staff within record companies, there are, broadly, two important aspects that are being assessed. These are considered by the music industry in all genres, but are arguably more acute and of greater significance within the production of country. The first is simply the amount of work that any artist will have to do to make themselves available to fans: while engaging in other activities such as recording, performing, touring, being interviewed and visiting radio stations, will a performer have the temperament, and be willing and prepared, to offer a smile, a few words and handshake? Second, can an artist establish and maintain a point of identification between themselves and the lives of their fans, a connection that will be taken to be genuine or authentic, of some shared interest, lifestyle or mutual understanding?[18]

The first point can be illustrated through another quote from Eddie Reeves, General Manager of Warner Reprise, talking about how he perceives the pressures that can be placed on country artists by the expectations of fans:

> It's not easy to be a successful country artist....You know, it's kinda cool for rock artists just to turn their back on the audience and turn their back on the media and turn their back on the record company and say, 'Everybody go screw yourself – I'm cool.' Then it can sell. It's just the opposite in country music because country music is more about family values, it's more about respect and the whole system. It's everything opposite to what that rock idea is about. So that's how it works and we just realize that's the kind of the thing that's here. It's

one of the things that makes it wonderful...I'm glad I'm working with our artist roster and not Burbank's artist roster.[19]

The country performer is not expected to be a detached, aloof, temperamental artist struggling for their art in a world of their own or speaking out and challenging the system (of record production in particular or society more generally). Country artists are expected to fit in and bond with their record company as part of the country community. They are not expected to challenge or critique the practices of the music industry and their individual labels, in the way that artists such as George Michael, Prince, John Lydon and Sinéad O'Connor have. The 'rules' of the genre require them to be ordinary, down-to-earth, everyday family people with all the contradictory impulses that this might imply. Yes, they can get drunk and miss some shows and commit adultery. But they cannot challenge the system of the music industry and the values through which a country genre culture has produced a particular type of music business.

The connection between fan and artist is, at the same time, part of a further bond established with record industry personnel (who are also fans). It is this that also informs and gives a tangible presence to the sense of community, to the proud but defensive stance towards the New York and Los Angeles attitudes. It is this that is integral to the emotional structures that are generated as the music industry meets and meshes with the broader genre culture.

But this also gives rise to dilemmas and contradictions when artists cannot continue to maintain this, through success, through deviations from the family way or through a desire for musical experimentation. Tensions arise when artists seek to change or wish to challenge or move away from the assumptions of country culture. Here, a sense of identification is important as both a real (at the concert, Fan Fair) and imaginary (on video, in a magazine) connection between artists, fans and record company people. It is important during concrete human encounters and relationships, but it is also important within the context of marketing and media presentation. The two are not separate but are intricately interwoven. Walt Wilson, General Manager of Capitol in Nashville, referred to this issue and his sense of frustration that artists will not always maintain the bond that they have established with their fans. He was particularly concerned about Garth Brooks when I spoke to him in the middle of 1996:

Garth is in a unique situation because he started his career as a member of his fans. He said, 'I'm with you. I'm amongst you and I'm gonna sing for you and we're all gonna have a great time and I'm not gonna change. I'm a farmer from Oklahoma.' And just in the past couple of years he's got to the point where I'm not sure that a lot of his fans really understand where he's coming from and I think he's made some bad comments. You know, when he says, 'I have more money than my grandkids will ever need,' well, you don't tell that to your fans. I mean, he doesn't need to tell them that. He just needs to still stay among them, and when he said that I think a lot of people went, 'Hold on here.' And then recently, when he said, 'I only sold four million records and if I don't sell any more I may retire.' You don't tell people that. You don't talk to common people, the common country music fan, and say things like that, because they can't relate to that, and what happens is that it puts you to a level where they think you're far superior than they are and when he then comes back and says, 'But I'm still a common man,' they say, 'No, you're not and we don't believe that any more.'[20]

The key issue that Wilson is emphasizing here is that of authenticity. Peterson (1997) has provided one of the most extended empirical elaborations of the specific ways in which authenticity is central to the production and circulation of a particular musical genre, showing in detail the components (accent and styles of singing voice, instrument, clothing, body movement, lifestyle, etc.) that have come to signal an authentic country performer, and how these have changed as the authentic has been continually reinvented or 'fabricated'. Drawing on ideas about the invention of tradition and construction of signs and images within the media, Peterson has highlighted the artifice of country genre codes that are often taken to be spontaneous natural reflections of a particular way of life.

However, the type of reasoning tends here to imply that this is somehow false, that something has been exposed, that as audiences we have been deceived by fabricated authenticities, invented traditions and media manipulations. There is obviously an important issue here, and Garth's problem may well have been what Wilson also referred to as 'media training' – i.e. presenting the right image, speaking during interviews in a way that maintains the 'common' stance. But there is more than this at stake. The problem is not so much that the 'authentic' can, and has been, continually constructed or fabricated. The decisive question is about how the authentic is experienced. If, following Michael Pickering's (1997) argument, we take it that experience is not only a legitimate but an integral source of historical and sociological enquiry in the study of any cultural form and practice, then we really need to address some key questions about the experience of authenticity.

Authenticity may well be manufactured, but this is only part of the story. Authenticity is also a concept and a sentiment, a feeling which connects the 'fabrications' of the industry with the lived realities of fans and artists. There is more than deceit here, more than manufactured poses, contrived nasal voices and put-on sentimentality lulling consumers into a state of false consciousness. It is here where beliefs about 'family', 'community' and the 'common people' need to be taken seriously and connected to the industry's fabrications. Country music's discourses of the common people, community and family are central to any understanding of the *experience* of authenticity and how this mediates the relationship between fan, performer and record company executive – whether physically present or separated across time and space and connected through cables, telephone lines or satellite beams.

Authenticity is neither true nor false. It is not simply about codes, fabrications and artifice any more than it is about the spontaneous organic unmediated expression of human art and mutual understandings. It is about relationships and, usually these days, overtly socially, technologically and spatially mediated relationships. Authenticity mediates social relations that have been 'disembedded' out of their immediate experiential contexts of face-to-face interaction by the modern music media and provides a glimpse of how actual experience does connect (in whatever naive or knowing way) with the invented tradition or codified real.[21]

It is through beliefs and sentiments about the family, community and the common people that Garth Brooks is 're-embedded' into the lives of his fans and the people he works with in the music industry. Country genre culture is still to a great extent grounded in the experience of white, rural, blue-collar, working-class life. It is this that notions of the 'common people' seek to signal, and, as Raymond Williams (1983) once pointed out, 'the common' has two simultaneous meanings: an affirmation of something that is shared and ordinary, and a more derogatory perception of something that is equally ordinary, but vulgar – which is perhaps why executives from New York continue to feel uncomfortable when they visit Nashville.

Chapter 6

The Latin music industry, the production of salsa and the cultural matrix

Like other genres, salsa is a deceptively simple word that refers to an identifiable category of music which is internally diverse and historically changing, and also to a broader series of extra-musical social practices and cultural associations. Like all music it can be studied in formal terms as a genre with specific identifiable stylistic traits, melodic phrases, rhythmic patterns, harmonies and instrumental-vocal exchanges, and these can be learnt by musicians wishing to perform salsa (Gerard and Sheller, 1989). As with the other genres covered in this book, salsa can also be approached in anthropological or sociological terms as a dynamic social practice created across analytic distinctions such as production/consumption and culture/politics.

A number of writers have carefully listened to the constituent parts of the salsa mixture and traced their historical lineage and connections to the cultural identities and modes of expression of populations in Cuba, Puerto Rico and New York (Duany, 1984; Boggs, ed., 1992; Manuel, 1995a). Locating salsa within the context of such Caribbean connections and cross-currents, Angel Quintero Rivera (1998) has also charted the broader historical context within which salsa has emerged as an unfinished mixture of European melodic patterns, African derived rhythms and African-American blues and jazz styles. As these labels refer to sounds which are already the result of preceding mixtures, it is not surprising that salsa has been called a 'mixture of mixtures' (Quintero Rivera and Manuel Alvarez, 1990), one which continues to blend with other performance practices.

Quintero, like other writers, has also stressed the political context within which salsa emerged. During the late 1960s and early 1970s salsa became integral to the cultural political agenda of activists struggling for social, economic and political recognition in the Americas and Caribbean, whether articulated to a specifically working-class Puerto Rican agenda or to notions of pan-Latino consciousness (Duany, 1984; Padilla, 1989). As salsa has moved out from these points of origin, it has also been embraced as a music that addresses broader issues of identity for populations in Latin America, the Caribbean, Spain and the Canary Islands (Padilla,

1989; Estupiñán, 1994). As salsa has travelled further across the world it has connected with the experiences and practices of Latin and non-Latin populations in numerous other places, inspiring musicians, dancers and listeners as far apart as Britain, Germany, Japan and Israel (Bechdolf, 1997; Hosokawa, n.d.; Román Velázquez, 1998).

At the same time, salsa has become a marketing category within a set of business practices that often represent a stark contrast to some of its political meanings and cultural associations. Here, salsa functions as a commercial label for positioning recordings in record stores, for constructing charts and designing marketing campaigns. In the first part of this chapter I will outline how the major record labels manage the production of contemporary salsa within distinct Latin divisions and how this is informed by and contributes to the broader series of social divisions across which commodified Latin identities are created. Following my discussion of rap and country music, I shall also highlight how the cultural world of Latin music and the genre culture of salsa are kept at a distance from the dominant interests and prevailing agendas within the main offices of the music corporations. I shall then discuss how salsa has moved out from its containment as a commodity within specific production systems, and outline the dynamics through which a 'salsa matrix' of production–consumption relations is created, generated through a range of emotional investments, knowledges and social practices which cannot be reduced to any simple music industry logic or model of Latina/o commodification. I shall start my discussion by locating salsa as a subdivision of 'tropical' within the broader category of Latin music.

TROPICAL MUSIC AND THE LATIN RECORDING INDUSTRY

The term 'tropical' has many meanings and associations which are contested and conceived of in contrasting ways in different places. Geographically, 'the tropics' refers to the region of the Earth's surface between the Tropic of Cancer and the Tropic of Capricorn, the part of the world which receives more light than any other area of the planet. Certain species of plant and animal can be found only in this region and hence are labelled accordingly, as tropical plants or tropical fish, for example. Certain maladies are also labelled 'tropical diseases' and these can be countered by tropical medicine. Certain foods may become relabelled on their travels, such as the numerous 'Tropical China' or 'Tropical Chino' restaurants and take-outs that can be found in Puerto Rico.

The application of the term 'tropical' does not simply involve a neutral process of geographical labelling. It can also carry connotations of exoticism, the romantic stereotype of beaches, plants, animals, people and a world of difference. The tropical species are, after all, collected and exhibited by those who usually do not live in the tropics. The term 'tropical', as it has been applied to a range of people and things, often connotes a type of exoticism, whether referring to the tropical art deco of Miami's South Beach, the labelling of literature or the descriptions and imagery of male and female sexuality. As Frances Aparicio and Susana Chávez-Silverman (eds) (1997) have suggested, 'tropicalization' can involve a similar mixture of romanticism, denigration and mystification to that Edward Said analysed in his work on Orientalism. Various traits, beliefs and images are 'tropicalized' and are internalized and reproduced, but these are also re-appropriated (redefined), transcultured and resisted by those living with this label (Aparicio and Chávez-Silverman, eds, 1997).

The category of tropical music is just one part of this complex and contradictory process. Initially, tropical was adopted as a musical category during the 1940s and 1950s and was used to make a commercial distinction between what was then called 'Cuban music' and the music being produced in other regions of the Caribbean coastline: for example, music from parts of Mexico, Venezuela, Panamá and Colombia that was considered to be stylistically distinct to music made inland. Tropical has also been used as a way of signifying a shared sense of Caribbean musical identity across linguistic, geographical, political and economic divisions – a proud affirmation of 'our tropical music' (although this is, more often than not, a music industry promotional device). The same label can, of course, connote a type of exoticism. This is most apparent when tropical recordings appear on the shelves of stores in Japan, the United States, France or Britain with images of idyllic beaches, palm trees and bikini-clad women, or when music from this region becomes part of a 'roots' package for world music aficionados.

Within the music industry and its organizational divisions, tropical positions salsa music and personnel along with genres such as cumbia, originally from Colombia, and merengue and bachata, both originally from the Dominican Republic, and separates these from other Latin subgenres such as Tejano, Tex-Mex and regional Mexican. In terms of market information and the organization of promotion and sales teams, tropical music is associated with recordings purchased in the Caribbean, New York, Florida and the East Coast generally, while the other genres are considered more relevant in Texas, California and the Mexican border regions. A further process of sublabelling separates staff to work with Latin pop (with artists such as Luis Miguel and Ricky Martin), and Latin rock (or *rock en español*), which is particularly popular in Mexico, Argentina and Chile. However, there is a sense in which these divisions are far from stable and static. As Maribel Schumacher, President of Marketing for Time-Warner's WEA Latina division, observed when speaking of how staff within record companies perceive the musical preferences of Latin people in the United States:

> What's happening in the US Hispanic market is that we're beginning to see signs of Hispanic homogeneity or amalgamation. That is to say that we're beginning to see that the West Coast is playing and buying some tropical music and that the East Coast is playing, on the radio, and buying Mexican regional music. So maybe ten years from now we might be addressing the US Hispanic market very differently than we are now....Television has done a lot. Spanish language television has done a lot to bring all the different cultures together. There are a couple of key television programmes on Saturday and Sunday that have the highest ratings in the US Hispanic market [*Sábado Gigante* and *Siempre Domingo*] and those programmes are watched by the Mexicans, the Nicaraguans, the Cubans, the Puerto Ricans, the Argentineans....So, what does *Sabádo Gigante* do? It features a Mexican banda group next to a merengue band, or a pop-rock artist like Miguel Bose next to a balladeer like Luis Miguel – and, it gets away with it.[1]

The broad and changing 'Latin music market' is thus a conjunction of two distinct but overlapping and interacting entities shaped by culture, geography, politics and commercial business practices. There is a distinct Latin music market within the United States: what some people working for record companies call a 'sub-market'. In turn, this is connected to the music market of Latin America.

Since the middle of the 1980s both the US 'Hispanic' and Latin-American markets have been viewed as increasingly attractive by the music industry. The reason is not too difficult to discern. Along with other industries which began making similar noises, *Music Business International* excitedly informed its executive readers that 'Hispanics' spend 'more per capita' than other consumers in the United States and quoted an official estimate that there would 'be 40m Hispanics in the United States' by the year 2000 (Ochs, 1993), although according to many people within the music industry this figure was already an underestimate. At the same time, the growth and increasing 'stability' of the economies of Latin America was attracting the major record companies, who were beginning to set up or re-establish a number of offices in 'regional operations centres'. Here again this activity was supported by reference to official trade figures; for example, *Billboard* reported that 'the Latin-American market' grew by 33 per cent in 1994 alone and that Brazil and Mexico had finally entered the 'top ten legitimate music markets' (Clark-Meads, 1995, p. 3).

Due to these cultural and commercial connections, the production of salsa, tropical and US Latin music more generally should really be understood within the context of the Americas as a whole. Historically, since early in the twentieth century, much of the music from Latin America that has been sold in the United States has derived from 'field recordings' produced in Mexico, South and Central America and the Caribbean. Although sometimes 're-exported' back to these regions, it was more often sold as 'ethnic' music in the USA.[2] In addition, many sounds now recognized and labelled as tropical 'classics' were recorded during the 1940s and 1950s in Cuba or by Cuban musicians in Mexico, and sold as 'Cuban music', a category that record companies ceased using (denying many of salsa's roots) following the 1959 Revolution and the economic blockade of Cuba by the United States (Perez, 1986).

When, during the 1980s, the major labels began to consider the possibility that Latin-American nations might be becoming 'stable' or 'legitimate' markets, this was primarily in terms of selling more repertoire in Latin America (and hence extracting further revenues) in addition to the region's role as a 'source' of music and artists. Further afield, the Latin music market could also encompass music fans and performers in France, Italy, Spain and Portugal. Although the full range of these political dynamics, cultural connections and commercial arrangements is beyond the scope of this chapter, it is worth stressing that the production of Latin music is increasingly occurring across and within two corporate constructions: Latin culture imagined as a 'niche market' within the United States, and Latin culture constructed as a regional market within a so-called 'global' economy. Hence, I am only really dealing with one specific part of the cultural–commercial grid within which Latin music is produced and distributed.

NO STATIC AT ALL: THE CHANGING SALSA STYLE AND BUSINESS

Although there is some dispute about when the term 'salsa' was first used, and while there is debate about the novelty of the music and rhythms that were labelled in this way, there is broad agreement that the systematic use of the term 'salsa' as a commercial category is associated with Fania Records, a company initially operated alone by band leader Johnny Pacheco from 1964 and then more 'entrepreneurially' by Jerry Masucci after 1967. The Fania boom years were from the late 1960s to the end of the 1970s. In 1975 it was estimated that Fania accounted for over 80 per cent of all salsa record sales in the US and Puerto Rico (Flores, 1987).

The company's fortunes dramatically declined at the beginning of the 1980s. There were a number of reasons for this. In part, it was due to a change in aesthetic style that no longer favoured the sound that Fania had championed and recorded. For a number of observers, within and without the music industry, the early 1980s marked a point of aesthetic and commercial decline for salsa. It was during this period when *salsa romántica*, or sensual salsa, emerged, a style often criticized for lacking the political critique and instrumental innovations of the earlier recordings. However, there were more than aesthetic changes at stake. The company was affected by major artists leaving, sometimes acrimoniously, for other labels. Fania Records were also affected by a general slump in the Latin music business and currency problems in various Latin-American nations, particularly in Venezuela, which by the end of the 1970s was one of Fania's most significant markets.[3] Although the compact disc has enabled the company to reissue the old material, Fania ceased to become significantly involved in recording new salsa artists from early in the 1980s.[4]

With the exception of Cesar Rondon's (1980) detailed book on salsa that includes an account of the recording history of Fania Records and their artists, Peter Manuel is one of the few writers who has explicitly considered the role of the recording industry and the commercial arrangements of salsa's production. In a number of articles, Manuel (1991, 1995a, 1995b) has developed an account of the post-Fania salsa music industry and identified the 1980s as a significant moment of change. Manuel has woven a number of threads into what is ultimately a rather simple and pessimistic argument about the 'stasis of the salsa scene' and the appearance of what he has rather disdainfully called 'salsa lite' and 'ketchup'. Before discussing the industry further I shall take a few paragraphs to critique the main components of his argument.

Manuel's (1995a) first point is about recording techniques. He claims that the live band of musicians who learned their skills in clubs and recorded quickly and spontaneously without overdubs has been replaced by slick well-regulated multi-tracked recordings which lack spontaneity. Such an argument fails to acknowledge how the club experience has shifted to one organized around the playing of recordings (rather than live bands), in which the creativity of DJs such as Jesús Cintronnelle and Ramón Rivera in mixing and manipulating different tracks has maintained a sense of improvization and spontaneity. This shift has relocated 'improvization' on to a different terrain from that of the apparently spontaneous 'live' interaction between musicians and dancers.

Second, Manuel adopts a distinctively masculine discourse when criticizing what he has explicitly characterized as the feminization of salsa. Manuel writes of *salsa romántica* as 'sentimental', of the performers as 'cuddly', and contrasts it with 'aggressive, proletarian' *salsa caliente*. To support his argument he quotes from Jorge Manuel López who recalls that 'salsa used to be all about the timbales and bongó, but now it's all about sweet and elegant words, and the girls like it much more than the earlier, macho salsa' (Manuel, 1995a, p. 91). For Manuel, this is symptomatic of the way in which salsa has become 'irrelevant to many young Latinos' who

are drifting towards other genres such as rock or rap. What such an explanation does not acknowledge is that these aesthetic changes have been
accompanied by a reconstitution of the salsa audience and that this has
allowed more women to enjoy the genre.[5] Frances Aparicio's (1998)
detailed ethnographies of the different ways in which people listen to salsa
suggests that women were listening to and often reinterpreting the macho
salsa from the beginning, but were perhaps not so publicly visible and
acknowledged. Aparicio's research provides a challenge to, and also an
acknowledgement of, the gendered separation of musical experiences
whereby men are often associated with the 'public' and 'live' and women
with the recorded and 'private'. This is an ideological division that once
informed much writing on rock music and has been challenged by feminist
musicologists such as Susan McClary (1991), but Manuel reproduces this
in his narrative of salsa.

Related to this, Manuel's position seems to be that of a romantic political aesthetic of male proletarian urban resistance (an orientation that has
characterized much writing about music and subcultures in Britain and the
US). Relevant as this may have been to the early 1970s, the music has
undergone changes in modes of performance and contexts of reception
that are directly related to changes in social context: salsa has left the
barrio and gone out into a broader world. The growing Latin populations
of the United States (and those producing and consuming salsa) are no
longer so easily defined by one geographical, generational, social and political experience. This change was registered in an article in the *Los Angeles
Times* that identified changes in the constitution of the music audience as
involving a transition from an 'older, blue-collar, Spanish-speaking population to a younger, bilingual market' (Ramirez, 1996, p. B5). These shifts of
class, education and language are used by the music industry to construct a
particular idea of the music market, and should not be taken as a transparent indication of reality. However, they suggest that changes in salsa
practices are related to the way in which producers and their audiences are
drawn from a variety of geographic and social locations. There is also an
indication of greater overlap and interaction with other styles as younger
people live a more 'bi-cultural' experience.

That salsa can no longer be identified with the urban barrio and male
worker does not mean that it is no longer 'political'. When salsero Marc
Anthony took to the stage in front of 20,000 people at New York's
Madison Square Garden in September 1998 and performed draped in the
flags of the Dominican Republic and Puerto Rico, he was simultaneously
raising awareness of, generating cash for and inspiring solidarity with
those in the Caribbean who had suffered the consequences of Hurricane
Georges. Like the actions of performers such as Peter Gabriel or Bruce
Springsteen, it was a typical example of the (often uneasy) way that
popular music and political activity intersect – not directly solving issues,

but bringing people together and raising awareness and cash aid. It was certainly not indicative of salsa lite.

While Manuel's cultural pessimism is misleading and premature, he clearly has a point about the way that the music industry seeks to deal with salsa in a very particular and restricted way. But Manuel portrays this process in terms reminiscent of the old mass culture thesis. He argues that 'the majors, in classic monopoly-capitalist fashion, have tried to homogenize the market by promoting common-denominator Latin pop and sentimental ballads, rather than catering to the country's various Hispanic groups' (1995a, p. 90). Such an argument seems to contradict Manuel's other claim that musical styles such as Spanish language rap and merengue have had an impact on salsa's popularity (sounds that are also distributed by the major companies to different parts of the 'Latin market'). More fundamentally it misrepresents the way that the major companies are dealing with the various genres and audiences that constitute what has been labelled as a 'Latin market'. As a number of executives in the music industry acknowledged when I interviewed them, and as trade magazines have continually pointed out, while it might be desirable to try and find a pop artist who can cross barriers between different Latin groups, there is not one 'homogenous market'. Try as it might, the industry is certainly not able to make one.

There is not one unified US Latin market but a series of specific sub-genres and audiences, formed as a result of the way the corporate structures of musical production are uneasily connected to Cuba, Puerto Rico and the Caribbean regions of Latin America on the east, and to the Latin populations of California, Texas and Mexico in the west. The major pop artists able to cross these grids (such as Luis Miguel, Selena and Gloria Estefan) are the exceptions. As I will shortly argue, an assessment of the salsa music industry requires a more nuanced critique than simply that of the 'homogenization' of culture.

The homogenization argument is itself contradicted by considering the products released by the music industry (and putting to one side the continuing life of salsa through performances and the playing of old recordings in both domestic contexts and public spheres). This indicates a greater plurality of styles and practices within the salsa category than the thesis of homogenization or 'salsa lite' would imply. Drawing explicitly on the terminology through which recordings are defined in broad commercial terms by the industry, it is possible to identify a number of distinct styles: 'old school' (now reappreciated as *salsa gorda*), bands and artists who maintain an older style with few concessions to modern arrangements or subjects but continue to release recordings (e.g. El Gran Combo, Sonora Ponceña, Fania All Stars); *salsa romántica* – continuing in the style of the 'sensual' salsa that gained momentum during the 1980s (e.g. Gilberto Santa Rosa, Jerry Rivera); 'soulful salsa' (although there is a certain amount of disagreement about whether this is something different to romantic salsa), which is more blues and r 'n' b inflected, makes more use of synthesizers and is particularly influenced by the arrangements and production of Sergio George (this might refer to an artist such as Victor Manuel); this in turn merges into 'dance club salsa', a clumsy label for the music of artists such as La India and Marc Anthony who came out of the dance club scene in New York and whose music exhibits the influences of r 'n' b, hip hop and the salsa mixing techniques developed and deployed by DJs in dance clubs and for radio.

It is also possible to identify a strand of what I would call 'salsa pastiche' here, not only in the way that La India has moved from hip hop to salsa to jazz and back to salsa, but also in projects such as the *Tropical Tribute to The Beatles* put together for the artists of RMM Records. At the same time there are varying types of 'salsa synthesis', with salsa interacting with other styles, such as merengue, rap and rock (evident in the recordings and performances of groups such as Jayuya and DLG). This is a trend that is also apparent in recordings made since the late 1980s in Cuba, which, according to Augustin Gurza (1996), represent a new 'progressive vanguard of salsa music' (identified artists include Los Van Van, Irakere and NG La Banda).

This is only one very general way of identifying different artists and is based on commercially available recordings alone. I am not presenting these as a definitive typology, but to make the point that the 'salsa scene' has been far from static, as suggested by Manuel. Salsa is not only aesthetically alive, it is considered dynamic enough for significant sections of the music industry to invest in. Regardless of sneering aesthetic judgements and despite prophesies of impending decline, by the middle of the 1980s the major companies were increasing their investment in Latin music and salsa.

THE RECORDING INDUSTRY, LATIN MUSIC AND THE PROBLEM OF LEGITIMATE MARKET KNOWLEDGE

Although RCA and Columbia have a historic 'tropical' catalogue that includes classic recordings made in Cuba and Mexico during the 1930s and 1940s, there was little evidence that such a heritage was informing the commitment of major label practices by the late 1960s and early 1970s. During this time the major labels were deriving the bulk of their revenue from rock, pop and soul and most were dealing with Latin music and musicians through short-term ad hoc low-investment deals with small independent companies. An example was CBS's arrangements to distribute only certain recordings from Fania Records' catalogue, particularly The Fania All Stars, who were adept at creating some imaginative fusions of salsa, rock and soul and hence, according to the ears of the majors, had greater potential to 'cross over' to listeners outside the Latin audience.[6]

The 1980s were not only a time of aesthetic and cultural change; the middle of this decade also marked a significant moment of transition in terms of how the major companies began dealing with Latin music in general and tropical music in particular. The major companies of the time – EMI, CBS (shortly to be purchased by Sony), PolyGram, BMG, Warner (WEA) – began creating distinct Latin departments and then acquiring catalogues to boost their market share and profile. Such activities were informed by the belief that the Latin populations of the US were beginning to represent a distinct market with an increasing disposable income.

The Latin division was thus lined up alongside other genres within each major label's portfolio of artists. However, the Latin divisions were not established in an effortless way but with the characteristic changes of direction and reorganization that are such a feature of the music industry. When first established as a distinct department, Latin music was considered something of a wild cat by the major labels. According to some personnel I have interviewed, it was frequently labelled a dog. For example, PolyGram opened a Latin department in New York City in the middle of the 1980s, then quickly closed it down. The company then reopened a new Latin division in Miami at the end of the 1980s with the renewed hope that it would become a cash cow.

Unlike rap, rock and country, which account for a considerable part of the US music market, salsa is a category of tropical music which, in industry terms, is very much a niche market. As music corporations all have limited resources to distribute among the genres within their portfolio, this means that resources have to be struggled for. Each department seeks to represent its own interests as more significant and attempts to justify its claims for more resources through the presentation of individual sales figures, market share statistics, radio play figures and so on. These types of statistic are not only used during marketing and promotional campaigns and distribution struggles. They take on an additional significance as they are used during the negotiations and interdivisional battles over scarce resources.

On this point the Latin division is immediately at a distinct disadvantage. The key figures here are the official sales statistics which are collated, verified and published by the RIAA (the Recording Industry Association of America), the trade body that oversees, represents and lobbies Congress on behalf of the music industry. Up until 1997 the RIAA had not published or officially verified the statistics for the sales of Latin music in the United States. Although agreeing to consider this possibility during 1996, by the middle of 1997 they had made 'no decision regarding the release of figures for the Latin music market'.[7] In past annual reports profiling the US music business, Latin music had been included in the category of 'other' (unlike rock, rap and country, for example). Officially, up to 1997 Latin music accounted for less than 1 per cent of the music sales in the US/Puerto Rico. However, staff I spoke to in record companies suggested that a more reasonable unofficial figure was somewhere between 4 and 7 per cent. To this can be added the fact that Latin music has been more pirated than other genres, contributing to its lack of representation in official sales figures. For many years there has been a huge illegal trade in pirated recordings of Latin music sold at 'swap meets' and 'flea markets'. An industry report of pirate recordings confiscated in the United States during 1995 indicated that 60 per cent were Spanish language recordings.[8] Hence, much Latin music that is circulated and purchased does not appear in the official industry statistics.

In a similar way, the Soundscan system, used to record all point-of-purchase sales of musical recordings in over 80 per cent of US retail outlets, under-represents the sales of salsa music. This is significant because these figures are used by *Billboard* to create the charts, and these in turn have an impact upon what retailers are prepared to stock and what various media may cover and programme. There are two notable problems here. First, many Latin stores in the United States are small-scale family operations, unlike the megastores and chains such as Tower Records and Sam Goody. These small retailers have generally not installed the machinery for recording sales or do not wish to have their trade subject to such scrutiny. Hence, many Latin music purchases do not appear in the official statistics.

A second problem is that there are very few Soundscan machines in Puerto Rico. This means that salsa, for which Puerto Rico is one of the major markets, is more under-represented than other Latin genres such as Tejano, Tex-Mex and regional Mexican genres. According to José Behar, then President of EMI Latin, Puerto Rico can regularly achieve sales of between 100,000 and 200,000 per recording.[9] Yet, a greater quantity of sales of these other genres is reported, particularly through machines installed in stores in Los Angeles and Texas. According to staff I spoke to at Sony Discos and PolyGram Latino,[10] the official sales statistics published by Soundscan and upon which the *Billboard* charts are based record only about 20 per cent of the sales of salsa.

Although Latin divisions have their own methods for collecting sales data, such statistics do not carry the same weight within the corporation and staff face the problem of legitimate market knowledge. When trying to convince corporate headquarters to allocate more resources to the Latin division, or when trying to persuade retailers to stock more recordings, staff involved in managing tropical music have to rely on their own figures. These statistics do not have the same aura of legitimacy as those produced, published and circulated by independent industry organizations. As Rigoberto Olariaga, National Sales Director of PolyGram Latino, explained: 'If it's not substantiated by the RIAA then it kind of takes a lot of the legitimacy away.'[11] Hence, the production of statistical data has significant consequences for individual divisions within the music companies. The rock division, for example, can present independently verified figures when lobbying for more resources. The Latin division often has to argue *against* the official statistics.

Apart from statistics, there is another type of knowledge which has a significant impact here: that is the cultural beliefs, values and everyday assumptions which guide the activities of personnel. As I have argued earlier in this book, these are inscribed into what are often taken to be straightforward business arrangements and part of the broader way in which culture produces a particular type of industry.

THE LOCATIONS OF SALSA PRODUCTION: MORE CULTURAL DIVISIONS AND BUSINESS DECISIONS

The Latin music divisions of the major labels must negotiate three distinct barriers: the structural location within the company, the distribution arrangements through which recordings are circulated and the geographical location of company offices. A consideration of the first of these, the structural location within the company, gives an indication of how the industry initially shapes the production and distribution of salsa by defining it as 'international' (basically as a 'foreign' music within the US).

Although salsa can legitimately be considered a US 'domestic' genre of music in that salsa and other Latin genres are produced and purchased within the US and its territories (most notably Puerto Rico), it is managed in separate Latin departments of the major companies that, with the exception of EMI, are located within the international divisions of the major corporations. This separation of companies into 'domestic' and 'international' divisions, and the allocation of workers, artists, genres and investment to each, is a characteristic that has a significant impact on the circulation of salsa. Although salsa and other Latin genres are produced and purchased within the US and Puerto Rico, knowledge of the music is significantly separated between different staff in the same company. There is a distinct divide between those working within the major offices of US music companies (who are able to formulate policies, set agendas and influence the allocation of resources) and those working in the Latin department or an out-of-house label.

This means that the activities of managing a considerable body of music that is produced and consumed in the US and Puerto Rico are located in sections of the major companies which do not report directly into head office in the US. So, for example, Sony Discos reports into the Latin American Region; WEA Latina reports into Warner Music Latin America which then reports into London; prior to the Universal merger PolyGram Latino reported into PolyGram Latin America which in turn also reported into London. Although EMI Latino reports into the domestic division, and while RMM has been able to operate out of New York City as an 'independent' label within UNI's Latin operation (again based in Miami), the recordings are distributed through a sales and retailing system which adds a further cultural–linguistic division to this corporate structural separation.

Sony is the only major record company which has, for many years, maintained a separate Latin distribution system. Sony Discos does not operate through the corporate Sony domestic distribution system, as do other majors, but through its own distribution company, an inheritance from the days of CBS, prior to Sony's management. The advantage of this is that specialist staff with knowledge of Latin music who can speak Spanish are recruited to deal directly with Sony's US retail accounts (approximately half are Latin accounts). Many observers working within the Latin music business feel that this is a clear advantage. During interviews, a number of staff referred to their frustrations as a result of the major companies having a Latin division of specialist staff, who then have to pass recordings over to a distribution division and its networks of field sales staff. These are workers who usually have little specialist knowledge of the music with which they are approaching retailers, and who do not speak Spanish. At the crucial point where recordings are to be sold into and positioned within the stores, they will be neglected in favour of more familiar music which requires less knowledge and expertise. Hence the structural divisions within the production division are reinforced by divisions of culture and language within the distribution division.

These problems are compounded by geographical divisions. When EMI Latino moved its headquarters from Los Angeles at the beginning of 1997 and when Universal opened a Latin music office in Miami during the same year, they joined the other major label Latin divisions who were already located in the city. Miami is considered to be a convenient base for a number of reasons. Economically, real estate and office space are cheaper than in New York and Los Angeles. In addition, Miami is at the intersection of transportation routes to the US, Caribbean and Latin America, important for the way in which the US Latin market is connected to the musicians and consumers of Latin America. As music companies interact closely with other media operations, so Miami is significant because of the Spanish language media that are concentrated in the city (production of radio, television and printed publications). Miami also boasts a number of good-quality recording studios. However, working from Miami adds a further physical distance between Latin personnel and staff in the main offices of the US record industry (in New York and Los Angeles).

Taken together, these divisions can create a formidable barrier between the main part of the US domestic company and Latin music personnel.

Staff in the Latin division find it difficult to influence the agendas that are being set at corporate HQ in the US and have little ability to persuade the company to take them seriously enough to invest time, money and skills in production and promotion. Here the organizational, geographical and language divisions combine to thwart attempts to sell Latin artists to a broader audience. The request from Latin staff for more investment in artists brings what has become a standard response: 'Sing in English' (even if the Latin division can show that there is a big demand for the artist singing in Spanish).

Back in 1977, the *New York Times* noted that, although 'Latin percussion instruments and Latin dance rhythms' had become 'an integral part of much contemporary pop', the music faced a significant 'business barrier'. The writer observed that attempts to 'expand distribution' were being hampered by 'the indifference of businessmen who know nothing about Latin music and would just as soon keep it confined to the cultural ghetto' (Palmer, 1977, p. 22).

Nineteen years later, and unaware of this article at the time, I interviewed Maribel Schumacher, who was then President of Marketing at WEA Latina. Her comments provided an echo of what was written in the 1970s. I asked her if she thought that the division between the Latin/international part of the company and the domestic division was a barrier to the way she worked. She responded:

> I don't know whether it's so much a question of structure, so much as people and attitude....We've always gotten the cold shoulder, you know, the Anglos don't want to know that Latin music will cross over. That's the bottom line. The bottom line is that they want to keep us in the ghetto, ghettoized. I don't think it's a case of structure, I think it's a case of human beings, of people believing in something and then creating the structure to make that happen. But if you have the structure and you don't have people who believe in what you're doing...

She ended with a shrug of the shoulders, indicating that even if there were a different structure there would still be the problem of 'people'.[12] As such, her comments indicate how structure and organizational arrangements intersect with cultural patterns and beliefs – how, in my terms, industry produces culture and culture also produces industry.

Hence it is not simply that there are particular organizational structures, it is that these are operated according to a particular type of knowledge through which the world is imagined in a particular way. Uncritically received cultural assumptions and common-sense ideas about a world of discrete markets and separate social worlds are inscribed into business practices. These are deployed systematically, ignoring all evidence to the contrary (which would, I suspect, produce a type of cognitive dissonance that would undermine the logic of the system), and this contributes to the separation of knowledge and experience.

In many ways the situation I am describing here is symptomatic of the relationships that uneasily connect the USA to Cuba, Puerto Rico and the Caribbean regions of Latin America on the east, and to the Latin populations of Texas, California and Mexico on the west. It's also indicative of institutional tensions between the English-language and Spanish-language cultures of the United States. In short, this is symptomatic of the treatment of Latin identity and people as a 'foreign' rather than an integral part of 'US culture'. As Raúl Fernández has noted during a discussion of Cuban music: 'the absence of the Latin in North America's music parallels the absence of Latin America in the construction of the United States "national character"' (1994, p. 111). Fernández is careful to note that this cannot simply be explained as a consequence of an 'imperial design', a point I would endorse. There are, after all, logical cultural and linguistic reasons for connecting Latin music production internationally to the regions of Latin America – but not for organizationally *dis*connecting it from North American culture.

These broader cultural political tensions are structured into what are often taken to be straightforward economic organizational practices. These are activities that are lived by those working within the industry as if they are merely responding to 'the world out there'. The immediate impact of this for creative practice is that it establishes a series of distinct barriers, erected between staff within music companies, and in turn between musicians and between different groups of consumers.

BETWEEN COERCION OF COMMODITY AND CREATIVE AUTONOMY: THE SALSA MATRIX

So far I have been placing most of my emphasis on how the recording industry limits and constrains the activities of those involved in the making and enjoyment of different genres of music. However, there is a certain moment when gaps, spaces and holes appear – a point when business structures and commercial systems of distribution cannot provide a complete account of how salsa, or any other genre, is circulated and given meaning. While salsa music may be marginalized within the US music industry structure, it is at the same time enjoying a life across a broader series of connections, affiliations and patterns of interpersonal relationships. In concluding this chapter I want to suggest that salsa is being made and re-made within a 'cultural matrix', which owes part of its existence to the recording industry, but which cannot simply be explained in terms of political economy nor by focusing on the cultural worlds of the corporate organization. Although the term 'salsa' was originally used as a commercial category by Fania Records and continues to be associated with New York City, I believe it is useful to think about the circulation of contemporary salsa through the concept of a 'salsa matrix', a term I intro-duce as a way of delineating the grids through which salsa moves and the dynamics which facilitate this process.

The salsa matrix is fundamentally shaped by the major commercial webs that connect music company offices and studios in New York City, Miami and Puerto Rico. It is within this triangle that a large amount of salsa composing, arranging, production, recording and manufacture takes place. This is in part for practical reasons, due to the availability and loca-tion of musicians, arrangers and studios and the desire to achieve what people in the industry often perceive to be the distinct and different 'New York sound' (more r 'n' b influenced, looser arrangements and using non-traditional instruments such as synthesizers) or 'Puerto Rican sound' (more conventionally arranged, with stricter use of rhythms and instruments). This production process is co-ordinated from offices in these locations, and most companies with an interest in acquiring new salsa recording artists have tended to concentrate their scouting efforts in these areas.

From here a further series of webs expand the salsa matrix. These are not quite as institutionally structured and initially connect the NYC–Puerto Rico–Miami triangle to other locations, primarily through regional offices. Most notable here is the salsa of Venezuela. This would include major artists such as Oscar D'León and, for many years, the influ-ential Rodven label that was acquired by PolyGram in 1995, moved from Venezuela and restructured and administered from Miami. Also important here is the salsa of Colombia, produced by major artists such as Joe Arroyo and Fruko. A further series of connections then branch out to salsa music-making in other regions of the United States (in Los Angeles and Chicago, for example). Connections to the major record companies are loosely maintained through a variety of contact networks, taking in regional promotional offices and a range of small labels.

The matrix then extends to Cuba, a connection that was denied and often rendered invisible and inaudible for a large part of the genre's history, certainly in economic terms, through the USA's economic blockade of the island. By the middle of the 1990s some of these ties had been loos-ened up despite the Helms–Burton law tightening the embargo in other respects, in part thanks to the struggles of those who had managed to work within the conditions of the blockade through various educational activities. In addition, the United States government gradually allowed more musicians to tour for cultural activities and the Cuban government relaxed its regulations that had stopped musicians negotiating with multi-national record labels.

For musical enthusiasts Cuba is heralded for its excellent musical conservatories, studio-recording facilities and the imagination of its musicians. With a new wave of artists explicitly labelling themselves salsa performers during the 1990s, and with events such as the hundred-hour continuous salsa event at La Tropica in Havana during March 1997 entering the *Guinness Book of Records*, many began believing that the excess of talent competing for musical recognition and the increasing cultural and commercial interest in the island would herald a new 'golden age' similar to that of the 1940s and 1950s (Varela, 1997). Certainly, personnel within the music industry, like other businesses, are putting structures into place and deals are being signed between major labels and local producers in anticipation that Cuba will eventually open up to US business and provide an attractive source of repertoire and, inevitably, a new market of consumers (Llewellyn, 1997).

As Rigo Olariaga of PolyGram Latino remarked when I asked about the potential influence of Cuba during an interview in June 1996: 'That's something like eight million people – we can't wait....The influence from Cuba is going to be mind-boggling....Just like Puerto Rico has been an incredible influence, and that's only three million people.'[13] And, as Ned Sublett of the label QBADISC rather apocalyptically proclaimed, perceiving even greater numbers of people: 'When the eleven million people on this island have purchasing power it will open up an astonishing world force' (Varela, 1997).

The possible commercial changes in Cuba may well redraw the map of the tropical music industry and reshape the salsa matrix and its grids connecting North America to the Caribbean, Central and South America. It may also render more visible further webs as the matrix extends to specific points in Europe, notably Spain, and particularly to the Canary Islands. Not only was the Spanish Society of Authors and Composers (SGAE) the first outside rights-collecting society given permission to open by the culture ministry, Cuban music has frequently found its way to Europe along the old colonial shipping routes to the Canary Islands. It is here that the Manzana label has been based, Europe's largest importer of Caribbean and Cuban salsa (Llewellyn, 1997).

A short distance from the Canary Islands, the bird or plane will soon connect with another significant point on the salsa matrix. If much is made of the African origins of salsa's rhythms then it should also be acknowledged that the music has, since it first appeared during the 1960s, returned and been re-appropriated. A process described as 'reverse transculturation' has occurred, whereby salsa has been re-made and re-integrated into the music of musicians performing in the Congo–Zaire (Angelero, 1992) and by bands in Senegal, the latter connection audibly symbolized in Africando's outstanding album *Trovador* (1993). Again such connections have been maintained by radio play, performances by travelling musicians and the circulation of cassette tapes, and formally established through affiliated companies in these regions.

The idea of a 'cultural matrix' thus suggests a broader salsa music 'industry' and is an attempt to identify the grids through which salsa is made and moves. I'm trying here to evoke a multi-faceted, multi-dimensional, coherent but disrupted process, identifiable but open to change. In thinking about this I have also drawn upon a number of related ways that the term 'matrix' has been used. First, I have drawn from the terminology deployed in the music industry, whereby an artist is perceived to have what is called 'matrix value' if they can be moved out from their home market. The assumption is that this can potentially bring a greater financial return for proportionately less further investment. This is clearly a motive, and influences the strategic movement of many musical styles across the world.

I have also drawn on Jesús Martín-Barbero's notion of the 'historical matrices of mass mediation' (1993, p. 85), a phrase he has used to highlight how cultural forms are created and understood through processes of change and numerous enculturations occurring over time. Martín-Barbero has also evoked the notion of 'cultural matrices' when highlighting the 'different modes of existence of the popular' (1987, p. 165), as cultural forms connect with multiple social identities and move through 'dimensions of conflict' shaped by such factors as ethnicity, region and religion. To this can be added Ulf Hannerz's spatializing geographical metaphor of the 'matrices of transnational cultural flow' (1996, p. 159) within which cultural mosaics are created, connecting together previously distinct cultures to form and re-form larger 'meta-cultures'.

More specifically, the term 'salsa matrix' has been used by Vernon Boggs (1992) when thinking about the historical trajectory and 'war of the word' that has followed salsa between New York City, Cuba, Colombia and Venezuela. Furthermore, the actual musical practice of making salsa has also been described through such a concept to emphasize how salsa is organized according to a 'cluster' of music elements based around a 'rhythmic matrix' rather than the type of rhythmic beat that is the organizing principle in much rock, pop and soul music (Robbins, 1990).

My use of the term 'cultural matrix' is an attempt to retain all of these meanings in a loose and evocative way (rather than as a theoretical 'model') in order to think about the contrasting dynamics through which popular music may travel across the world and through time out from its containment within systems of commercial categories. Musical recordings are not simply 'distributed' by the music industry but moved through complex cultural matrices of meanings, social practices and transformations on their way to meet new listeners, dancers and musicians. The idea of the cultural matrix is an attempt to suggest that a range of different dynamics are involved in the circulation of commodities, and that these cannot be reduced to any straightforward logic of the music business or capital, nor simply to the transformative creativity of musicians or active consumption of audiences. I am pointing to how a cultural matrix of production–consumption relations is created, which involves a range of emotional investments, knowledges and social practices, and how this cannot be reduced to any one simple creative logic or commercial pattern.

The way in which the recordings of a salsa artist are ultimately circulated around the world often owes little to the rational plans that are made within corporate offices and boardrooms. It is frequently a far more ad hoc affair, influenced by the actions of fans, friends, managers, promoters, disc jockeys, collectors, journalists and general music enthusiasts. Work by Roberta Singer (1983) and Ruth Glasser (1995) in the United States and Patria Román Velázquez (1996) in Britain is suggestive of how the movement of Latin music has been facilitated by the activity of enthusiasts, whether fans, musicians or DJs who acquire recordings (often on their travels or through specialist importers) and circulate them among like-minded people. Such circling may lead to an engagement in small-scale CD production, and the pursuit of licensing arrangements to obtain the rights to commercially distribute recordings which are being neglected by both the major companies and small labels. Unlike many of the habits of production and organizational routines I have referred to in this book, such activities involve a different set of cultural activities and degree of emotional investment along with a contrasting type of knowledge construction – practices which conceive of an audience as more than simply a market.

To illustrate this issue I will select just one example from a long history of this type of activity as an illustrative case that enables me to make a number of points in relation to the argument I am developing here. I will refer to a double CD compilation of recordings issued in 1996 by the London-based Soul Jazz label and entitled *Nu Yorica! Culture Clash in New York City: Experiments in Latin Music 1970–77* (SJR CD 29).

This is a compilation of tracks licensed from a number of different small companies and includes recordings by Cortijo, Eddie Palmieri, Grupo Folklorico and Cachao, among others. It comes with a forty-page booklet that provides detailed profiles of the musicians and tracks and an educative, informative and critical text that addresses the reader in a way that is rare in the packaging of commercial CDs. The booklet clearly tries to frame how the listener should appreciate the music that is presented. First, it provides considerable historical context, explaining how a diverse group of musicians came to be making Latin music in New York during the 1970s, with distinct sections about New York's immigration history, Puerto Rico's music and relationship to the US, and Cuba and the development of Afro-Euro Cuban music.

The booklet also contains a particular argument about the multi-cultural interaction that has resulted in the meeting of musical traditions, and specifically connects this to the music industry's difficulty in dealing with this and its aesthetic consequences. So, for example, the reader is presented with a particular critique of the salsa label: 'The main problem with the term "salsa" is that, although unifying a music for Latin America, it didn't unify the Latin music of New York.' Detailing the diversity of musicians playing 'Latin music' (Afro-American, Italian-Spanish, Afro-Filipino) the booklet argues that 'many of these musical experiments have become lost over time, slipping through the gaps between salsa, jazz, funk, Latin jazz and soul'.

This theme is developed in profiles of individual artists. For example, the reader and listener is told: 'Ocho are not to be found in the history books of salsa, not because of their music, but on account of the definition of "salsa" not being able to handle the complexities of New York culture.' In a similar way, the tracks 'Carnaval' and 'Gumbo' are presented from Cortijo's *Time Machine* album (original 1974) with the accompanying explanation: 'The style of music is still bomba and plena but it is filled with jazz stylings as African chants mix with Afro-American funk as well as the use of the Brazilian Cuica drum. The record was misunderstood at the time by nearly everyone, too Latin for the jazz market, too jazz for the Latin market.' Here the selection of music is connected to a critique of conventional music industry labels and their impact on the activities of musicians and perceptions of audiences.

While challenging conventional music industry marketing categories and highlighting the gaps in between, this is not a naive celebration of multi-culturalism. Also presented is a critique of the politics that has created such social conditions. Alongside the argument that 'music can break through racial barriers' is the warning that 'we should be aware that New York's history is one of structural racism' and reference is made to the experience of Native Americans, immigration quotas, the arrival of black people as slaves, the imposition of US citizenship on Puerto Ricans and the trade embargo against Cuba. The listener is encouraged to reflect on a context to musical creativity that has involved the wielding of considerable institutional power and acts of oppression.

In concluding this chapter by referring to one double CD which, through its production and presentation, seeks to contradict and challenge the divisive practices I have been referring to earlier, I should stress that I am not simply presenting an argument about the potentials of a small independent company against the cynical corporate majors. Enough research has shown that the 'indies' can be as exploitative, ruthlessly economically driven and as narrow in their aspirations and marketing techniques as the big major companies. What I wish to draw attention to here does not concern a type of company, but a type of practice. This CD, put together in a careful way with attention to historical and political detail, is a deliberate attempt to challenge the music industry labels that are used to classify creativity, divide living culture and separate social experiences. It is an example of commercial recorded music being circulated in a way that deploys a different type of logic, emotional investment and pluralizing knowledge to that found in much of the industry. In its own way it is contributing to the routes taken by music, the inspiration of musicians and the excitement of audiences, and perhaps adding new points and perspectives to the salsa matrix.

The practices that created this CD are within the 'circuit of capital', yet point to more than a strictly instrumentalist and economic logic. The 'logic' here foregrounds music as a form of intercultural communication and information. It provides intimations of other ways of doing things. It suggests a discursive practice that does more than convert us into markets, and hints of an alternative cultural logic, routes and categories. Alone this may do little to change the corporate system of musical production, but it may take a few bricks out of the walls that divide us.

Chapter 7

Territorial marketing: international repertoire and world music

At a music business conference in Liverpool during the early 1990s an anecdote was circulating about a new clause in recording contracts. Having introduced an amendment giving themselves the rights to any future sound carrier yet to be invented (following the lengthy royalty negotiations that were required to modify contracts when the introduction of CD caught the business unprepared), record companies were now including a clause which assigned them <u>the rights to any material circulated in territories beyond the Earth.</u> Music companies were not prepared to take the slightest risk that they might lose income as a consequence of future extraterrestrial travel opening up even more markets.

The wild cynical imagination of musicians or wild cynical music industry practices? Or a typical tale told in Liverpool? I was never too sure. Truth is beside the point. The significance of this story and its ability to circulate so freely in this way – and to be recalled years later by those who attended[1] – is testament to the issue it highlights: that of territory, a key term within the music industry. Staff speak of being 'treated as a territory' by their foreign corporate owners, particularly when long-distance management changes, staff cuts and office closures occur. Musicians routinely sign contracts assigning the 'territorial rights' to the US or North America with one company and complete a deal for 'the rest of the world' with another label. The reasoning guiding such a decision is the judgement that while some companies may dominate distribution and retail sales in the United States, they may be less skilled at getting recordings to the public in other parts of the planet. Small companies or independent labels also routinely license their recordings to different companies operating in a range of territories, defined as a nation or a region covering a number of different nation states.

In this chapter I will explore this theme by drawing on the ideas of Nestor García Canclini as a way of explaining <u>how territorialization is central to what are called 'global' marketing</u> strategies in the music <u>industry.</u> This is partly an attempt to move away from the term 'global', a word which has been incorporated into a number of discourses about

more DtG. Negus,
not so ma
tico Canclini dude ...
Territorial marketing   153

culture, politics and economics, and which has been subject to consider-able critique.[2] I do not wish to rehearse these arguments here, but focus on the issue of territory to consider the movement of music in a more specific way. In doing this I shall follow García's suggestion that the dynamics of cultural relations in the modern(izing) world are characterized by two distinct interrelated processes which he has labelled 'deterritorialization' and 'reterritorialization'. The first term, deterritorialization, refers to 'the loss of any "natural" relationship between culture and geographical and social territories'. This has been accompanied by a process of reterritorial-ization which involves the relocalization 'of old and new symbolic productions' (García Canclini, 1990, p. 288). García's ideas are developed from an analysis of art in Latin America and debates about the character and consequences of modernity. Here I want to draw on these ideas to think about the music industry and the construction and use of the cate-gories of international repertoire and world music. I shall highlight how the label of domestic repertoire defines a strategy of territorial confine-ment, how international repertoire involves an attempt to deterritorialize artists and their music and how world music entails an attempt to reterri-torialize both old and new recordings, to *re*localize the meaning of music.

OR
maybe
not
genealogic
to DtG

Central to such territorial strategies is the work of the record company international marketing department. Since they were first formed, the international marketing departments within the major record labels have exerted a growing influence on the acquisition, prioritizing and circulation of the music of recording artists. This has been particularly so since the middle of the 1980s when the major entertainment corporations began adopting so-called 'global' strategies and littering their advertising and annual reports with images of the planet Earth and one-world rhetoric. A further theme in this chapter concerns the way that 'international' has been transformed from an administrative departmental label to a category of music, and almost a genre label. My aim is to highlight how this has occurred and to pursue some of its consequences. In doing this I will high-light how the international department plays a central role in the territorial labelling of music and how this corporate entity attempts to influence the dynamics through which different types of music move, or do not move, across national boundaries.

THE INTERNATIONAL IMPERATIVE AND ACQUISITION POLICIES

The major record labels began setting up distinct international depart-ments during the late 1960s and early 1970s. The initial task of these entities was primarily administrative. Staff were appointed to co-ordinate the movement and marketing of artists between and across the different national territories in which the company was operating. So, for example, personnel were recruited or redeployed to make sure that staff in Britain were providing their Japanese colleagues with the necessary paperwork, recordings and promotional material to present an artist. Or these staff acted as intermediaries, facilitating the mutual exchange of recordings between different national territories and linking together workers in Spain and the United States, or Brazil and Portugal, for example.

Since this time, the international marketing departments have grown in size, significance and influence within the music industry. From previously having an administrative function they have increasingly come to play a major role in defining a company's international priorities, and in turn they have begun to exert an influence on how artists are acquired, produced and presented. One obvious reason for this is that international staff have become yet another occupational grouping within the music industry accorded the task of reducing uncertainty.

In Chapter 2 I referred to the problem of 'market anxiety' and how this impacts on the workings of record companies and the formulation of strategies. This market anxiety has been increasingly re-imagined as a 'global' problem for the corporations, particularly as the US share of the world music market has been declining over recent years and is predicted to continue to decline.³ According to business analysts within the music industry, the markets of Western Europe and North America contain more older people, whereas there are far more younger people in markets constructed as Latin America and South East Asia. However, there are economic uncertainties about how these regions will develop and questions about the repertoire implications. For example, what should companies do about the relative decline in English-language pop and the increasing popularity of Mandarin and Spanish language songs?⁴ This type of issue affects decisions about where to locate offices and how to judge the potentials of 'domestic' repertoire in different regions of the world. This anxiety has contributed to further waves of restructuring and organizational change, as companies have sought to deal with the world on a more regional basis in recognition of the potential revenues that can be gained from strategically co-ordinated international marketing. In turn, this also informs judgements about the 'international potential' of any newly acquired or existing artists, and hence the degree to which resources will be made available for investment in artists. The international potential of any new artist has become an important consideration when a company is assessing a new acquisition. When asked how much thought was given to the potential of any newly signed artist to achieve success outside the United States, Tommy Mottola, President of Sony Music, responded:

> Tremendous. It's one of the most important factors. I'll tell you why: when you look at the cost in the US of signing an artist with an

advance, recording that artist, doing one or two videos, all the additional marketing and promotion, tours, advertising, and merchandizing costs, the record company is going to spend well in excess of $1 million on any new artist on its first release. Even at one million albums, which is considered a major breakthrough for a brand-new artist, you're basically going to break even. Where are you going to make the money? Only one place. Outside of the US market. So when we think about signing a new artist, we always do it with a global strategy in mind.

(quoted in Newman, 1996, p. 1)

The international market, outside the United States, is attractive for the same reason that it appeals to Hollywood film producers and book publishers – it can provide the corporation (and musicians, directors and novelists) with extra income for proportionately less additional investment. It is through this sort of imperative that the international marketing department has come to assume an important position and become separated from other departments within the major labels. There are two divisions. First, and somewhat confusing in terms of terminology, it has become separate from the broad international administrative division (where US companies locate their Latin department or label, for example). Second, it has become clearly separate from other departments within the domestic division of the major labels (where companies locate their country or rock department or labels). Drawn ever closer to corporate headquarters, and in some companies working within the remit of corporate head office, the staff within the international marketing department have become the experts with whom those in a national territory (Japanese domestic) or label division (country music) must liaise and upon whom they rely for knowledge, guidance and admission to 'global' markets. The status of the international marketing department has increased since the late 1980s, the epoch when the major labels began deploying discourses of 'globalization' as a way of 're-imagining' the world.

In narrating the shift from international as an administrative, organizational designation to international as an aesthetic, evaluative category, I shall start by saying something about the world that is being imagined by the international marketing department.

RE-IMAGING THE WORLD AS GLOBAL

Despite the numerous references to the term within the music industry and in business more generally, there are not simply global markets waiting out there (on the planet) in some transparently obvious way. The 'global market' is an idea that is constructed in a specific way by the music business (and made up in a contrasting but similar manner by other industries). Staff in the major record labels have adopted a particular way of understanding what global markets are, producing knowledge about them, and distributing that knowledge within the corporation.

In re-imaging the world for 'global marketing', international staff have drawn upon an often taken-for-granted reservoir of knowledge and a particular set of experiences, and use these to understand and make assessments about the world of music. This includes aesthetic judgements about the instruments, tempos, rhythms, voices and melodies that are able to 'travel well'. It incorporates semiotic judgements about the type of images that are more suitable for an 'international audience'. It includes political judgements about areas of the world considered to be 'unstable' or where certain types of music are banned for moral or religious reasons. It includes economic judgements about the number of potential consumers who can be reached, and assessments about parts of the world where the corporation may have difficulty collecting revenue. It includes marketing judgements about the arrangements for the distribution of recordings (the availability of radio, retail outlets, television broadcasting) and the 'penetration' of the technologies of musical reproduction (tape machines and CD players). Finally, it includes pragmatic judgements about the popularity of various sound carrier formats (cassettes, mini disks or compact disks) and the existence of copyright law that will ensure that recordings broadcast by the media, played in public and circulated for purchase will generate rights revenue that will accrue to the corporation. Hence, the so-called 'global markets' tend to be those which have strictly enforced copyright legislation and highly priced CDs rather than cheaply priced cassettes (so Japan is an important global market, whereas India is not). In this way the 'global' is imagined in terms of a series of very particular criteria. These business-oriented criteria can be further illuminated by thinking about one of the most profitable categories of music within the recording industry: international repertoire.

THE GLOBAL MARKET AND INTERNATIONAL REPERTOIRE: MELODY, LANGUAGE AND ACCENT

The term 'international repertoire' gained increasing currency and usage in the organizational discourses of the recording industry during the 1980s. It is a term used regularly by personnel within the music business, reported in trade reports and corporate publications and frequently found employed in record stores in non-English-speaking countries. International repertoire is marketed to a 'global' market; the recordings are released simultaneously in all of the major territories of the world. In recent years, trade magazine *Music and Copyright* has calculated that sales of 'international repertoire' have accounted for approximately 41 per cent (1996) to 45 per cent (1995) of all recorded music sold outside the United States (with US repertoire making up 75 per cent of this total).[5]

The category of international repertoire can be contrasted with 'regional repertoire', recordings that are released in a broad area (such as Spanish-language popular music in Latin America or Mandarin pop in East Asia), and 'domestic repertoire', recordings released solely in one national territory. In practical terms international repertoire refers to a list of very specific artists. Staff in the international department at each major company, in collaboration with senior business affairs executives, have been accorded the task of drawing up a 'global' priority list of about fifteen to twenty artists and advising other sections of the company whether their artists are going to be admitted or not.

What guides the judgements that are made? How do staff decide which artists to admit and who to exclude? The most obvious immediate answer is that this question is resolved according to economic criteria. It is those artists who have previously achieved international success and who are releasing a new album who will have little difficulty attracting radio play and media coverage and gaining sales. After this, it is those artists who have already achieved success in a specific part of the world and who seem likely to be able to 'break out' from a territory. However, such spontaneous breaking is subject to considerable rationalization and ordering. It is also subject to the imposition of a number of very particular aesthetic codes and cultural judgements prior to any attempt at promotion. There are, after all, at any one moment, many artists with the potential to 'internationalize'. Here musical criteria and aesthetic judgements play an important part when senior staff are deciding who is to be prioritized.

In February 1996 I interviewed David McDonagh, Senior VP of International at PolyGram's New York office, and having mentioned my interest in rap production I asked him how he assessed acts for international priority. Like other international staff I have spoken to, he identified a very particular type of music and explained his reasoning as follows:

> The basic kind of music that has broad appeal internationally is kind of, like, pop music ballads. Ballads always work. It doesn't matter if it's Whitney Houston, Mariah Carey, Bon Jovi or whoever it happens to be. A ballad is always going to be something that will work in basically every country around the world. So, with hip hop or rap music there aren't too many artists that have ballads. So, already you're in a situation where what fundamentally is going to work anywhere doesn't happen too often as far as hip hop and rap is concerned....Occasionally a song comes along that basically can be seen as a pop song in terms of having that immediate type of appeal and it's still by a rap or a hip hop artist, but it just so happens that it's

I guess I never thought much about the marketing of US music abroad, just the marketing of "world music" in the US...

a song that has broader appeal. Warren G is an example with 'Regulate', which was, like, a sort of soft melodic type of song and it did have rapping throughout. It also happened to have a sample that was instantly recognizable....We currently have one song by LL Cool J, which has Boyz II Men on it, which is called 'Hey Lover' and that one is pretty much a ballad, and because it features Boyz II Men that immediately gives it more of a pop feel.[6]

David, like a number of people I interviewed, considered the rap tracks that had international appeal to be those which in aesthetic terms could be related to a slow ballad structure or which contained a highly distinctive melodic sample. Hence, 'Gangsta's Paradise' owed its success and international promotion as much to Stevie Wonder's heavily sampled slow melodic ballad 'Pastime Paradise' as it did to Coolio's rap, and, of course, its circulation on the *Dangerous Minds* film soundtrack album. In a similar way, the international success enjoyed by Sean 'Puff Daddy' Combs might be explained in terms of his ability to transform ballads into rap tracks while retaining their recognizably melodic structure, as he did successfully in re-signifying the Police's 'Every Breath You Take' into 'I'll Be Missing You'.

It is in these types of sound that the major labels will be more inclined to invest time and money for international promotion, and this has led to accusations that certain artists have recognized this and are wilfully sampling melodic songs and adding a small rap as a way of gaining wider promotion. While there may be an element of truth in this claim, the dynamics driving the changing aesthetic style of rap are far more complicated and informed as much by the blurring of boundaries between soul, r 'n' b, jazz and rap as they are likely to be driven by any short-term ploy to make a fast buck.

In addition to providing music that in some way can be likened to a melodic ballad, any potential international artist must sing their ballads or melodic rock songs with the right kind of voice. This was highlighted by an international director who remarked that in theory an artist could come from any place in the world as long as they sing 'in English without an accent'.[7] This point was also made on another occasion, specifically when talking about Japanese artists, by Stuart Watson, who was then Senior Vice President of MCA International.

The voice and language is crucial, particularly when consideration is being given to artists who may have achieved considerable domestic or regional sales and who may be given the opportunity to 'have a shot' at the international market. This is a common career strategy that is built into the marketing plans of artists whose first language is English. The aim is to move a performer from 'domestic' (Britain, for example) to 'regional' (Europe) to 'international' (the rest of the world and, if coming from

Britain, to the United States). For many record company executives, however, the dream is to 'internationalize' an artist whose native language is not English. In 1993, after two years of preparation, Watson had managed to persuade his colleagues within MCA Records to prioritize Mari Hamada for international promotion. The following details are included here because they provide an insight into the planning and strategic intent of such an aim; for highlighting a particular way of thinking about international strategies within the music industry.

Mari was born in Tokyo and recorded her first heavy rock album, *Lunatic Doll*, for Victor Musical Industries of Japan in 1983. By the end of the decade she had become a major performer in Japan, selling out large tours and being awarded platinum albums for record sales. In 1991 she joined MCA Records, which was subsequently purchased by the Japanese Matsushita corporation in 1992. Following Watson's cajoling from MCA's London-based international division, her new record company began developing a strategy aimed at transforming her from a domestic Japanese artist into an international performer with world-wide appeal. Details of the marketing strategy provide an indication of some of the dynamics of re-labelling in the music industry and how an attempt to deterritorialize is central to the construction and marketing of international repertoire.

Despite recording fourteen previous albums, and although her Japanese release was called *Anti Heroine*, her first 'international' release for MCA, in 1993, was rather blandly titled *Introducing Mari Hamada*. Although she had written many songs in the past, she co-wrote the songs for this album with Marc Tanner, a US writer and producer, and the album was produced by Steve Tyrell (who had previously worked with Linda Rondstadt and The Heights). The majority of the songs on the album were sung in English (unlike many of her previous Japanese releases) and, as Stuart Watson remarked, stressing her lack of accent and ability to pronounce the letter 'r' against stereotype assumptions about how Japanese performers sing in English: 'She rocks and rolls, she doesn't wok and woll.'[8] Oh boy...

The company's marketing plan quite deliberately played down her national origins. The primary 'public relations objective' was 'to enhance public awareness of Mari Hamada as a singer who is able to "transcend" the Japanese background and thrive in the international arena'.[9] The marketing and public relations strategy was based on presenting Mari in such a way that she would be perceived as 'international', rather than as a 'domestic' Japanese artist. Emphasizing her 'international lifestyle', the press release quoted Mari as saying,

> The more I work with international producers, musicians and engi-neers and the more I visit the US, Europe and other countries, the more I feel that music is borderless. I strongly believe that my music

can be appreciated in any country, and I hope that with this debut I can realise my dream to be successful around the world.[10]

The initial aim was to build on her success in Japan by popularizing Mari in Taiwan, Indonesia, Hong Kong and Singapore. However, the ultimate aim was to internationalize the artist, to present her around the world without any specific sense of a connection to a particular place. Watson stressed that it was important that the company did not approach colleagues in the United States immediately (mainly to avoid rejection at the start). As he enthusiastically explained, the aim was

> not to target America first, to target Asia Pacific first and then Southern Europe – the image-orientated markets of Italy, France and Spain. And then, after we've done that, go and get Australia and New Zealand, if we're lucky get Northern Europe, and last of all, with 500,000 sales behind us – America. Because America will then have to deliver because we've sold everywhere else.[11]

This example illustrates how an artist is re-labelled – specifically, how a 'domestic' artist is deterritorialized for international marketing and the very specific geographical 'logic' through which the company aims to build her international career, culminating with the final goal of success in the United States. Mari was indeed promoted in Asia Pacific, and in 1994 toured Europe as support act to Kim Wilde on her 'Hits Tour'. However, Mari did not and as yet (as I write in 1998) has not become an internationally successful artist. Her music has certainly crossed many national boundaries and is listened to by fans in different parts of the world. But my inquiries among popular music researchers in Japan, Australia, New Zealand, France and Italy during 1998 suggested that Mari was clearly not an international artist. Indeed, she was even considered to be rather passé in her 'home' territory.[12] Like so many music industry proposals and plans, the internationalization of Mari Hamada failed to occur, certainly not in the manner envisaged at the time.

It is possible to speculate about the reasons for her failure to internationalize and to suppose that, at the very moment when she was being primed for international promotion, Mari's rather bland adult-oriented rock was sounding out of date alongside the increasing international popularity of the more contemporary sound of 'alternative rock'. However, my concerns here are not with the reasons for her failure, but with the way in which she was re-presented. One of the immediate problems that Mari faced was the requirement that she first sing in English, and then sing with the right accent. The problems of language and accent are not faced simply by artists whose first language is not English. Language and accent also present barriers to artists from the United States who may not be prioritized due to such judgements. Most notably, rap and country artists rarely make it into the international category. According to international marketing staff I have spoken to in the United States, Britain and Japan, both rap and country are judged to be 'too dependent upon the lyrics' or 'the vocals' and are considered to foreground the voice and lyrical content in a way that people from other parts of the world 'can't relate to' or 'cannot identify with'.[13] Despite their being heard around the world, a judgement is made that the vocal and musical accents of rap and country are too distinct for international priority and promotion (and the concomitant investment involved). Ironically, many British artists are not considered to have the requisite 'global English' accent to join the international category, and since the early 1960s many British artists who have succeeded in the United States have done so singing with an 'American' inflexion and pronunciation to their singing.

Rap, country and British rock have certainly travelled the world, but they have often done so according to a quite different logic to that of the planned strategic international marketing which was attempted with Mari Hamada. When this does happen it is often due to the commitment of an artist's management or a local promoter, intermediaries who can play a part in attempting to influence the music label's strategy. To quote from David McDonagh again, when I asked him if it was possible to influence record company decision-making in any way:

> There could be some manager who just decides 'we want to go to Australia and spend a month there because our artist has always wanted to do that'. With that sort of information the Australian company might go, 'Well, we'll put the album out.' So there are a variety of ways, but ultimately if the people in the companies are not there supporting the music it makes it much more difficult…there are instances where maybe on paper it didn't make sense to go after something too hard, but it's the passion and enthusiasm that the people show at the other end that makes you want to give it a try.[14]

Artists may be pushed along like this, aided in their travels by the efforts of managers and the enthusiasm of their followers and friends within the music labels and media. This may pose a challenge to the stasis and inertia of the major labels and the unwillingness of staff to stick their necks out and act speculatively. Artists and their music may travel the world in a more ad hoc manner, in a similar way to the movements through the 'salsa matrix' discussed in the last chapter. But this is a still a long way from being prioritized and admitted to the category of 'international repertoire', a label which has become an institutionalized euphemism for the recordings of artists who sing conventional melodic songs in accent-free English and who have a number of ballads in their repertoire. Not surprisingly, most artists admitted to the priority list are from the United States and Britain. Yet, in theory, an 'international' artist may be drawn from any place, as long as they fit the musical and vocal criteria, and this can occur. Discussing this point, Stuart Watson identified the brief international success of Vanessa Paradis as 'a very interesting exception…a very rare one'. It was this sort of exception that led him to try and break Mari Hamada. It is this possibility that continually motivates artists to struggle for admission to the international category.

THE INCENTIVES OF THE INTERNATIONAL AGENDA

In drawing up a global priority list and making these aesthetic judgements, international marketing staff have begun to assume an important position and have become far more than administrators. They have played a part in constructing a musical label which sets an agenda for other personnel within the company who wish to have their artists admitted to this category. Just as performers in Nashville, for example, can attempt to tailor their recordings to suit the requirements of country music radio, so artists and their representatives within various sections of the major corporations attempt to make subtle and not so subtle changes in an attempt to be placed on the international priority list. The re-presentation of Mari Hamada was just one example. In this way international repertoire begins to function as a set of stylistic characteristics or a genre label within the corporation.

Rather than individual labels and departments approaching international staff with artists, the international division conducts a surveillance operation and places pressure on departments to 'think internationally' from the beginning. Rather than attempting to promote a diversity of existing artists, an approach is adopted that involves locating artists who fit the criteria (and ignoring those who do not fit this formula). Staff begin to 'know' who should and should not be admitted. Word filters throughout the companies and is formally passed down to artist and repertoire staff: 'The artists who will gain most success are those with "international appeal".'

It is not unusual to find that a label that started life as an administrative functional category has produced a musical genre – many 'administrative' or marketing terms have had similar consequences in the past. Rock 'n' roll, for example, initially introduced to refer to a diversity of regionally distinct styles in the United States, became a major commercial brand, and a variety of performers could gain admittance to this new category with minor modifications to their previous repertoire.[15] Salsa, initially coined in a similar way to place together a variety of performers drawing on distinct Afro-Cuban musical traditions, is another commercial category that new artists may use to self-define their music and that recording companies utilize in their repackaging of older recordings. Where 'international repertoire' differs, however, is in its origins. Terms such as rock 'n' roll, salsa, funk and jazz were drawn from their vernacular use within particular cultural traditions and then used by the music industry as a way of organizing catalogues. The term 'international' has been formulated within the corporate suite and then used to exert an increasing influence on acquisition policies, production and distribution practices and the styles adopted by performers.

While musicians may well be inspired to adopt the characteristics of a new musical style, it can be economically advantageous to be labelled in one way and not another. Being admitted to the category of international repertoire will result in increased financial investment. In the long term; if leading to success, it could mean admittance to an exclusive artist aristocracy. An artist prioritized for international promotion by a major record label is marketed and presented in a systematic way that involves the identification of key markets, the strategic geographical movement through these places and the support of a large promotional budget. The company establishes a clearly defined marketing plan, invests accordingly and promotes systematically through various targeted regional media. Staff in each regional office (whether Germany, Argentina, Japan or Australia) are given clear sales targets that they are expected to reach.

This can create a considerable amount of local frustration and tension, as staff in other territories often prefer to be working with their own artists than with a prioritized US or UK artist. As Kei Nishimura, General Manager of Business Affairs International at Toshiba-EMI, explained referring to a world-wide international priority list of approximately ten artists: 'Whether we like it or not, we have to go with all these artists.'[16] As Manfred Zunkeller recalled from his days as head of artist and repertoire for EMI Germany:

> I'll never forget one marketing meeting. The head of marketing and the head of sales were there. We were talking about a Diana Ross single, and the sales were very poor. There was a local guy called Andy Burg selling boxes and boxes of records. But everyone kept talking about Diana Ross, not about Andy Burg.
>
> (quoted in Pride, 1991, p. 16)

Whatever the perceptions of markets held by local staff, regardless of their commitment to their own artists and despite personal preferences that may predispose them to certain performers and not others, these personnel must ensure that attention is first devoted to the world-wide priorities. The international marketing department, drawn ever closer to the strategic planning staff at corporate head office, has ways of ensuring that these plans are implemented. One technique entails offering incentives: performance-related bonuses are awarded for exceeding sales targets, increasing market share and achieving high chart positions. At the same time, staff are routinely made accountable for not reaching established goals. The most common sanction is straightforward demotion or the termination of employment (the same consequence as not achieving specific goals in any record label division). Corporate headquarters also attempt to 'motivate' local staff in different territories, gaining their involvement in more subtle ways by offering access to artists, both backstage at events and in company offices.

In this way the success of a Mariah Carey, Elton John, Bon Jovi or Michael Jackson is prioritized and systematically implemented by the major company. Not only does this procedure entail the use of considerable financial resources, it also involves a particular type of economic-oriented instrumental rationality. The diversity of musical activity in the world is reduced to a specific type of 'market' activity and a coercive management practice is deployed to enforce people, spread out in different offices around the world, to work in a particular way to ensure that international priorities do become successful. It is in this way that record companies attempt to deterritorialize their major artists and their music, a practice motivated by an anticipation of the rewards that can be gained from sales on the 'international market'. This is a major dynamic and powerful influence, exerting considerable pressure within the music industry. However, there are also other labelling practices at work; some artists are being *re*territorialized.

RETERRITORIALIZATION AND WORLD MUSIC

As Steve Jones (1993) has noted, 'world music' began to gain currency at a moment that saw the increasing use of the international category and the adoption of 'global' strategies by the music industry. World music is a label that has been used since the late 1980s to refer to an eclectic mixture of styles, rhythms and sounds, and like so many musical categories it initially emerged to resolve a marketing dilemma within the entertainment industries. The category was formulated following a meeting in London of staff drawn from various small labels who wished to construct a market space to place a diversity of music, variously labelled as 'ethnic', 'traditional' or 'roots', which was increasing in popularity.

If international repertoire is constructed in such a way that an artist can, in theory, be taken from anywhere and sold to anywhere else (the negation of places), then world music involves the affirmation of place. It involves the reterritorialization of old and new 'domestic' repertoire and its recategorization as 'world' music. Artists are selected from the 'domestic' repertoire of specific localities (Bulgaria, West Africa, South America) and repackaged, re-labelled as 'world music' and distributed to consumers in other particular places, for whom this label has a particular meaning (for people in Japan, Britain, the USA and Canada, France, Australia, New Zealand, for example). World music is clearly not music from the 'world', but a narrow selection of sounds from *somewhere else* in the world. In some instances it involves the re-labelling of domestic artists as world music within the same national territory, as happened with the Aboriginal band Yothu Yindi (Mitchell, 1996).

If the successful marketing of international repertoire requires the development of an accent and sound that cannot be placed, then world music requires accents, languages and sounds that can definitely be 'placed'. By this I do not mean that such sounds and accents materially exist in or are intrinsically connected to particular places, but that the sounds of specific instruments, musical tones, rhythmic patterns and voices signify a sense of geographical place via various musical semiotic codes and connotations that have developed historically and which are usually recognized by listeners as 'verbal-visual associations' (Tagg, 1987). As Stephen Feld has observed, people rarely hear musical sounds that are 'totally new, unusual and without some experiential anchors' (1984, p. 6). Sounds are recognized, and geographical place is one of the main ways in which music is located.

Music has no *necessary* belonging to specific places, but certain sounds have come to *signify* particular places ('Zimbabwean' guitar patterns, 'Bulgarian' folk styles, 'Irish' melodies, 'Latin' rhythms). These musical codes are decoded and recognized as such by listeners. Of course, the British fan of hard rock, rap or techno may not recognize the place of many world music sounds any more than the salsa fan in Puerto Rico will recognize the association of the sounds of Portishead and Tricky with the English city of Bristol. But sounds *are* recognized as such by the 'interpretive communities' (Fish, 1980) who have acquired the competence to 'know' these sounds and who constitute the audience that is targeted for the selling of world music. In contrast to world music, the international repertoire of artists such as Dire Straits, Elton John or Madonna is less easily located and more easily open to local appropriation (which is not to deny that critics frequently locate this generically as 'western' or 'Anglo-American'). It was the attempt to promote Mari Hamada as an international artist (rather than a world artist) that led to an attempt to construct a non-accented and non-placeable sound and identity.

As the territorial significations that are encoded within the musical sound may not necessarily be recognized by consumers, the record companies provide information to assist in the placing of the artist. This can be found in all aspects of the marketing and mediation process. For example, in 1994 EMI, recognizing the amount of 'domestic' repertoire that the company had accumulated in its various subsidiaries, announced the introduction of a new 'Hemisphere' series through which its artists were to be re-labelled as 'world music'. The first releases were recordings from Brazil, Mali, the Andes and Central Africa. To 'educate' listeners, each release was accompanied by detailed explanatory liner notes and 'a map highlighting the source of repertoire' (Duffy, 1994, p. 40).

This emphasis on the place of world music was very soon routinized and institutionalized. It could be seen regularly in press reviews. To take one example: at the end of 1993, the British newspaper *The Independent* produced a critical review of 'the albums of 1993'. Under 'rock and pop', the following artists were featured; Bjork, Crowded House, Cypress Hill, Donald Fagen, Fluke, Shara Nelson, Willie Nelson, Smashing Pumpkins, Paul Westerberg and Neil Young. Although including vague references to the popularity of some of the artists in the US and Europe, there was no reference to the national origins of the artists, no reference to the fact that Bjork is from Iceland, Crowded House from New Zealand/Australia, Smashing Pumpkins from the USA and Neil Young from Canada. In contrast, under the world music category, every artist (with the exception of a compilation album of calypso music) was identified with their national origins: Etoile de Dakar (Senegal), Sam Mangwana (Zaire/Angola), Shaggy (New York), Jean-Fritzner Delmont (a Parisian exile from the Francophone Caribbean), Pete Rodriguez (Puerto Rico), Muzsikas (Hungary), George Dalaras (Greece), Bernado Silva (Spain) and Detty Kurnia (Indonesia).[17]

As domestic artists are reterritorialized and re-labelled as world music, so an emphasis on their origins becomes integral to their presentation to people outside their home domestic market. This is one of the central practices in the development of world music as a marketing category and commercial strategy. For world music artists, place became central to their presentation, not only because they are often found filed under their country of origin in retail stores, but because this aspect is emphasized in their individual presentation. So, for example, the cover of Salif Keita's critically acclaimed and commercially successful album *Soro* (1987) featured images of the artist in performance playing percussion instruments, and also a photograph of the artist sitting with a group in a canoe emerging out of some trees and marshland into a lake. The liner notes attempt to reduce any misunderstanding or ambiguity about the location that might be signified by this imagery. As the listener hears the album, he or she can read that 'Salif Keita is one of the most remarkable stars in Africa today. From the West African state of Mali and of noble birth he is a direct descendent of Soundjata Keita, the warrior king who founded the empire of Mali in 1240' (Yamotei, 1987).

The packaging of world music in this way has often been viewed as a rather cynical ploy by the music industry. Rick Glanvill has referred to the 'trade in world music' as 'reminiscent of the colonial trade patterns' with the 'music of South America, Africa and Asia being mined as a raw resource' (1989, p. 64). Simon Frith has noted how world music was defined in terms of 'an existing rock ideology that valued the "authentic" above the "plastic" ', which in turn was connected to 'first-world anxieties' and romantic notions of the innocence of pre-capitalist music (1991, pp. 282–4). Paul Gilroy has observed how world music makes use of an enduring 'logic of authenticity...[to] make non-European and non-American musicians acceptable in an expanded pop market place' (Gilroy, 1993, p. 99).

There is no doubt that the presentation of world music often involves an exoticism and romanticization of music from 'other' places (Goodwin and Gore, 1990). The repackaging is not for people who live within these territories, but for those outside who may have no immediate experience of them. Similar tendencies may be found in the selling of world cinema, world literature and world travel as well as in the marketing of everyday products such as coffee or 'exotic' rain-forest shower gels. However, it would be misleading to suggest that everyone involved in the marketing of world music is cynically exploiting talent with just one aim, or that promoting an artist in terms of their place always means constructing an exotic sense of 'otherness'. Such an assumption also ignores the multiple motivations of musicians, who may be willingly or reluctantly contributing to this process. Working practices and the beliefs through which they are guided and understood are not so coherent or predictable. The activities of people working for companies producing world music are informed by many motives and these cannot be collapsed into any one logic.

Many are enthusiasts working for small labels, ardent devotees who perceive world music to be an indication of a kind of emergent global culture brought about by increasing cosmopolitanism and who hear this as a direct challenge to the narrow range of aesthetic styles admitted to the international repertoire category. Such an opinion has been regularly voiced in editorials in *Rhythm Music Magazine* (RMM). To take one example:

> As 'world music' becomes more than a catch-all term, as people in America and throughout the world get more and more in touch with the tremendous variety the planet has to offer, this magazine will have an ever more important contribution to make...it remains our intention to cover all genres of music from the unique vantage point of 'world music' listeners. These listeners are intelligent and cosmopolitan in their outlook and tastes. I've seen someone at the sales counter in a large record store, buying Miles Davis, the

Either/Orchestra, the Master Musicians of Jajouka, the Dagar Brothers, Elliott Carter's String Quartets, Steve Reich, Bob Marley, Sinatra and the Rolling Stones – all at once! For listeners like this, old barriers, boundaries and stereotypes no longer apply.

(W. Russell, 1993, p. 4)

However, other fans and workers within the music and media business are more reflexively aware of the elements of romanticism and mythologizing that might have become an integral element of their music preferences. *New York Times* music critic Jon Pareles defended 'big world music' against the sampling and blending of various 'raw materials' that was leading to what he heard as studio-manufactured 'small world music'. As he wrote in a review,

I'm a diehard fan of world music from specific places and times, music that grew out of local traditions and survived while sustaining its heritage. Part of my attachment is probably sentimental: an idealization of the exotic and primitive and rare, and a willingness to ignore the paradoxes of listening to a jungle-healing ritual, on a CD, to escape the pace and commercialism of music-as-usual.

(Pareles, 1996, p. H34)

This type of dilemma has been acknowledged by a number of writers. As ethnomusicologist, musician and producer of world music recordings Stephen Feld has observed:

Musical appropriation sings a double line with one voice. It is a melody of admiration, even homage and respect, a fundamental source of connectedness, creativity, and innovation...yet this voice is harmonized by a countermelody of power, even control and domination, a fundamental source of asymmetry in ownership and commodification of musical works.

(Feld, 1994, p. 238)

The making and marketing of the sounds of musicians as world music is unavoidably caught up in this asymmetry and the power imbalances through which the modern music industry moves. But it provides hints of something more, a glimpse of briefly realized solidarities between musicians and listeners stretched out across the globe. As Deborah Pacini Hernández (1993) has highlighted, many recordings are accompanied by detailed information and documentation which, like the Latin music CD profiled in the previous chapter, seek to contextualize the music within an educational discourse – an attempt to counteract its abstraction as a commodity freed from any roots and responsibilities. Attempts have been made to frame the reception of world music recordings in such a way as to encourage an 'attentiveness to musical, social or political change occurring elsewhere' (Guilbault, 1997, p. 31). Such efforts are clearly not made during the packaging, marketing and selling of international repertoire. Like rap, country and salsa, world music is a label that is more than a commercial category. Yet world music travels an ambiguous route, between the mythical search for authentic redemption and a quest for purity, and a type of reflexive post-exotic listening which is aware of the territorializing strategies of the music industry, media and the way in which the musical identity has been constructed. The same sounds take both routes simultaneously and cannot be reduced to one or the other.

NEW FRONTIERS, OLD HORIZONS AND A DIFFERENT DREAM OF GLOBAL CIRCULATION

I want to conclude by making four distinct points that arise as a consequence of the processes I have been narrating in this chapter and that also build on the discussion of genres in earlier parts of this book. My first point concerns the pressures that are placed upon and the temptations presented to musicians, as a result of the corporate organization of musical production and pursuit of specific commercial strategies. All performers are encouraged to compete with one another, from their earliest days of gaining exposure in small clubs, through the fierce competition to acquire a recording contract and arguments about positions on concert billings and label rosters, to subsequent struggles to get records into the charts and to gain further investment for promotion. The anecdotes about such struggles are legend, particularly in popular biographies. This chapter has highlighted the pinnacle which such competition sets its sights upon and has sketched the territories through which artists must struggle to join an international elite. As I pointed out in Chapter 2, the major record labels have a limited amount of resources to allocate to different genres and artists. Hence, staff engage in continual interdepartmental rivalry and lobbying for recognition and greater investment. Resources are allocated to those artists who will bring the greatest return on investment. The top return on investment is produced by 'global' artists performing international repertoire, yet very few musicians are admitted to this priority list. Those who are admitted, and who are not immediately ejected for failing to hit the required sales targets, can become part of a highly mobile international pop aristocracy. These artists will receive greater investment, will realize larger sales and hence will be able to obtain bigger advances and higher royalty rates. Needless to say, this will have a significant impact upon their lifestyle. All this attracts artists who, whether willingly or reluctantly, struggle against each other to be admitted to this category. The pressures and conditions that produce these rivalries cannot be neglected when considering the conditions of creativity. This is an integral part of the creative environment which any major global artist will inhabit. The pressure on musicians to churn out the same old familiar material and maintain their position is enormous, at least for those musicians who value and wish to maintain such a position within a musical aristocracy.

In contrast, most recording artists will stay within their own generic category and many will remain within their own national container. Some may gain regional promotion. So, for example, rock singer-songwriter Shakira from Colombia has been marketed in North America, the Caribbean, Central and South America and Southern Europe, and Singaporean Dick Lee enjoys success in Japan and South East Asia. Others may remain resolutely 'domestic', being allocated minimal resources and administered for promotion in one nationally defined territory. This leads to my second point. Many artists remain decidedly 'local', not because their music has no intrinsic appeal outside its specific base and not because it is never actually heard outside a locale. It remains local or national or 'domestic' because the resources are not invested within and across national territories and because organizational structures do not allow the artist to cross over to different regions *within* the corporation. Here I should add that an artist has to 'cross over' within the corporation (from staff to staff, from department to department) before they can start crossing over to other territories, media systems and musical categories. In an increasingly 'global' world, such artists may find their recording contract terminated and their local career quickly curtailed if there is a slight drop in their sales. After all, there is always another competitor waiting in the wings who may, just possibly, have more 'international potential'.

These constraints lead me to my third point and a further consequence. The definition of certain artists as non-international prior to any attempt actually to promote them internationally leads to a type of defensive reaction. Staff dealing with the numerous genres and artists that are excluded tend to retreat into a defensive genre bunker. It is not simply that they have been denied resources and routes to wider promotion, although this may partly explain any frustrated retreat. It is also an act of defiance and gesture of not wishing to compromise or 'cross over'. As the major labels have tried to make themselves more 'global' they have played an active part in contributing to national and local fragmentation. The pursuit of international repertoire and investment in this category has contributed to a process of aesthetic fragmentation. Artists, audiences and industry personnel remain within their genre boxes, unheard by those listening within different genre containers. This may result in a process of dynamic uncompromising musical development within a genre category, or it may lead to generic formularism and uninspired mannerism. It will certainly not facilitate or contribute to any creative fusions, meetings or blendings with musicians and audiences from other genres.

My fourth point comes with a twist. Despite all of these corporate constraints, there is an increasing amount of popular music moving across the world and it is travelling in ways which are not directed, controlled or understood by the major entertainment corporations. The three musical genres featured in this book – rap, country and salsa – and numerous others that I have mentioned in passing or which I have not had the space to feature on these pages, are travelling the world, performed by musicians, circulated by enthusiasts, despite being denied admittance to the exclusive international priority list. Such dynamism is not sustained by an identifiable corporate 'culture industry' but instead by the cultural *industry* of enthusiasts, fans and musicians. As Raymond Williams once pointed out, while the term 'industry' has come to signify the 'institutions for production or trade', it can also be used to refer to 'the human quality of sustained application and effort' (1983, p. 165). This is industry as an effort of will, as a dynamic human quality rather than as a bureaucratized institution. Much music is moving across the world through human cultural industry and not as a result of institutional corporate strategy. This point is important, and is usually neglected by those writers who present overtly mechanistic or deterministic models of the music industry and who neglect the fact that human industry is part of organizational industry.

While an elite group of artists are internationally successful *because* of the investment, resources and promotional techniques of the major labels of the music industry, there are many others who are internationally successful *despite* the music industry. Again I wish to stress the importance of this point because it suggests different dynamics to the 'global' movement of music; all sounds do not move according to the same 'logic'. A simple and basic contrast I would draw is between the well-organized and in many respects imperialist strategies and struggles through which a major superstar is distributed, and the more ad hoc and chaotic 'matrices of transnational cultural flow' (Hannerz, 1996) through which the recordings of a blues singer, a salsa performer, a rap or jazz artist are circulated around the world. Many recordings move across the world despite the plans, priorities and prejudices of the major corporations. This is facilitated by the activity of enthusiasts whose actions contribute to the formation of music industries but whose cultural industry is far from institutionalized. Much more research is needed to understand the intricate patterns which may be involved here, but the dynamics are certainly less coherent and institutionalized than the formal relationships established between independent and major record labels.

The active seeking out of recordings, of bringing musicians across borders, of engaging in dialogues with other enthusiasts, can in a modest way pose a challenge to the music industry labels that are used to classify creativity, divide living culture and separate social experiences. Much of this industry still involves the circulation of music as a commodity but it is moved in a way that deploys a different type of logic, emotional investment and pluralizing knowledge to that found in much of the institutional industry.[18] It points to more than a strictly instrumentalist and economic logic. To return to my own refrain from the end of the previous chapter (also for any narrow-minded reader who skipped the last chapter just as they might avoid the Latin genres in a record store): the 'logic' here foregrounds music as a form of intercultural communication and information. It suggests a discursive practice that does more than convert us into markets and hints of an alternative cultural logic moving across existing commercial categories and corporate structures. Alone this may do little to change the corporate system of musical production, but it might take a few bricks out of the walls which divide us.

P.151

Chapter 8

Walls and bridges: corporate strategy and creativity within and across genres

When we hear our favourite performer singing to us, whether we are driving through open spaces in the country or immersed in the sounds of a personal stereo on a crowded bus or train, it is easy to forget the business context within which popular music is recorded and circulated. When the musician's artistry connects directly with our own lives and everyday concerns, it is perhaps inevitable (and probably necessary) that we suspend belief and knowledge of how the music we are listening to has come to be heard in this way. Yet the mundane mediations of the music industries are important, and have a direct impact on the songs that come to be recorded and the way we get to hear them. The musician's art and the listener's pleasure occur within specific circumstances, and my central aim in this book has been to explore how musical creativity can be realized within and across the cultures of production shaped by the modern recording industry. In doing this I have highlighted how record companies manage creativity by incorporating musical genres into the techniques of portfolio management. I have also sketched the different ways that broader genre cultures intersect with and become an influential part of the industry of cultural production.

In the early part of the book I placed more emphasis on how entertainment companies use corporate strategies to exert control and enforce accountability. I focused on portfolio management as one of the key strategies deployed by the major record labels and highlighted how this is used to deal with three key issues. First, it provides a means of managing problems of risk arising from uncertainties about whether or not new and existing artists will deliver what is expected and, if they do, whether the products will continue to be purchased and accrue catalogue value. Second, it enables the corporations to divide a company's catalogue into distinct departments, with specific staff and resources allocated to work particular repertoires, defined according to genre categories. Departments or labels must then compete against each other to justify their claims for a share of corporate resources. Third, portfolio management enables the company to monitor and account for the activities of personnel in each division through financial indicators which are used when making judgements about the 'success' of their mix of genres and departments. Different company units and staff can then be rewarded with performance-related bonuses and the allocation of more resources, or punished by being removed from post or through the closure of specific departments or labels.

In addition to portfolio management, I also discussed various techniques aimed at 'knowing' the consumer and highlighted how an ideal consumer is imagined and constructed, an entity bearing a tenuous connection to the activities it attempts to describe. Central to consumer strategies is the work of the distribution division. Three further issues are also significant here. First, the distribution divisions of the major record labels occupy an important position within the corporate structure of the music industry. The distribution divisions perform a key monitoring role, deploying a series of rewards and sanctions when controlling the number of recordings being manufactured and released by company labels and departments. Second, the distribution divisions are the repositories of knowledge about artistic trends and music listening habits and have come to exert an increasing influence over the decision to acquire both artists and labels, and over judgements about contract renewal. The third important point I highlighted here concerns the knowledge and practices of distribution sales staff. This can have a significant impact on the availability of different types of music. To recall one example I discussed earlier, the wider distribution of Latin music in the United States is hampered by a fragmented retail sector composed of many small family-run stores, a lack of genre knowledge, and poor Spanish-language skills on the part of major label distribution staff (this is an issue which may be of relevance when considering the distribution of other genres in parts of the world where distinct language communities are associated with specific musical styles).

My discussion of salsa was part of the central section of this book where I also focused on rap and country when explaining how the formal separation of genres within music organizations is uneasily connected to a broader series of social divisions and tensions. Expanding on my critique of 'the jargon of corporate identity' in Chapter 3, I argued that the genre cultures that arise from the intersection of record label units with surrounding social formations render notions of unique 'company culture' a decidedly mythical and superficial concept for understanding the interplay of music genres and corporate cultures. In each of the chapters devoted to specific genres, and through their cumulative argument, I stressed the significance of genre cultures as an unstable intersection of music industry and media, fans and audience cultures, musician networks and broader social collectivities informed by distinct features of solidarity and social identity (rap alliances and affiliations; country community and family; regional and pan-Latin identities). While not wishing to overemphasize the media of communication, I also highlighted the significance of various occupational intermediaries such as radio station personnel, retailers, DJs and 'street promotion' people, and pointed to a number of variations between genres. For example, country is highly dependent upon radio, to the extent that contracts can be terminated, albums re-recorded or artists not acquired if radio play cannot be achieved as a primary marketing route. In contrast, rap relies on complex interconnected networks of mediations through performances, posters, magazine articles, community events, parties, the actions of DJs and word-of-mouth chains, all prior to any attempt to gain radio play. Salsa, partly marginalized within the United States, is frequently circulated through various cultural matrices, in which touring musicians, friends, enthusiasts, managers and local promoters can have a significant influence on the wider distribution of the music.

Through these chapters and in the latter part of the book, I have tried to show how, simultaneously, the recording industry establishes specific control strategies and dominant agendas while a considerable amount of musical production, distribution and consumption is beyond the immediate influence and understanding of the corporations. This is particularly so when considering the international movement of music and the 'global' strategies of 'international marketing'. A major tension here arises from the way that artists are usually located within genre departments and separate media routes for 'domestic' distribution, but are then called upon to 'transcend' their genre origins and to produce sounds which can be accommodated to various aesthetic agendas, media systems and promotional routes favoured by international marketing staff. As only a very small number of artists will ever be prioritized for international marketing, most have to carve out their own routes and pathways via the combined cultural industry of their supporters, or remain defiantly or apathetically locked in a genre box. In discussing this issue I suggested that we think of 'industry' as not only the institutional routines of commerce and trade, but as the concerted actions of human endeavour – the human 'cultural industry' that is often far removed from the formal procedures followed in media organizations.

In following this general narrative I have sought to stress the conditions within which musical creativity can be realized, shaped as much by formal organizations, occupational roles and corporate production techniques as by the broader genre cultures across which music is made, circulated and given meaning. I have argued that an environment is generated where certain ways of making music (some combinations of sounds, words and images) come to be produced and appreciated as 'creative'. This is always political (in sociological terms) before anyone can even begin to claim aesthetic merit for some sounds and not others (and engage in textual politics). The dynamics of cultural production always result in the privileging

of certain practices, products, sectors, producers and publics over others and, simultaneously, the separation of these from one another.

This clearly has consequences for those of us who wish to encourage democratic participation in cultural production and broad access to the products that are made available. But the political questions, and any potential policies that we may wish to advocate, do not simply depend upon finding ways of dealing with 'the industry', occupational tasks or administrative concerns, nor the issues arising as a consequence of 'owner-ship' (corporate control, monopolies and oligopolies) in any simple sense. Apart from the fact that 'control' is often more tentative than it might appear (as I have stressed in much of this book), the implication of my argument is that we also need to understand how industries are formed within a broader context or, to return to my refrain; how culture produces industry. For example, the possibility of gaining access to, participating in and becoming formally recognized as a cultural producer (whether in the domains of literature, painting, music, clothing design, theatre, film or other practice) is clearly dependent upon presenting a 'marketable' product. But it is also informed by patterns of power and prejudice arising from the way in which the formation of particular industries has been shaped by such factors as class, gender relations, sexual codes, ethnicity, racial labels, age, political allegiances, family genealogy, religious affilia-tion and language. Depending where you are in the world, some of these may appear to be more significant than others. In making this point, I do not wish to reduce the production of culture to a series of social variables or bodily distinguishing marks, but to emphasize the way in which broader social divisions are inscribed into and become an integral part of business practices, informing what are often assumed to be basic commercial deci-sions. The reason why one singer and not another may gain a recording contract is not only dependent upon the judgements of accountants and the expertise of producers with an ear to 'the market' (the public). It is shaped by the cultures of production, the culture within the industry and the industry within culture: there are multiple mediations between the appearance of 'talent' and its recognition by an 'audience'.

This point leads me to a further question, and this concerns the contri-bution of recording industry personnel – the people who derive their livelihood from the production of popular music and who claim a partic-ular mediating role in 'the creative process'. I started the research for this book assuming that entertainment corporations and record labels occupy a significant position between artist and audience and, as such, are a crucial site for studying the dynamics of music and images in formation, for understanding the mediations and modifications that concretely connect the intentions of artists with the interpretations of their listeners and viewers. This idea had grown out of my previous research on the music industry (Negus, 1992) in which I had focused in a more detailed way on how record label staff work quite consciously in attempting to stabilize and frame the meaning of any musical work through a direct engagement in the production and encoding of audio and visual characteristics (contributing to sound recording, image presentation and video production). I began the research for this book thinking that I might further illustrate this process through a series of case studies that would show in detail how the content of popular music is modified, transformed and stabilized by identifiable staff within the producing organizations. However, while I have traced and pinpointed how music is framed and shaped in particular ways through very specific practices and industry strategies, I have come to reassess my assumptions about the 'contribution' of music business personnel and their position within this process.

Although record companies have considerable power to direct or define the way popular music is produced and reaches the consumer, they are continually having to concede a lot of 'control' to those artists who become successful. Most established artists struggle to reach a position whereby they own their own master recordings and license their artwork to a record company for a limited number of years, with precise clauses governing what the company can and cannot do with it. In addition, many small companies, representing newer artists, attempt to attain a similar position to that of the major artists. In the case of both established artists and new acts operating through a smaller company, the expertise of accountants and lawyers and the skills of producers have contributed to a situation whereby a production company (operated by artist or entrepreneur) creates a product that is then licensed to a major company, which has been given this product because of its ability to distribute recordings. Indeed, major record companies are increasingly acknowledging that their skills are not so much in the area of making a 'creative' contribution by fiddling with the sounds and images (as artists have complained for numerous years). Instead, record companies are stressing their ability to understand how to distribute music to consumers.

Although a few prominent music industry executives have been recognized for their constructive interventions into daily music production, most personnel are engaged in less 'defining' and 'transforming' of the product (and hardly ever see the inside of a recording studio or comment on a 'demo'). Instead, a large part of what they are doing relies on the deployment of more conventional business management techniques. Some staff might be reasonably described as 'gatekeepers' (or perhaps 'doorkeepers') in the sense that they make a decision to let an individual, band or recording enter through a door. As the new faces travel along the corridor they will meet the occupational intermediaries, who are less engaged in opening and closing doors and more involved in passing information backwards and forwards along a chain. Other workers are less tied to the office routine and can be viewed as 'cultural intermediaries', in the terms suggested by Pierre Bourdieu (1986), spending their time socially engineering a connection and point of identification between the lifestyle of a singer and the habitus of their listeners. Meanwhile, other staff are performing an activity that one senior executive compared with that of a 'traffic cop' – conducting a type of 'policing' operation, making sure all the elements are travelling on the right routes and in the right direction (and handing out tickets to those not obeying the laws of the road). In tandem, other executives are required to act as 'editors', planning release schedules, deciding which tracks are more suitable for 'domestic' or 'international' album releases, and often scrutinizing (mainly rap) lyrics in response to local political pressures. Meanwhile, and more conventionally, producers, arrangers and songwriters are playing a far more important role in defining the musical texts of rap, country and salsa. Perhaps it is important not to lose sight of this fact, particularly when navigating into and out of the corridors, offices, desks, filing cabinets and boardrooms of the recording industry.

In making this last point I do not mean to imply that staff in record companies have no impact on 'creativity'. However, I do think that the role of record companies in the 'creative' process needs formulating in a careful way – this if only to avoid the twin tendency of either portraying workers in the music industry as unthinking cogs in a mechanized bureaucracy, or viewing individual personnel through misty humanistic lenses as they make a voluntaristic contribution to popular art. As I have highlighted in this book, while the industry does provide a structural context and set of business practices which frame and shape how music and artists are 'processed', the industry is also itself constituted out of the available 'texts', their potential meanings and the practices through which they have been created. In this way, an everyday (often conservative) social aesthetic connects with and shapes the politics of the industry. This interaction is not easily understood, but is necessary for a fuller understanding of cultural production. In terms of the specific details in this book, I have argued that the genre cultures of rap, rock, salsa or country are playing a part in 'producing' the industry as much as the industry is 'producing' these musics.

In thinking through these issues, and in introducing a note of scepticism about the contribution (or, at least, the influence) of music industry staff, I should again stress that it has not been my intention to provide an answer to what creativity *is*. Creativity is a changing social activity that is realized, understood and appreciated within specific conditions, and as such is a potentially fluid, historically changing, geographically variable, dynamic practice that cannot be 'defined' or tied down in any simple way. I have not focused on the specific notes a keyboard player selects, the sequence of strings which a guitarist strikes or the vocal gymnastics of any singer (these have been well elucidated by other writers). Instead, I have been focusing on the organizational grids and genre cultures of the modern music industry as a way of thinking about the specific circumstances through which any recorded work or musical practice can be realized and received as creative in the first place. I now want to conclude by briefly opening up some of these issues further and relating my approach in this book to some specific social judgements about creativity, connecting some of the ideas presented here to the work of writers who are concerned about music-making specifically, or cultural practices more generally, and whose writings are indicative of general understandings of what creativity entails.

One writer who has been particularly concerned about musical creativity in everyday life is anthropologist Ruth Finnegan. She has conducted extensive detailed research among 'invisible' musicians – those amateur, semi-professional, relatively unknown enthusiasts who play music week in, week out, in orchestras, choral societies, rock and jazz bands, folk groups and brass bands. The musicians Finnegan has studied are mostly people who are playing music for the pleasure of the experience, rather than those who are overtly attempting to gain a recording contract and 'make it' in the music business. However, most of their musical learning occurs in relation to existing records, sheet music and the well-known songs that are circulated by the recording industry. Hence, it would be misleading to think that such musicians are 'outside' or independent of the music business, or that they are only tenuously connected through their consumption and appropriation of various products (instruments, amplifiers, recordings, etc.). Such musicians are an integral grouping or formation within genre cultures, and contribute to the maintenance and modification of musical styles and conventions, mediating both contemporary and 'classic' popular songs and giving them ongoing meanings within a broader context.[1]

In discussing these musicians Finnegan draws on Howard Becker's writings about 'art worlds' and argues that such musical practices provide continual opportunities for 'fulfilment and creativity'. This, she suggests, is a practice that involves working within conventions: 'Artistic practices are not totally constrained, for there is both the opportunity for fulfilment and creativity through using the established conventions, and sometimes room – though at a cost – to innovate and change them' (Finnegan, 1997a, p. 129).

One of the points that interests me about Finnegan's approach here is the way in which she separates creativity from innovation. This is a contrast with much of the everyday usage of the term, discussed back in Chapter 1, whereby creativity and innovation are often treated as synonymous. Her argument also raises questions for the claim that maverick, unconventional, independent labels provide the most creative environment for innovative musicians. Finnegan has made a very similar point in a related study of how personal experience is 'actively enstoried' – how, as individuals, we create a sense of our own identity through a variety of self-narratives. Under the subheading of 'personal creation – cultural convention' Finnegan discusses the 'creative' personal stories that people produce to provide a sense of meaning to their lives and, with a debt to theorists of speech communication and linguistics, she locates these creative tales firmly within the context of a series of everyday narrative codes and genre conventions:

> Self-narratives are a medium through which individuals at every level play a creative role in formulating both their own identities and, by extension, the culture in which they are participants....Self-narratives may at first sight seem too personal to contain recurrent stylistic or thematic patterns. But life stories or personal narratives do seem to form a recognized genre in our culture. It is an 'informal' and often unwritten one, it is true. But the existence and – as it were – artistry of generic conventions are not confined to examples which have been visibly written down or formally published.
>
> (Finnegan, 1997b, p. 77)

Finnegan is making a broader claim here than her point about musical creativity. She is suggesting that a sense of creative fulfilment is gained from social practices (making music being just one) and more generally creating social meanings, within identifiable and recognizably familiar genre codes and conventions, ideas that are known and understood but not necessarily formally recorded or written down.

From my perspective, Finnegan has identified a key aspect of the 'creative process', particularly as this applies to making and listening to music: she has highlighted how genre conventions are integral to creative pleasures and the organization of both the production and the consumption of music. This is why listeners and musicians continue to gain pleasure and fulfilment from the sounds, words and images of recognizably familiar musical genres, whether rock, rap, salsa or country. These creative pleasures are experienced and realized despite the judgements of those who may think that such conventional listening and music-making is a sure sign that a musical form has died or been rendered static. This is why genres continue and do not collapse, as many critics predict (or would wish). As I have stressed throughout this book, genres are more than musical labels: they are social categories. When someone performs or listens to a 'trite and clichéd' country ballad or feels moved by sentimental 'salsa lite' or plays one more time with rock's 'tedious beat and cries for freedom', they are not responding intellectually or simply aesthetically to tired musical codes, but emotionally, within the context of multiple recognitions, reverberations and appropriations that are generated by and come with belonging to particular genre cultures.) From one perspective, these genre cultures are undoubtedly contributing to the perceived 'stasis' generated by the music industry, but for those more closely involved they produce subtle changes and provide certainty and security.

There is another view of the creative process. If, for some musicians, a sense of creative fulfilment is realized in working within changing conventions, for others this produces no satisfaction at all, but a sense of frustration. The same can be true of listeners. Some people spend their listening lives within particular genre worlds, resistant to crossing the boundary to other genres (continually looking for the latest new rock band or merenguera, and knowing their exact route through a music store). Other listening lives are characterized by a restless desire for musical discoveries, a sonic quest which involves the continual abandonment of once-cherished performances and a search for new notes and rhythms, bending sound, as aesthetic conventions and broader genre cultures shift and change.

The tensions and consequences of what I'll call the fulfilment–frustration axis are central to the dynamics of musical creativity, and this leads me to another meaning of the creative experience. This is creativity as arising out of a sense of frustration with conventions and a desire to break the codes and genre rules and move across the boundaries of genres. This impetus to break out and seek new combinations has also been recognized and identified by a number of writers.

Ulf Hannerz is one such writer who, in contrast to Finnegan's creative conventions, has given his discussion of this issue the subheading of 'creative confrontations'. Drawing on anthropology and literary criticism, Hannerz is concerned with a more extensive 'generative cultural process' (as Finnegan is concerned with broader patterns of creative fulfilment) and emphasizes the consequences of the 'coming together of distinct flows of meaning' (1996, p. 61). Hannerz believes that creativity is realized when boundaries are broken, when meanings (of sounds, words, images, people, things) that were previously separate are brought together, creating in the process a new synthesis or hybrid. He quotes Salman Rushdie's often repeated remark, a comment made when discussing the book that caused him so much grief:

> The Satanic Verses celebrates hybridity, impurity, intermingling, the transformation that comes of new and unexpected combinations of human beings, cultures, ideas, politics, movies, songs. It rejoices in mongrelization and fears the absolutism of the pure. Mélange, hotch-potch, a bit of this and a bit of that is how newness enters the world.
>
> (cited in Hannerz, 1996, p. 65)

This is not only a more familiar view of creativity (as being about newness and innovation), but it suggests that it occurs through the novel combination and coming together of existing elements (musical sounds, words, people, things) to create something different. This is a process of creativity which involves musicians and listeners rebelling against the inhibiting effects of genre labels, or perhaps just accidentally meeting through the holes in the musical barbed wire. If much of the fulfilling routine creativity of everyday life involves working within conventions, then it also seems that many of the inspired creative moments occur as a result of frustration with conventions and the desire to break the rules of the genre, or simply from taking a different route and momentarily refusing the habitual and familiar tracks.

In this respect, much creative musical practice also occurs as a consequence of the dynamic tension created by another axis of musical creativity – what I'll call the axis of recognition–rejection. Musicians live with the constant desire for recognition and the constant threat of rejection. From the earliest days of stepping out on stage in a pub, club or community event (and hoping that people will stay, listen or dance and not leave the room or retreat to the bar) to the hours spent playing recordings to friends and to people within the music business, and then waiting for the response to that first radio play, musicians' lives are balanced on an axis of recognition–rejection. There is much more than any simple dichotomy between art and commerce involved here; music is about communication first and making money second (certainly for most people playing music in the world at any one moment). This is, of course, directly connected to the fulfilment–frustration axis. Playing within the conventions of a genre may bring fulfilment and recognition; breaking the conventions of a genre may lead to rejection and no obvious new synthesis; but breaking the conventions may also lead to fulfilment and recognition. It is an uncertain and unpredictable world, but one option at least appears to be safer than the other.

At a most basic level, recognition and rejection are accorded by an audience. Dancing, listening, applauding, buying a home-produced recording – these are audible and visible signs that musical communication is taking place, and a tangible part of any bonds and affective ties within genre cultures. At one time music could only be experienced during face-to-face encounters between audiences and musicians. The modern music industry is now the mediator of such experiences, and the portfolio management of genres has an obvious limiting impact upon what recognition–rejection and frustration–fulfilment have come to mean and be experienced as – recasting this in terms of a band or singer being dropped from a catalogue or not even admitted to the repertoire roster. A pattern of recognition–rejection and of fulfilment–frustration which has its origins in processes of musical communication and social exchange has clearly been translated or transformed into a logic of commodification. While this is obviously not a total process of co-optation (as I have emphasized in the latter part of this book – music is always escaping from attempts to tie it down to commodity alone), it has resulted in a number of highly distinct, identifiable and institutionalized boundaries, erected between listeners, musicians and workers within the music industry.[2]

One consequence of these divisions is that creative practice and discourses about creativity have come to be fragmented into genre-specific codes and conventions, boxed into social containers which either do not meet or meet under conditions of mutual incomprehension or contempt – 'I don't understand your music' or 'I don't like your music; it is boring/repetitive.' Such everyday statements are more than musical judgements. As Simon Frith (1996) has argued in his work on popular discrimination, such aesthetic judgements imply ethical agreements and disagreements, moral evaluations and assessments. The feelings that accompany aesthetic pleasure and displeasure are simultaneously emotional, sensual and social. Moving within or across musical genres is more than a musical act: it is a social act. More than a struggle for new musical relationships and sounds, it can also involve a desire for new social relationships and harmonies. Crossing genre worlds and bringing new genre cultures into being is not only an act of musical creation, it is also an act of social creation, of making connections, of creating solidarities.

Musicians are notoriously individualistic, continually questing for 'autonomy' and 'independence' and desiring the 'freedom' to pursue their own whims. Yet at the same time musicians are continually contributing to solidarities in a way that dissolves any simple individual/collective dichotomy or pattern of us/them musical discrimination. The practices of musicians and their fans are continually bringing about such possibilities within, between and across genres. The boundaries are there to be broken, the solidarities to be established.

Notes

1 Culture, industry, genre: conditions of musical creativity

1 It is worth pointing out that the term 'critical' is far from straightforward, has frequently been overused as a prefix and is often employed rhetorically in the games of positioning engaged in by some academic writers. Despite the insights provided in their article, Golding and Murdock also use this device to make a rather crude distinction between 'critical' and 'administrative' organizational research and in doing so misrepresent the work of radical scholars working within the field of organizational studies as much as they ignore the uncritically reproduced 'critical' orthodoxy (and genre conventions) of much political economy.

2 A key figure in the development of this trajectory of theorizing has been Herbert Schiller, who has persuasively argued that patterns of corporate ownership have had an impact on public debate and the form, content and practices through which modern culture is created. For his argument about the 'corporate takeover of public expression' see Schiller (1989); for an argument about the emergence of a form of 'transnational corporate culture domination' within international business see Schiller (1991), and for arguments about how control of the entertainment media leads to forms of 'information inequality' see Schiller (1996). For a clear outline of the connections between a political economy of communication/culture and the work of Karl Marx see the writings of Nicholas Garnham (1990). For a series of studies of the control of the press and broadcasting, mainly in Britain, see the work of Peter Golding and Graham Murdock (Murdock and Golding, 1974, 1977; Golding, 1990). For a more international perspective see Armand Mattelart (1991) and Vincent Mosco (1996).

3 Most notably Harker (1980), but see also the Introduction to Frith (1988).

4 One of the most influential formulations of this type can be found in Theodor Adorno and Max Horkheimer's critique of the culture industry (1979), first published in German in 1944. A more formal sociological model (an 'organization-set analysis of cultural industry systems') was developed by Paul Hirsch (1972), who proposed a 'filter-flow' model of music production whereby artistic creators provided the 'raw material' that was then processed and passed through the system to the public. For a further discussion and critique of this type of approach see Ryan and Peterson (1982) and also my extended critique of musical and cultural production (Negus, 1996, Chapter 2; Negus, 1997).

5 For discussion of the history of recording and importance of small record companies and the growth of subgenres and numerous promotional activities, see Garofalo (1997) and Laing (1969). For a critique of the post-Fordist approach to cultural production and the way that assumptions from this have influenced writings on the music industry, including my own first book, see Hesmondhalgh (1996a, 1996b).

6 Bourdieu's work on the 'field of cultural production' is mainly concerned with European high culture, nineteenth-century French novelists in particular and Flaubert specifically. Despite the insights this provides into the struggles of novelists and the social production and recognition of their art within a given period, it is unclear how such an approach might be used to understand twentieth-century mass-mediated popular culture, and the role of entertainment corporations which are not so clearly tied into localized class/habitus positions, as in Bourdieu's (1993, 1996) detailed case studies of Flaubert.

7 An argument that informs Iain Chambers' approach to popular music. For example, see his discussion of the history of British and US pop (1985) and his account of 'world music' (1994). For a more thorough discussion of the complex of human actions that are condensed into the simple term 'consumption' and the range of representations that can become attached to commercial 'commodities', see Mackay (ed.) (1997).

8 The culture of organizations will be covered in more detail in Chapter 3. For a useful collection of articles which draws together many approaches and critical assessments of this range of literature, specifically in relation to cultural production, see du Gay (ed.) (1997).

9 The idea of the culture of production was originally developed during numerous conversations with Paul du Gay, particularly when we were both working on our Ph.D. studies between 1989 and 1992, and when collaborating for the Open University's course on *Media, Culture and Identities* (1994–6). Du Gay's (1996) work on subjectivity at work and the way in which management deploys various techniques to encourage workers to take on or assume specific identities intersected with ideas I was developing from my own research on the music business (Negus, 1992).

10 For a more extended discussion and critique see Negus (1997).

11 For insights into this issue see Hofstede (1991), Salaman (1997), Smircich (1983).

12 For useful accounts of the meanings of advertising see Williamson (1978) and Jhally (1990).

13 I should also note here that in my experience of interviewing numerous people in the music industry, staff in record companies rarely use a concept of creativity in the way in which fans, journalists and musicians might. If and when the issue arises or is introduced, it is often in terms of an agnostic, and I think a partly 'professional', belief that 'art' or 'creativity' is what those involved in particular genres (artists, audiences, critics, mediators) decide it is at any particular time. Staff within the recording industry are well aware that they have a direct impact on how creativity can be realized, given meaning and contested, but, perhaps not surprisingly, being immersed in other more pressing day-to-day concerns, they find it difficult to reflect upon the issue in a critical way. When asked direct questions about creativity many will only offer platitudes or corporate rhetoric ('our company provides the most sympathetic environment for creative artists', etc.). Hence, a further assumption guiding my approach here is that ideas about creativity cannot be pursued very far by asking direct questions to those within the music business. Instead, I wish to

open up this issue by moving slightly more obliquely between what goes on in the music industry and ideas about what creativity might entail.

14 For examples of this type of literature see C. Humke and C. Schaefer (1996) 'Sense of Humor and Creativity', *Perceptual and Motor Skills*, Vol. 82, No. 2, pp. 544–7 on indicators of creativity; J. Rodriguez-Fernandez (1996) 'Is "Sudden Illumination" the Result of the Activation of a Creative Center at the Human Brain?', *Perspectives in Biology and Medicine*, Vol. 39, No. 2, pp. 287–309 on the 'location' of creativity within the brain; C. Hale (1995) 'Psychological Characteristics of the Literary Genius', *Journal of Humanistic Psychology*, Vol. 35, No. 3, pp. 113–35 on the psychological characteristics of the 'lone genius'; and a partial critique of this approach in A. Montouri and R. Purse (1995) 'Deconstructing the Lone Genius Myth: Toward a Contextual View of Creativity', *Journal of Humanistic Psychology*, Vol. 35, No. 3, pp. 69–103.

15 See for example R. Epstein (1996) 'Capturing Creativity', *Psychology Today*, July–August, Vol. 29, No. 4, pp. 41–7.

16 On this point I wish to acknowledge useful conversations with Havelock Nelson of *Billboard* (in New York City, 27 February 1996) and Marcus Morton at EMI (in Hollywood on 24 April 1996).

17 In Simon Frith's excellent chapter on 'Genre rules' (1996) he only comes to the issue of 'transgression' towards the end of this chapter, and then briefly in passing.

18 Unfortunately for English readers, the vast majority of Quintero Rivera's work on salsa is currently only available in Spanish. Some key works in Spanish relevant to this discussion of musical practice include Quintero Rivera (1997, 1998) and Quintero Rivera and Manuel Alvarez (1990). For useful articles on the sociology of music in English see Quintero Rivera (1992, 1994).

19 Translated, by me, from Spanish: 'manera de hacer música', 'libre combinación de ritmos, formas y géneros afrocaribeños tradicionales' 'en su libre combinación evitaba o evadía su posible fosilización en fórmulas'.

20 How, under what conditions and within which historical circumstances this might occur, however, is an issue beyond the scope of this discussion here. Any attempt to theorize genre as transformative would surely need to engage with concepts of power, if only to comprehend the forces which keep genre codes in place and which also facilitate their transcendence.

21 The distinction between indies and majors has been used by a number of writers to explain the source of creativity and changes in popular music (see for example Chapple and Garofalo, 1977; Gillett, 1983). This approach has been criticized by a number of writers, including me, and I do not wish to rehearse these arguments here (see Frith, 1983; Negus, 1992; Hesmondhalgh, 1996, 1998). The battle of talented artists against the ruthless individual executive often informs books that seek to 'expose' the industry, one of the most persuasive and useful sources being Dannen (1990). The distinction between subcultures and the mainstream has also been used to identify creative changes within popular culture more generally (most notably by Hebdige, 1979). For a sustained critique of this position see Thornton (1995).

2 Corporate strategy: applying order and enforcing accountability

1 For a discussion of the use of techniques of 'overproduction' see Hirsch (1972). For the indies versus majors debate see Chapple and Garofalo (1977), Frith

(1983), Gillett (1983), Laing (1985), Lee (1995), Hesmondhalgh (1996a, 1996b), Negus (1996).

2 An idea that informs Dannen (1990).

3 Such a notion informs Bruce Haring's *Off the Charts: Ruthless Days and Reckless Nights Inside the Music Industry*, Birch Lane Press, 1996, despite his brief reference to the new management strategies of the 1990s.

4 Peterson's 'dialectical' theory of changes in country music style seems to verge on this in some respects; see Chapter 6.

5 See, for example, S. Fried, 'Bad Vibe in Tune Town', *Vanity Fair*, February 1995, pp. 66–73/117.

6 This approximation is according to a range of both officially published and unofficial figures circulated within the industry. Exactly what percentage each company accounts for is a particularly elusive statistic. While senior executives often boast that their company has the greatest market share, most company accountants are very secretive about the actual figures that might validate such claims. Trade magazine *Music and Copyright* calculated the 1996 company shares for sales in the 'world soundcarrier' market as follows: BMG 12 per cent, EMI 14 per cent, PolyGram 16.5 per cent, Sony 15.5 per cent, Universal 6 per cent and Warner Music 15 per cent (with the remaining 21 per cent attributed to other companies collectively categorized as independents). See 'PolyGram Again the World Leader in 1996 Soundcarrier Sales', *Music and Copyright*, No. 117, 16 July 1997, p. 1. In terms of the United States, market share figures are annually reported by Soundscan and in *Billboard*. The 1997 figures for shares of the US album market were as follows: Warner Music 18.9 per cent, Sony 13.7 per cent, PolyGram 13 per cent, EMI 12.6 per cent, Universal 12.1 per cent, BMG 11.8 per cent, with other 'independents' accounting for 17.9 per cent (although this included music produced by the Disney Corporation's record division); source: *Billboard*, 1 January 1998, pp. 78–80. The acquisition of PolyGram by Universal immediately disrupted these patterns and sent industry analysts reaching for their calculators to suggest that, for the period January–March 1998, the combined share of the new corporation would be 22.4 per cent, above Sony, who at 19.5 per cent were pushing ahead of Warner at 17.8 per cent ('Morris Poised to Take Reins at Uni/PolyGram', *Billboard*, 20 June 1998, p. 1/93).

7 For an insight into some of the chaos and tensions caused by such continual changes, see a passionate attack on the conglomerate use of 'human chess pieces' which appeared as a large font editorial in *Billboard*, 23 December 1995, under the title 'Industry Infighting is Self-Sabotage'. See also Zimmerman (1995).

8 It is also worth bearing in mind that Sony view music as important software for their hardware even if the revenues of the music company are less significant for their overall profits.

9 These cuts are discussed in D. Midgley (1994) 'Thorn EMI's Fissile Future', *Management Today*, August, pp. 24–8.

10 'EMI Music: In Search of Growth in Interactivity and Stability in the US' *Music and Copyright*, No. 51, 12 October 1994, pp. 12–14. *Music Business International World Report 1995* reported that, back in 1986, music accounted for just 9 per cent of Thorn-EMI's 'income'. By 1994 the music division was accounting for 41 per cent of group 'turnover' and nearly two-thirds of pre-tax profits (Spotlight Publications, 1995, p. 408).

11 As reported in Dane (1995).

12 For details see L. Buckingham (1997) 'Out of Tune With Uncle Sam' *Guardian*, 31 May, p. 26; A. Rawsthorn (1997) 'EMI Cuts Costs in America' *Financial Times*, 28 May, p. 21.

13 'Ich bin ein Amerikaner' *The Economist*, 18 June 1994.

14 'BMG Entertainment is the Fastest Growing Bertelsmann Division' *Music & Copyright*, No. 61, 15 March 1995, pp. 12–13.

15 See *Music and Copyright* No. 61, op. cit., and D. Mollner (1995) 'Zelnick Looking to Boost BMG's RCA Label, Pump up Core Business', *Variety*, 9 January.

16 Clive Davis quoted in D. Jeffrey (1996) 'Well-Rounded Acts Bring Arista Record Year' *Billboard*, 13 January, pp. 3–14.

17 Quoted in *Spotlight*, BMG in-house magazine, No. 2, Fall 1995, p. 2.

18 As reported in *Music Business International World Report 1995*, Spotlight Publications, p. 384.

19 See Dane (1995) and 'WMG Faces Restructuring as Time-Warner Reshapes Itself' *Music and Copyright*, No. 60, 1 March 1995, pp. 12–14.

20 See 'WMG Faces Restructuring as Time-Warner Reshapes Itself' *Music and Copyright*, No. 60, 1 March 1995, pp. 12–14.

21 It is worth pointing out that Sony and CBS had been operating a joint venture in Japan for about twenty years prior to this purchase.

22 'Sony Still Waits for the Benefits from Hardware–Software Synergy' *Music and Copyright*, No. 57, 18 January 1995, pp. 8–10. See also Negus (1997) for further discussion of this issue and additional references.

23 Reported in Dane (1995).

24 Suggestions of a 'U-turn' back to technology rather than software are made in *The Economist* 'Back to Basics', 9 December 1995, p. 86. The indication that Sony was 'diversifying' – but within the technological area, into cellular phones, PCs and batteries – is made in Michiyo Nakamoto and Louise Kehoe (1995) 'Seeing a Need for a Change of Focus' *Financial Times*, 15 November 1995, p. 28.

25 'A Brighter Future?' *The Economist*, 13 August 1994.

26 Details can be found in G. Edmondson (1994) 'Philips Needs Laser Speed' *Business Week*, 6 June 1994, pp. 18–19.

27 Particularly when companies were bidding for Virgin Records, see D. Hamilton (1994) 'Matsushita's MCA Reaction Masks Anxiety' *Wall Street Journal*, 18 October, p. 5.

28 'MCA Music Entertainment: Set for Steady Growth under Bronfman?' *Music and Copyright*, No. 64, 26 April 1995, pp. 12–13.

29 For further discussion of this issue see J. Trachtenberg (1996) 'Jimmy Iovine Spins More Gold at Interscope' *Wall Street Journal*, 22 February 1996, pp. B1–3; C. Morris (1996) 'MCA Purchases 50% of Interscope' *Billboard*, 2 March, p. 13/84.

30 Seagram had judged that profits on wines and spirits had been declining while profits on entertainment products (although less predictable) had been increasing. The company therefore sold its interest in Tropicana Juice to Pepsi to help finance the purchase of PolyGram. Reported in 'Seagram Profits Double on Gain From Stock Sale' *San Juan Star*, 13 August 1998, p. 112.

31 Reported in 'Morris Poised to Take Reins at Uni/PolyGram', *Billboard*, 20 June 1998, p. 1/93.

32 'Why Can't BMG, EMI and PolyGram maintain 14% of the US Market?' *Music & Copyright*, No. 50, 28 September 1994, pp. 3–4.

33 Personal interview with Dennis Petroskey, Corporate Communications, BMG, New York City, 6 March 1996.

34 In reading my account of corporate strategies in the music industry, you should bear in mind the cautionary note of Bob De Wit and Ron Meyer, who have remarked that many 'companies seldom formulate and publish a complete strategy statement', and they also note that what 'sometimes gives the appearance of a consciously formulated strategy...may be the natural result of compromise among coalitions backing contrary policy proposals or skilful improvisatory adaptation to external forces' (1994, pp. 41–2). In researching for this book I have followed De Wit and Meyer's suggestion that 'strategy' needs to be deduced from considering various sources and observing company behaviour rather than by reference to strategy statements or the like.

35 Personal interview with Bob Merlis, Director of Media Relations, Warner Music Inc, Burbank, 25 April 1996.

36 In writing this section I have drawn on information in De Wit and Meyer (1994) and Purcell (1989) and from material sporadically and anecdotally recounted in various trade magazines, in addition to formal interviews.

37 Insights into this process were provided by Fran Nevrkla, Director, Commercial and Business Affairs, Warner Music, London, during a meeting on 5 January 1996.

38 I wish to acknowledge the very helpful insights and information about this issue, within the music business in general, provided by Anne Latora, Senior VP Financial Administration, PolyGram Group HQ, New York City, during an interview on 29 March 1996.

39 See T. Jones (1995) for an account of the historical processes whereby accounting knowledge became a way for remote owners to judge the performance of companies without needing to monitor day-to-day work.

40 Personal interview, Nashville, 30 May 1996.

41 For further discussion of this point in relation to business in general see Armstrong (1989).

42 Personal interview, Nashville, 30 May 1996.

43 Sony, for example, have a panel of 8,000 people that has 'been in place since 1973' (when the company was CBS), with members changed every two to three years.

44 Particular thanks to Keith McCarthy and Linda Greenberg, both at Sony Music Entertainment, Lynn Franz at PolyGram, and Barbara Nuessle at Chilton Research for talking to me in depth about some of these methods and for allowing me to view or take away various bits and pieces of research data.

45 Personal interview, New York City, 9 April 1996.

46 For a longer discussion of this see Negus (1992).

47 It is within the distribution division where most market research departments are located.

48 I would like to acknowledge the insights provided by Curt Eddy, VP Field Marketing, PolyGram Group Distribution, when I spoke with him in New York City on 1 February 1996.

49 For an insight into such issues see D. Jeffrey (1996) 'Musicland Posts Weak 1995 Results, Retailer Plots Strategy to Improve Performance' *Billboard*, 10 February 1996, p. 3.

50 The most common strategies of independents include:

   1 Getting finance through joint ventures 'within' a major company which will allow the small label to jointly own their master tapes.

2   Diversification of musical catalogue so as not to be dependent upon one sub-genre (i.e. rap labels diversifying into other areas of r 'n' b).

3   Further diversification into other areas of entertainment (pursued by Def Jam who had a joint venture with PolyGram) or into retail, equipment and studio interests (pursued by Zomba).

For an insight into some of the details of business strategies of smaller labels see M. Snyder (1995) 'Urban Entrepreneurship: Young Mavericks Make Noise with Their Own Labels' *Billboard*, 3 June 1995, pp. 22–3; A. Sandler (1995) 'Big Labels Ride Black Music Bandwagon' *Variety*, 26 August 1995, Vol. 360, pp. 13–15; Z. Schoepe (1996) 'Zomba Acquires Hilton Sound' *Billboard*, 17 February 1996, p. 51. See also Gray (1988), Hesmondhalgh (1996a, 1996b, 1998) and Lee (1996).

51   All quotes here come from a personal interview with Nelson Rodríguez, New York City, 27 February 1996.

52   Personal interview, New York City, 28 March 1996.

53   Personal interview, New York City, 6 April 1996.

54   Personal interview, Nashville, 30 May 1996.

3 Record company cultures and the jargon of corporate identity

1   An opinion held by many people. The comment here was made by Michael Rosenblatt who previously worked for WEA and was Senior VP Artist and Repertoire at MCA when I interviewed him in New York City on 6 February 1996.

2   Personal interview with Bob Merlis, Director of Media Relations, Warner Brothers Records, Burbank, 25 April 1996.

3   Although it is worth noting that many insights are available in an anecdotal and diffuse form in various case studies of record companies, and implicitly inform various accounts of the history of the music industry; see, for example, Sanjek (1988) and Garofalo (1997).

4   Reported in 'Morris Poised to Take Reins at Uni/PolyGram', *Billboard*, 20 June 1998, p. 1/93.

5   This comment and others here are taken from 'Going Hollywood: PolyGram's Levy Puts Music Firm Further Into Moviemaking' *Wall Street Journal*, 15 June 1995, p. 9/1.

6   Phrase used during meeting at *Billboard*'s London office, 2 November 1995.

7   There are certain parallels with the type of charismatic political leadership and authority analysed by sociologist Max Weber early in the twentieth century. As Weber observed, charisma does not provide 'security of office' and is always under review (will the person 'lose their touch'?) and poses continual problems of succession.

8   For further discussion of this issue see Negus (1997).

9   'Why can't BMG, EMI and PolyGram maintain 14% of the US Market?' *Music & Copyright*, No. 50, 28 September 1994, p. 3–4.

10 All quotes from personal interview, New York City, 19 March 1996.

11 Personal interview, New York City, 25 March 1996.

12 Personal interview, New York City, 6 February 1996.

13 Personal interview, London, 15 November 1995.

14 Personal interview, New York City, 2 February 1996.

15 See, for examples of this type of reasoning, J. Kotter and J. Heskett (1992) *Corporate Culture and Economic Performance*, Free Press. See also P. Anthony (1994) *Managing Culture*, Open University.

4 The business of rap: between the street and the executive suite

1 Notable here is Tricia Rose (1994a) who notes the importance of independent labels and the significance of video in the distribution of rap. She is also careful to acknowledge that the commercial marketing of rap has produced a contradictory situation whereby the music is affirmative of black identity, yet can also be used by corporations such as McDonald's, Coke and Nike in ways that are directly connected to anxieties about US cultural imperialism. Rose (1994b) has also discussed rap in relation to the general contractual arrangements operating within the music industry, particularly in an interview with Carmen Ashurst-Watson. Also notable here is Reebee Garofalo's (1997) discussion of the music industry and rap in his history of popular music, and Nelson George's coverage of rap within the context of his critique of the music industry and its role in the 'death of rhythm and blues' and formation of post-soul culture (1989, 1992).

2 A useful collection of essays is Adam Sexton (ed.) (1995).

3 An argument proposed by Ann Marlowe who has stated that:

> For some time now the problem with capitalism hasn't been that it doesn't work but that it's no longer fun. Opposition culture has failed to make good on this....The business of rap is just business, yet it looks like fun.
>
> (1995, p. 223)

4 Discussed at length in relation to Atlantic and Stax Records in Wade and Picardie (1990).

5 For a more detailed discussion of this report see George (1989).

6 Personal interview, New York City, 27 February 1996.

7 See Reynolds (1996) and Rosen (1996). See also Clark-Meads (1996) for a discussion of Capitol redefining their 'core business'.

8 These types of changes are discussed in Sandler (1995).

9 Referred to by J.R. Reynolds in 'Confab Covers Urban Industry Issues' *Billboard*, 18 May 1996, p. 20.

10 Backgrounds of various producers, artists and entrepreneurs are discussed in Fernando Jr (1995).

11 Most notable here is the well-publicized East–West NYC–LA dispute which, in the early to mid-1990s, became focused in a series of highly public confrontations between those associated with Death Row Records and Bad Boy Records.

12 Most notably C. Delores Tucker, Chairwoman of the National Political Congress of Black Women, and William Bennett (previously Ronald Reagan's Secretary of Education) put pressure on Time-Warner shareholders. Likewise (then) Senator Bob Dole continually accused Warner Music and other labels of 'putting profits ahead of common decency' and 'glamorizing violence'. For a perspective on this and its impact from within the industry see Nunziata (1995). One immediate consequence was that Michael Fuchs, Chairman CEO of Warner Music Group, announced that the company would form label groups made up of an A and R person, label head, someone from business

affairs and legal personnel to judge the suitability of future releases, with particular attention paid to lyrics. On this point see Jeffrey (1995). In addition, when MCA purchased Interscope, the label that had been distributing recordings by Death Row Records, Doug Morris, CEO of MCA Music Entertainment, publicly announced that the company had an option 'not to release any music it deems objectionable' (Morris, 1996).

13 This was most explicitly raised by a senior executive at a major corporate group when explaining how the company would strategically assess the value of different musical genres. It was an off-the-record interview.

14 Personal interview, Paul Robinson, Associate General Counsel, Warner Music Group, New York City, 13 February 1996.

15 This is acknowledged within the industry, but I was unable to obtain any verifiable figures.

16 This was again an off-the-record interview.

17 For discussion of recruitment from rock subculture into the industry, see Chapple and Garofalo (1977) and Frith (1983).

18 Personal interview, Joe Levy, *Details Magazine*, New York City, 22 March 1996.

19 Personal interview, New York City, 19 March 1996.

20 Personal interview, New York City, 5 April 1996.

21 Personal interview, New York City, 6 February 1996.

22 Greg Peck, a former VP of Black Music at Warner Music, quoted in Reynolds (1995, p. 26).

23 Personal interview, Universal City, Los Angeles, 6 May 1996.

24 Personal interview, EMI, Los Angeles, 24 April 1996.

25 All similar to many referred to in textbook guides to marketing; see, for example, Kotler (1994).

26 Personal interview, Terri Rosi, VP Black Music Marketing, BMG Distribution, New York City, 11 April 1996.

27 Personal interview, Terri Rosi, VP Black Music Marketing, BMG Distribution, New York City, 11 April 1996.

28 Telephone interview, 15 April 1996.

29 For an argument about the co-optation of rock, see Chapple and Garofalo (1977). For a discussion of the way in which rock has been central rather than peripheral, or oppositional, to the development of the modern recording industry, see Frith (1983).

5 The corporation, country culture and the communities of musical production

1 As Richard Peterson (1997) has pointed out, the term 'hillbilly', applied to the music by the record industry, was a pejorative term used to refer to someone who was unschooled, rough, simple-minded and from the backwoods of the Appalachian mountains, a point that is perhaps significant for the later way in which record industry headquarters would look down on Nashville and country.

2 Also on this point see Peterson's (1978) discussion of attempts by various artists, in alliance with the Country Music Association, to protect real country music from the encroachments of pop.

3 Peterson only deals with this issue through the rather vague remark that 'the oedipal conflict between generations provides a wellspring of innovation' (1997, p. 230).
4 Personal interview, Eddie Reeves, Nashville, 20 May 1996.
5 Personal interview, Joe Galante, Nashville, 30 May 1996.
6 Personal interview, Scott Siman, Nashville, 10 June 1996.
7 'Artists of the Year', *Gavin Report*, 15 December 1995, p. 16.
8 Thanks particularly to Tim Dubois, Walt Wilson and Rick Sanjek for their insights into this issue.
9 All quotes here from personal interview, Nashville, 4 June 1996.
10 For details about some of the recordings and artists that have fallen victim to this situation see Bob Allen (1991) 'Five Country Albums You'll Probably Never Get to Hear' *Journal of Country Music*, Vol. 14, No. 1, pp. 18–26.
11 The Telecommunications Bill passed by the House and Senate in February 1996 reduced the role of government in the regulation of telecommunication practices and relaxed ownership legislation which had previously placed a limit on the number of stations that could be owned by one company, allowing companies to own multiple transmission systems simultaneously (telephone and cable television, for example). For further discussion of this issue see Sanjek (1998).
12 Personal interview, Nashville, 10 June 1996.
13 A number of people are acutely aware of this. During 1997 and 1998 staff at the Country Music Foundation were working on an anthology of black country artists. This was released by Warner Brothers as a three-CD compilation entitled *From Where I Stand: The Black Experience in Country Music*.
14 Personal interview, Nashville, 10 June 1996.
15 Personal interview, Nashville, 30 May 1996.
16 Personal interview, Nashville, 20 May 1996.
17 For further discussion of this issue see Lewis (ed.) (1992) and Chapter 1 in Negus (1996).
18 For further general discussion of this see Chapter 4 in Negus (1992). In relation to the culture of country, see Peterson (1997).
19 Personal interview, Nashville, 20 May 1996.
20 Personal interview, Nashville, 4 June 1996.
21 I am drawing here on Anthony Giddens' (1990) discussion of the 'disembedding' and 're-embedding' of social relationships across space and time, outlined in his arguments about globalization and the 'consequences of modernity'.

6 The Latin music industry, the production of salsa and the cultural matrix

1 Personal interview, New York City, 4 April 1996.
2 For a further discussion of this point see Glasser (1995).
3 I would like to acknowledge helpful insights provided by Victor Gallo, General Manager of Key Productions, who were managing the Fania catalogue, during a personal interview in New York City, 28 March 1996.
4 However, it is perhaps significant that the company established a new label called Nuevo Fania in the latter part of 1996 as a means of acquiring the rights to and distributing the recordings of contemporary Cuban artists, a development tragically disrupted by Jerry Masucci's untimely death in January 1998.
5 Interviews with recording industry personnel suggested that far more women were purchasing *salsa romántica* than the 'old school' recordings. However, it

should be acknowledged that this is a music industry assumption based on a particular set of experiences and perceptions of the world. I am unaware of any research evidence which may verify this.

6 For discussion of Fania All Stars Recordings and arrangements with CBS see Rondon (1980).

7 Personal correspondence, John Ganoe, Recording Industry Association of America, 6 May 1997.

8 See 'Fonovisa Makes Gains Against Piracy' *Billboard*, 24 February 1996, p. 6/104, and 'Fonovisa Decries RIAA In Piracy Fight' *Billboard*, 24 February 1996, pp. 36–7.

9 'A Small Island of Grand Opportunities' *EMI Latin Times* (in-house magazine), July/August 1996, p. 2.

10 Personal interviews with Rigoberto Olariaga of PolyGram Latino and Harry Fox of Sony Discos, both in Miami on 20 June 1996.

11 Personal interview, Miami, 20 June 1996.

12 Personal interview, New York City, 4 April 1996.

13 Personal interview, Miami, 20 June 1996.

7 Territorial marketing: international repertoire and world music

1 Thanks to Sara Cohen for remembering this with me.

2 For general discussions and debates about globalization see M. Featherstone (ed.) (1990) *Global Culture*, Sage; A. Giddens (1990) *The Consequences of Modernity*, Stanford University Press; P. Hirst and G. Thompson (1996) *Globalization in Question*, Polity Press. For specific discussions of globalization in relation to culture, media and communication see A. King (ed.) (1991) *Culture, Globalization and the World System*, Macmillan; S. Braman and A. Sreberny-Mohammadi (eds) (1996) *Globalization, Communication and Transnational Civil Society*, IAMCR/Hampton Press; A. Sreberny-Mohammadi, D. Winseck, J. McKenna and O. Boyd-Barrett (eds) (1997) *Media in Global Context: A Reader*, Arnold. For a specific discussion of the music industry in Europe see Negus (1993).

3 Exact figures vary, depending on the source, but see, for examples and further discussion of this issue: M. Cox (1993) 'We Are The World', *Wall Street Journal*, 26 March 1993, p. 7; P. Dwyer, M. Dawson and D. Roberts (1996) 'The New Music Biz' *Business Week International Edition*, 15 January 1996, pp. 1/20–5.

4 For a discussion of how MTV has responded to this by introducing MTV Latino and MTV Mandarin, among other programmes in Hindi, Portuguese and Japanese, see M. Levison (1995) 'It's An MTV World' *Newsweek*, 24 April 1995, pp. 44–9.

5 'Local repertoire grew to 54 per cent of sales outside the US in 1996' *Music and Copyright*, Vol. 111, 23 April 1997. Figures for 'domestic' and 'regional repertoire in Latin America' were collapsed into one category of 'domestic' at 54 per cent; the remaining 5 per cent was accounted for by music defined as 'classical'.

6 Personal interview, New York City, 15 February 1996.

7 Personal interview with Mike Allen, International Director, PolyGram, London, 11 May 1993.

8 Personal interview with Stuart Watson, Senior Vice President, International, MCA Records, London, 9 June 1993.

9 'Public Relations for Mari Hamada', Mary Chiang Associates Ltd/MCA Records, 8 April 1993, p. 2.

10 'Introducing...Mari Hamada', press release, MCA Records, March 1993.

11 Personal interview with Stuart Watson, Senior Vice President, International, MCA Records, London, 9 June 1993.

12 Here I would particularly like to acknowledge the help of Shuhei Hosokawa and Masahiro Yasuda.

13 These comments were made during off-the-record conversations, hence they are unattributed.

14 Personal interview, New York City, 15 February 1996.

15 A point made by Laing (1969). See also Garofalo (1997).

16 Personal interview, Toshiba-EMI, Tokyo, 16 September 1993.

17 'Big Hits, No Plugs; The Albums of 1993', *The Independent*, 23 December 1993, p. 23.

18 What I am pointing to here are the cultural dynamics through which music enjoys a life as more than that of commodity, but 'within' the networks of the music industry. Hence, my discussion here is intended as one step towards delineating different types of economic and cultural practices as a challenge to the idea that industrial musical production simply involves one process or dynamic (rational, calculative and homogenizing). At the same time I am trying to identify possibilities for more speculative, pluralizing and informative forms of social practice and musical knowledge production. This is also in part an effort to overcome the analytic division (which has continued to inform many discussions of popular music) between an 'inside' (production) of determinism and constraint against an 'outside' (consumption) of appropriation and free will. Following Stuart Hall's (1983) 're-reading' of Marx, this is also an attempt to retain some notion of a 'circuit' of production–consumption relations that are dislocated, unstable and being broken, but continually being re-made through the reproduction of capitalist social relations.

8 Walls and bridges: corporate strategy and creativity within and across genres

1 Here it is important to remember that popular songs, both new and ancient, are continually mediated by amateur musicians playing in a variety of settings; in this way, songs become more than simply their recordings and these musicians contribute, in an oblique way, to the sales of the original recordings.

2 Reebee Garofalo has raised this point on a number of occasions in relation to the fragmentation of audiences through radio broadcasting and marketing methods, for example arguing that 'the audiences for hard rock, salsa and rhythm and blues are often mutually exclusive and divided neatly (and at times antagonistically) along racial and cultural lines' (1986, p. 81). See also Garofalo (1997).

Bibliography

Adorno, T. (1991) *The Culture Industry, Selected Essays on Mass Culture*, ed. J. Bernstein, London: Routledge.

Adorno, T. and Horkheimer, M. (1979) *Dialectic of Enlightenment*, London: Verso.

Anderson, B. (1983) *Imagined Communities*, London: Verso.

Angelero, A. (1992) 'Back-to-Africa: the "reverse" transculturation of Salsa/Cuban popular music' in V. Boggs (ed.) *Salsiology: Afro-Cuban Music and the Evolution of Salsa in New York City*, New York: Excelsior, pp. 301–5.

Aparicio, F. (1998) *Listening to Salsa: Gender, Latin Popular Music and Puerto Rican Cultures*, Hanover, NH: Wesleyan University Press.

Aparicio, F. and Chávez-Silverman, S. (eds) (1997) *Tropicalizations, Transcultural Representations of Latinidad*, Hanover, NH: Dartmouth College/University Press of New England.

Armstrong, P. (1989) 'Limits and possibilities for HRM in an age of management accountancy' in J. Storey (ed.) *New Perspectives on Human Resource Management*, London, Routledge.

Bechdolf, U. (1997) 'Dancing to Latin American Music: Exoticism or Creolization of Cultures?' Paper presented to 'Popular Music: Intercultural Interpretations', Ninth Conference of International Association for the Study of Popular Music, July 1997, Kanazawa, Japan.

Becker, H. (1974) 'Art as Collective Action', *American Sociological Review*, Vol. 39, pp. 767–76.

——(1976) 'Art worlds and social types' in R. Peterson (ed.) *The Production of Culture*, London: Sage, pp. 41–56.

Billig, M. (1995) *Banal Nationalism*, London: Sage.

Boggs, V. (1992) 'Salsa's Origins: Voices from Abroad', *Latin Beat*, Vol. 1, No. 11, pp. 26–31.

——(ed.) (1992) *Salsiology: Afro-Cuban Music and the Evolution of Salsa in New York City*, New York: Excelsior.

Bourdieu, P. (1986) *Distinction. A Social Critique of the Judgment of Taste*, London: Routledge.

——(1993) *The Field of Cultural Production*, Cambridge: Polity.

——(1996) *The Rules of Art*, Cambridge: Polity.

Buckingham, L. (1997) 'Out of Tune With Uncle Sam', *Guardian*, 31 May 1997, p. 26.

Chambers, I. (1985) *Urban Rhythms, Pop Music and Popular Culture*, London: Macmillan.

——(1994) *Migrancy, Culture, Identity*, London: Routledge.

Chapple, S. and Garofalo, R. (1977) *Rock 'n' Roll is Here to Pay*, Chicago: Nelson Hall.

Clark-Meads, J. (1995) 'IFPI Says Sales in Latin Markets Up 33%' *Billboard*, 19 August 1995, p. 3.

Clark-Meads, J. and White, A. (1996) 'Roger Ames New President of PolyGram Music Group', *Billboard*, 6 April 1996, p. 6/94.

Cline, C. (1996) 'Indie Country', *Twanging!*, No. 7, April, pp. 1–2.

Cusic, D. (1995) 'Country Green: The Money in Country Music' in C. Tichi (ed.) *Readin' Country Music: Steel Guitars, Opry Stars and Honky Tonk Bars: The South Atlantic Quarterly*, Vol. 94, No. 1, Winter, pp. 231–41.

Dane, C. (1995) *UK Record Industry Annual Survey*, Weston-super-Mare: Media Research Publishing.

Dannen, F. (1990). *Hit Men. Power Brokers and Fast Money Inside the Music Business*, London: Random House.

De Wit, B. and Meyer, R. (1994) *Strategy: Process, Content, Context*, Minneapolis/St Paul: West Publishing Company.

Deal, T. and Kennedy, A. (1988) *Corporate Cultures*, Harmondsworth: Penguin.

DeCurtis, A. (1995) 'Dre Day', *Vibe*, December, pp. 92–4.

Duany, J. (1984) 'Popular Music in Puerto Rico: Toward an Anthropology of Salsa', *Latin American Music Review*, Vol. 5, No. 2, pp. 186–216.

Duffy, T. (1994) 'EMI Spans the Globe in New World Music Series', *Billboard*, 5 February 1994, p. 40.

du Gay, P. (1996) *Consumption and Identity at Work*, London: Sage.

——(ed.) (1997) *Production of Culture/Cultures of Production*, Open University/London: Sage.

Edwards, T. and Stein, J. (1998) 'Getting Giggy With a Hoodie: Young Black Designers are Giving Urban Fashions Street Appeal', *Time*, Vol. 151, No. 1, pp. 71–2.

Ellison, C. (1995) *Country Music Culture*, Jackson: University Press of Mississippi.

Estupiñán, L.M. (1994) 'Canarias, Decana Español de la Salsa', *El Manisero*, No. 2, April–May 1994, pp. 10–14.

Fabbri, F. (1982) 'A theory of music genres: two applications' in P. Tagg and D. Horn (eds) *Popular Music Perspectives*, Gothenburg and Exeter: IASPM.

——(1985) 'Patterns of music consumption in Milan and Reggio Emilia from April to May 1983' in P. Tagg and D. Horn (eds) *Popular Music Perspectives 2*, Gothenberg and Exeter: IASPM.

——(1989) 'The system of Canzone in Italy today (1981)' in S. Frith (ed.) *World Music, Politics and Social Change*, Manchester: Manchester University Press, pp. 122–42.

Fabrikant, G. and Weinraub, B. (1996) 'Having Gotten the Part, Bronfman Plays the Mogul', *New York Times*, Money and Business, 4 February 1996, Section 3, p. 1/13.

Feiler, B. (1996) 'Gone Country', *New Republic*, 5 February 1996, pp. 19–24.

Feld, S. (1984) 'Communication, Music and Speech About Music', *Yearbook for Traditional Music*, Vol. 16, pp. 1–18.

——(1994) 'Notes on World Beat' in C. Keil and S. Feld (eds) *Music Grooves*, Chicago: University of Chicago Press, pp. 238–46.

Fernández, R. (1994) 'The Course of U.S. Cuban Music: Margin and Mainstream', *Cuban Studies*, Vol. 24, pp. 105–22.

Fernando Jr, S.H. (1995) *The New Beats: Exploring the Music Culture and Attitudes of Hip-Hop*, Edinburgh: Payback Press.

Finnegan, R. (1997a) 'Music, performance and enactment' in H. Mackay (ed.) *Consumption and Everyday Life*, London: Sage, pp. 113–58.

——(1997b) 'Storying the Self: personal narratives and identity' in H. Mackay (ed.) *Consumption and Everyday Life*, London: Sage, pp. 58–112.

Fish, S. (1980) *Is There a Text in This Class? The Authority of Interpretive Communities*, Cambridge, Mass.: Harvard University Press.

Fitzgerald, T. (1996) 'Uknowhowsheduit', *Beat Down*, Vol. 4, No. 2, pp. 22–3.

Fligstein, N. (1990) *The Transformation of Corporate Control*, Cambridge, Mass.: Harvard University Press.

Flippo, C. (1996) 'The Gold Rush May Be Over, But Country is Still Flourishing in '96', *Billboard*, 28 December 1996, pp. 36–7.

Flores, A. (1987) 'Once-hot Biz of Salsa Sound is a Cold Note', *New York Daily News*, 14 July 1987, pp. 1/6.

Frith, S. (1983) *Sound Effects, Youth, Leisure and the Politics of Rock 'n' Roll*, London: Constable.

——(1988) *Music for Pleasure*, Cambridge: Polity.

——(1991) 'Critical response' in D. Campbell Robinson, E. Buck and M. Cuthbert (eds) *Music at the Margins; Popular Music and Global Cultural Diversity*, London: Sage.

——(ed.) (1993) *Music and Copyright*, Edinburgh: Edinburgh University Press.

——(1996) *Performing Rites. On the Value of Popular Music*, Oxford: Oxford University Press.

García Canclini, N. (1990) *Culturas Híbridas, Estrategias para Entrar y Salir de la Modernidad*, Mexico: Grijalbo.

Garnham, N. (1990) *Capitalism and Communication: Global Culture and the Economics of Information*, London: Sage.

Garofalo, R. (1986) 'How Autonomous is Relative: Popular Music, the Social Formation and Cultural Struggle', *Popular Music*, Vol. 6, No. 1, pp. 77–92.

——(1993) 'Black popular music: crossing over or going under?' in T. Bennett, S. Frith, L. Grossberg, J. Shepherd, G. Turner (eds) *Rock and Popular Music: Politics, Policies, Institutions*, London: Routledge pp. 231–48.

——(1994) 'Culture Versus Commerce: The Marketing of Black Popular Music', *Public Culture*, Vol. 7, No. 1, pp. 275–88.

——(1997) *Rockin' Out, Popular Music in the USA*, Needham Heights, Mass.: Allyn and Bacon.

Gavin Report (1996) 'Texas Radio and the Americana Beat', *Gavin Report*, No. 2096, 15 March 1996, pp. 29–30.

George, N. (1989) *The Death of Rhythm and Blues*, London: Omnibus.

——(1992) *Buppies, B-Boys, Baps and Bohos*, London: HarperCollins.

Gerard, C. and Sheller, M. (1989) *Salsa, The Rhythm of Latin Music*, Temple, Ariz.: White Cliffs Media Co.

Giddens, A. (1990) *The Consequences of Modernity*, Stanford, Ca.: Stanford University Press.

Gillett, C. (1983) *The Sound of the City*, London: Souvenir Press.

Gilroy, P. (1993) *The Black Atlantic, Modernity and Double Consciousness*, London: Verso.

Glanvill, R. (1989) 'World music mining: the international trade in new music' in F. Hanly and T. May (eds) *Rhythms of the World*, London: BBC Books.

Glasser, R. (1995) *My Music Is My Flag: Puerto Rican Musicians and Their New York Communities 1917–1940*, Berkeley, Ca: University of California Press.

Golding, P. (1990) 'Political communication and citizenship: the media and democracy in an inegalitarian social order' in M. Ferguson (ed.) *Public Communication: The New Imperatives*, London: Sage.

Golding, P. and Murdock, G. (1996) 'Culture, communications, and political economy' in J. Curran and M. Gurevitch (eds) *Mass Media and Society*, London: Arnold, pp. 11–30.

Goodwin, A. and Gore, J. (1990) 'World Beat and the Cultural Imperialism Thesis', *Socialist Review*, Vol. 20, No. 3, pp. 63–80.

Gorden, A. (1997) 'It All Adds Up', *The Source*, January, p. 98.

Gray, H. (1988) *Producing Jazz*, Philadelphia: Temple University Press.

Gregory, K. (1983) 'Native-View Paradigms: Multiple Cultures and Culture Conflicts in Organizations', *Administrative Science Quarterly*, Vol. 28, No. 3, pp. 359–76.

Gubernick, L. (1993) *Get Hot or Go Home, Trisha Yearwood: The Making of a Nashville Star*, New York: St Martin's Press.

Guilbault, J. (1997) 'Interpreting World Music: A Challenge in Theory and Practice', *Popular Music*, Vol. 16, No. 1, pp. 31–44.

Gurza, A. (1996) 'Salsa Wars', *LA Weekly*, 29 April–2 May 1996, pp. 53–5.

Hall, S. (1983) 'The problem of ideology, Marxism without guarantees', in B. Matthews (ed.) *Marx: 100 Years On*, London: Lawrence and Wishart, pp. 57–84.

——(1997) 'The work of representation' in S. Hall (ed.) *Representation: Cultural Representations and Signifying Practices*, London: Sage, pp. 13–74.

Hannerz, U. (1996) *Transnational Connections, Culture, People, Places*, London: Routledge.

Harker, D. (1980) *One for the Money: Politics and Popular Song*, London: Hutchinson. 784·0941/HAR

Hebdige, D. (1979) *Subculture, The Meaning of Style*, London: Methuen.

Hennion, A. (1982) 'Popular music as social production' in D. Horn and P. Tagg (eds) *Popular Music Perspectives 1*, Gothenberg and Exeter: IASPM, pp. 32–40.

——(1983) 'The Production of Success: An Anti-Musicology of the Pop Song', *Popular Music 3*, pp. 158–93.

——(1989) 'An Intermediary between Production and Consumption; the Producer of Popular Music', *Science, Technology and Human Values*, Vol. 14, No. 4, pp. 400–24.

Hesmondhalgh, D. (1996a) 'Flexibility, Post-Fordism and the Music Industries', *Media, Culture and Society*, Vol. 18, No. 3, pp. 469–88.

——(1996b) *Independent Record Companies and Democratisation in the Popular Music Industry*, Ph.D. thesis, Goldsmiths College, University of London.

——(1998) 'The British Dance Music Industry: A Case Study of Independent Cultural Production', *British Journal of Sociology*, Vol. 49, No. 2, pp. 234–51.

Hirsch, P. (1972) 'Processing Fads and Fashions: An Organizational Set Analysis of Cultural Industry Systems', *American Journal of Sociology*, Vol. 77, No. 4, pp. 639–59.

Hofstede, G. (1991) *Cultures and Organizations*, London: McGraw-Hill International.

Hosokawa, S. (no date) *'Salsa no tiene frontera': Orchesta de la Luz or the Globalization and Japanization of Afro-Caribbean Music*, unpublished manuscript.

Jackson, K. (1996) 'America's Rush To Suburbia', *New York Times*, Section E, 9 June 1996, p. 15.

Jeffrey, D. (1995) 'Warner's Fuchs Pledges Scrutiny', *Billboard*, 14 October 1995, p. 1/91.

Jhally, S. (1990) *The Codes of Advertising*, London: Routledge.

Johnson, R. (1997) 'PolyGram: The Hits Just Keep on Coming. Racial Tensions at Record Label', *Fortune*, Vol. 36, No. 12, p. 40.

Jones, S. (1993) 'Who fought the law? The American music industry and the global popular music market' in T. Bennett, S. Frith, L. Grossberg, J. Shepherd, G. Turner (eds) *Rock and Popular Music: Politics, Policies, Institutions*, London: Routledge, pp. 83–98.

Jones, T.C. (1995) *Accounting and the Enterprise*, London: Routledge.

Kotler, P. (1994) *Marketing Management; Analysis, Planning, Implementation and Control*, New Jersey: Prentice Hall.

Laing, D. (1969) *The Sound of Our Time*, London: Sheed and Ward.

——(1985) *One Chord Wonders; Power and Meaning in Punk Rock*, Milton Keynes: Open University.

Lash, S. and Urry, J. (1994) *Economies of Signs and Space*, London: Sage.

Lee, S. (1995) 'Re-examining the Concept of the "Independent" Record Company: The Case of Wax Trax! Records', *Popular Music*, Vol. 14, No. 1, pp. 13–32.

Lewis, L. (ed.) (1992) *The Adoring Audience; Fan Culture and Popular Media*, London: Routledge.

Llewellyn, H. (1997) 'Vibrant Sounds of Cuba Spreading to the World: Cuban Music Industry Showing Signs of Life', *Billboard*, 3 May 1997, p. 1/78.

McClary, S. (1991) *Feminine Endings: Music, Gender and Sexuality*, Minneapolis: University of Minnesota Press.

Mackay, H. (ed.) (1997) *Consumption and Everyday Life*, London: Sage.

Malone, B. (1985) *Country Music, USA*, Austin, Tex.: University of Texas Press, second edition.

Manuel, P. (1991) 'Salsa and the music industry: corporate control or grassroots expression?' in P. Manuel (ed.) *Essays on Cuban Music*, Lanham, Md: University Press of America, pp. 157–80.

——(1995a) 'Salsa and beyond' in P. Manuel (ed.) *Caribbean Currents*, Philadelphia: Temple University Press.

——(1995b) 'Latin music in the new world order: salsa and beyond' in R. Sakolsky and F. Wei-Han Ho (eds) *Sounding Off! Music as Subversion/Resistance/Revolution*, New York: Autonomedia, pp. 277–86.

Marcus, G. and Fischer, M. (1986) *Anthropology as Cultural Critique*, Chicago: University of Chicago Press.

Marlowe, A. (1995) 'The hermeneutics of rap' in A. Sexton (ed.) *Rap on Rap: Straight-Up Talk on Hip-Hop Culture*, New York: Delta, pp. 220–4.

Martín-Barbero, J. (1987) *Procesos de Comunicación y Matrices de Cultura*, Naucalpan, Mexico: Ediciones G. Gili.

——(1993) *Communication, Culture and Hegemony, From Media to Mediations*, London: Sage.

Mattelart, A. (1991) *Advertising International: The Privatization of Public Space*, London: Routledge.

Miège, B. (1989) *The Capitalization of Cultural Production*, New York: International General.

Mitchell, T. (1996) *Popular Music and Local Identity; Rock, Pop and Rap in Europe and Oceania*, Leicester: Leicester University Press.

Morley, D. and Chen, K.H. (1996) *Stuart Hall: Critical Dialogues in Cultural Studies*, London: Routledge.

Morris, C. (1996) 'MCA Purchases 50% of Interscope: Gangsta Rap Issue Minimized by Execs', *Billboard*, 2 March 1996, p. 13/84.

Mosco, V. (1996) *The Political Economy of Communication*, London: Sage.

Murdock, G. and Golding, P. (1974) 'For a political economy of mass communications' in R. Milliband and J. Saville (eds) *The Socialist Register, 1973* London: Merlin.

——(1977) 'Capitalism, communication and class relations' in J. Curran, M. Gurevitch and J. Woollacott (eds) *Mass Communication and Society*, London: Arnold, pp. 12–43.

Neale, S. (1980) *Genre*, London: British Film Institute.

——(1990) 'Questions of Genre', *Screen*, Vol. 31, No. 1, pp. 45–66.

Negus, K. (1992) *Producing Pop: Culture and Conflict in the Popular Music Industry*, London: Edward Arnold.

——(1993) 'Global Harmonies and Local Discords; Transnational Policies and Practices in the European Record Industry', *European Journal of Communication*, Vol. 8, No. 3, pp. 293–316.

——(1995) 'Where the Mystical Meets the Market; Commerce and Creativity in the Production of Popular Music', *Sociological Review*, Vol. 43, No. 2, pp. 316–41.

——(1996) *Popular Music in Theory*, Cambridge: Polity Press/Wesleyan University Press.

——(1997) 'The production of culture' in P. du Gay (ed.) (1997) *Production of Culture/Cultures of Production*, London: Open University/Sage, pp. 67–118.

Nelson, H. (1994) 'Rap: In an Ever-Shifting Climate, Rap Holds Steady and Grows Strong', *Billboard*, 26 November 1994, p. 25/46.

Newman, M. (1995) 'Music City Musings: Labels Abound, but Songs (and Duos) at a Premium', *Billboard*, 21 October 1995, p. 16.

——(1996) 'Global Strategy Critical for Sony Executives Mottola and Bowlin', *Billboard*, 18 May 1996, p. 1.

Nunziata, S. (1995) 'The Year in Business', *Billboard*, 23 December 1995, p. YE-10.

Ochs, E. (1993) 'Latin Crossover That's Set to Shake the World', *Music Business International*, Vol. 3, No. 11, pp. 23–4.

Olivier, C. (1995) 'PolyGram's Hollywood Dream', *Corporate Finance*, September, pp. 30–5.

Pacini Hernández, D. (1993) 'A View From The South: Spanish Caribbean Perspectives on World Beat', *The World of Music*, Vol. 35, pp. 48–69.

Padilla, F. (1989). 'Salsa Music as a Cultural Expression of Latino Consciousness and Unity', *Hispanic Journal of Behavioural Sciences*, Vol. 11, No. 1, pp. 28–45.

Palmer, R. (1977) 'Can Salsa Escape the Cultural Ghetto?' *New York Times*, 23 January 1977, Section 2, part 2, p. 22/29.

Pareles, J. (1996) 'A Small World After All. But is that Good?' *New York Times*, 24 March 1996, p. H34.

Parker, A. (1997) 'Wu-Wear Urban Clothing Chain Opens Store in Norfolk Va', *Virginia Pilot*, 2 May 1997, p. 5.

Payton, T. (1997) 'Set It Off', *The Source*, January, p. 96.

Perez, B. (1986) 'Political Facets of Salsa', *Popular Music*, Vol. 6, No. 2, pp. 149–60.

Peterson, R. (1976) 'The Production of Culture. A Prolegomenon' in R. Peterson (ed.) *The Production of Culture*, London: Sage, pp. 7–22.

——(1978) 'The Production of Cultural Change: The Case of Contemporary Country Music', *Social Research*, Vol. 45, No. 2, pp. 293–314.

——(1995) 'The Dialectic of Hard-Core and Soft-Shell Country Music' in C. Tichi (ed.) *Readin' Country Music: Steel Guitars, Opry Stars and Honky Tonk Bars: The South Atlantic Quarterly*, Vol. 94, No. 1, Winter, pp. 273–300.

——(1997) *Creating Country Music, Fabricating Authenticity*, Chicago: University of Chicago Press.

Peterson, R. and Kern, R. (1995) 'Hard-Core and Soft-Shell Country Fans', *Journal of Country Music*, Vol. 17, No. 3, pp. 3–8.

Philips, C. (1996) 'Charting Sony Music's Future', *Los Angeles Times*, Business, 5 May 1996, pp. D1/D4.

Pickering, M. (1997) *History, Experience and Cultural Studies*, London: Macmillan.

Powell, K. (1996) 'Live From Death Row', *Vibe*, Vol. 4, No. 1, February, pp. 44–50.

Pride, D. (1991) 'European Equalizer', *Music Business International*, Vol. 2, No. 1, p. 21.

Purcell, J. (1989) 'The impact of corporate strategy on human resource management' in J. Storey (ed.) *New Perspectives on Human Resource Management*, London: Routledge.

Quintero Rivera, A. (1992) 'Ponce, the danza and the national question: notes towards a sociology of Puerto Rican music' in V. Boggs (ed.) *Salsiology: Afro-Cuban Music and the Evolution of Salsa in New York City*, New York: Excelsior, pp. 43–58.

——(1994) 'The camouflaged drum: melodization of rhythms and maroonage ethnicity in Caribbean peasant music' in G. Béhague (ed.) *Music and Black Ethnicity: The Caribbean and South America*, New Brunswick: Transaction Books, pp. 47–64.

——(1997) 'Prácticas Musicales y Visiones Sociales, Apuntes Sobre la Sociología de las Músicas "Mulatas" ', *La Cansión Popular*, Vol. 12, pp. 181–4.

——(1998) *Salsa, Sabor y Control: Sociología de la Música 'Tropical'*, Havana: Premio Casa de las Américas, Mexico: Siglo Veintiuno.

Quintero Rivera, A. and Manuel Alvarez, L. (1990) 'La Libre Combinacion de las Formas Musicales en la Salsa', *David y Goliath, Revista del Consejo Latinoamericano de Ciencias Sociales*, Vol. 19, No. 57, pp. 45–51.

Ramirez, M. (1996) 'Joining the Party: Multinational Giants See Great Potential in Latin Music', *Los Angeles Times* (Washington Edition), 12 March 1996, p. B5.

Reynolds, J. (1995) 'Rap Confab Assembles Nation', *Billboard*, 11 November 1995, p. 26.

——(1996) 'Capitol Records Setting a Bad Example', *Billboard*, 9 March 1996, p. 18.

Robbins, J. (1990) 'The Cuban Son as Form, Genre and Symbol', *Latin American Music Review*, Vol. 11, No. 2, pp. 182–200.

Román Velázquez, P. (1996) *The Construction of Latin Identities and Salsa Music Clubs in London: An Ethnographic Study*, Ph.D. thesis, Leicester University.

——(1998) 'El Desarrollo de un Circuito Salsero y la Construcción de Identidades Latinas en Londres', *Revista de Ciencias Sociales*, Nueva Epoca, No. 4, pp. 53–79.

Rondon, C.M. (1980) *El Libro de la Salsa*, Caracas, Venezuela: Editorial Arte.

Rose, T. (1994a) *Black Noise: Rap Music and Black Culture in Contemporary America*, Hanover, NH: Wesleyan University.

——(1994b) 'Contracting Rap; An Interview with Carmen Ashurst-Watson' in A. Ross and T. Rose (eds) *Microphone Fiends*, London: Routledge.

Rosen, C. (1996) 'Capitol Moves Urban Division to EMI: 18 Staffers Laid Off', *Billboard*, 9 March 1996, p. 3.

Rubin, M. (1997) 'Secrets of the Ch-Ching', *Spin*, October, pp. 95–102.

Russell, R. (1996) 'Edge of the Row', *Music Row Magazine*, Vol. 17, No. 10, June, p. 25.

Russell, W. (1993) 'Editorial, Information Please', *Rhythm Music Magazine*, September, p. 4.

Ryan, J. and Peterson, R. (1982) 'The product image: the fate of creativity in country music songwriting', in J. Ettema and D. Whitney (eds) *Individuals in Mass Media Organizations: Creativity and Constraint*, London: Sage, pp. 11–32.

Salaman, G. (1997) 'Culturing production' in P. du Gay (ed.) *Production of Culture/Cultures of Production*, London: Sage, pp. 235–84.

Samuels, D. (1995) 'The rap on rap: the "Black music" that isn't either' in A. Sexton (ed.) *Rap on Rap: Straight-Up Talk on Hip-Hop Culture*, New York: Delta, pp. 241–52.

Sandler, A. (1995) 'Big Labels Ride Black Music Bandwagon', *Variety*, 28 August 1995, Vol. 360, p. 13.

Sanjek, D. (1995) 'Blue moon of Kentucky rising over the mystery train: the complex construction of country music' in C. Tichi (ed.) *Readin' Country Music: Steel Guitars, Opry Stars and Honky Tonk Bars: The South Atlantic Quarterly*, Vol. 94, No. 1, Winter, pp. 29–55.

——(1997) 'One Size Does Not Fit All: The Precarious Position of the African-American Entrepreneur in Post WW2 American Popular Music', *American Music*, Vol. 15, No. 4, pp. 535–62.

——(1998) 'Popular music and the synergy of corporate culture' in T. Swiss, J. Sloop and A. Herman (eds) *Mapping the Beat, Popular Music and Contemporary Theory*, Oxford: Blackwell.

Sanjek, R. (1988) *American Popular Music and Its Business*, Oxford: Oxford University Press.

Schiller, H. (1989) *Culture, Inc. The Corporate Takeover of Public Expression*, Oxford: Oxford University Press.

——(1991) 'Not Yet the Post-Imperial Era', *Critical Studies in Mass Communication*, Vol. 8, pp. 13–28.

——(1996) *Information Inequality*, London: Routledge.

Schumacher, T. (1995) 'This Is a Sampling Sport: Digital Sampling, Rap Music and the Law in Cultural Production', *Media, Culture and Society*, Vol. 17, pp. 253–73.

Scott, A. (1994) 'Dornemann: Embracing Danger, Avoiding Risk', *Music Business International*, Vol. 4, No. 3, pp. 9–13.

Sexton, A. (ed.) (1995) *Rap on Rap: Straight-Up Talk on Hip-Hop Culture*, New York: Delta.

Siehl, C. and Martin, J. (1990) 'Organizational culture: a key to financial performance?' in B. Schneider (ed.) *Organizational Climate and Culture*, San Francisco: Jossey-Bass.

Singer, R. (1983) 'Tradition and Innovation in Contemporary Latin Music in New York City', *Latin American Music Review*, Vol. 4, No. 2, pp. 183–202.

Smircich, L. (1983) 'Concepts of Culture and Organizational Analysis', *Administrative Science Quarterly*, Vol. 28, No. 3, pp. 339–58.

Snyder, M. (1996) 'Artist Support Groups', *Billboard*, 8 June 1996, p. 30/44.

Stephenson, W.H. and Coulter, E.M. (eds) (1995) *A History of the South: Vol. XI, The New South 1945–1980*, Baton Rouge: Louisiana State University Press.

Tagg, P. (1987) 'Musicology and the Semiotics of Popular Music', *Semiotica*, Vol. 66, pp. 279–98.

Tate, G. (1996) 'Is Hip Hop Dead?' *Vibe*, Vol. 4, No. 2, March, p. 35.

Thornton, S. (1995) *Club Cultures: Music, Media and Subcultural Capital*, Cambridge: Polity.

Tichi, C. (1994) *High Lonesome: The American Culture of Country Music*, Chapel Hill: University of North Carolina.

UNESCO (1982) *Culture Industries: A Challenge for the Future of Culture*, Paris: UNESCO.

Varela, C. (1997) *Cubadisco '97 – Cuba's New Free Market Salsa*, www.salsasf.com/features/Cubadisc.html.

Vincent, R. (1996) *Funk, the Music, the People and the Rhythm of the One*, New York: St Martin's Press.

Wade, D. and Picardie, J. (1990) *Music Man, Ahmet Ertegun, Atlantic Records and the Triumph of Rock 'n' Roll*, New York: W.W. Norton.

Whalen, J. (1994) 'Rap Defies Traditional Marketing', *Advertising Age*, No. 65, 12 March 1994, p. 12.

Williams, R. (1961) *Culture and Society*, Harmondsworth: Penguin.

——(1965) *The Long Revolution*, Harmondsworth: Penguin.

——(1983) *Keywords*, London: Fontana.

Williamson, J. (1978) *Decoding Advertisements*, London: Marion Boyars.

Willmott, H. (1993) 'Strength is Ignorance; Slavery is Freedom: Managing Culture in Modern Organizations', *Journal of Management Studies*, Vol. 30, No. 4, pp. 515–52.

Yamotei, N. (1987) Sleeve notes for *Soro*, Salif Keita, Stern Records 1020.

Zimmerman, K. (1995) 'Year of Turmoil', *Music Business International*, October, pp. 18–22.

Index